The Royal and Russian Navies

Manchester University Press

RUSSIAN STRATEGY AND POWER

SERIES EDITORS
Andrew Monaghan and Richard Connolly

EDITORIAL BOARD
Julian Cooper, OBE
Emily Ferris
Tracey German
Michael Kofman
Katri Pynnöniemi
Andrei Sushentsov

To buy or to find out more about the books currently available in this series, please go to: https://manchesteruniversitypress.co.uk/series/russian-strategy-and-power/

The Royal and Russian Navies

Cooperation, competition and confrontation

David Fields and Robert Avery

MANCHESTER UNIVERSITY PRESS

Copyright © David Fields and Robert Avery 2025

The right of David Fields and Robert Avery to be identified as the author of this work has been asserted in accordance with the Copyright, Designs and Patents Act 1988.

Published by Manchester University Press
Oxford Road, Manchester, M13 9PL

www.manchesteruniversitypress.co.uk

British Library Cataloguing-in-Publication Data
A catalogue record for this book is available from the British Library

ISBN 978 1 5261 8458 0 hardback
ISBN 978 1 5261 8459 7 paperback

First published 2025

The publisher has no responsibility for the persistence or accuracy of URLs for any external or third-party internet websites referred to in this book, and does not guarantee that any content on such websites is, or will remain, accurate or appropriate.

EU authorised representative for GPSR:
Easy Access System Europe, Mustamäe tee 50, 10621 Tallinn, Estonia
gpsr.requests@easproject.com

Typeset
by Deanta Global Publishing Services, Chennai, India

From David:

My love and thanks go to my family, Jessica, Polly, Ellie and Alex who have suffered my obsession with Russia for far too long and endured the stresses and strains of Moscow life twice. Without your love and patience this book would not have been possible and so it is dedicated to you, and also to Agnes and Wilf, with heartfelt gratitude.

From Robert:

My dedication of our book is to those attaches and interpreters who made it work – and their Russian teachers.

Captain David Fields Royal Navy (Ret'd); Robert Avery OBE

Figure 0.1 The authors on board HMS *Invincible* with Soviet destroyer *Bezuprechny* in the background. July 1990. © Author – Robert Avery.

2000

'Acting Russian President Vladimir Putin, in an unexpected gesture to the West, suggested in a television interview today that Russia would consider joining NATO, if the Western alliance agreed to treat Russia as an equal partner.'[1]

2022

'The era of cooperation with the West is irrevocably over, interaction with unfriendly countries is possible only on a "one-off, transactional" basis.' Alexei Drobinin, Director of the Foreign Policy Planning department of the Russian Foreign Ministry.[2]

Notes

1 D. Hoffman, 'Putin Says "Why Not?" to Russia Joining NATO', *Washington Post*, 6 March 2000, www.washingtonpost.com/archive/politics/2000/03/06/putin-says-why-not-to-russia-joining-nato/c1973032-c10f-4bff-9174-8cae673790cd/ (accessed 12 February 2023).
2 'V MID RF zayavlyayut o nevozmozhnosti vozvrashcheniya k prezhnemu sotrudnichestvu s Zapadom', *Interfax*, 3 August 2022, www.militarynews.ru/story.asp?rid=0&nid=578756&lang=RU (accessed 23 August 2022).

Contents

List of figures	page x
List of tables	xiv
List of testimonies	xvi
List of first-hand accounts	xvii
About the authors	xviii
Foreword	xix
Preface	xxii
Acknowledgements	xxviii
List of abbreviations	xxx
1 A concise history of the Russian Navy	1
2 Pre-1988 UK–Russia naval relations	5
3 1988–99 From confrontation to cooperation	17
4 1999–2010 Back towards confrontation	77
5 2010–14 Collapse of cooperation and return to confrontation	103
6 What did the two navies learn about each other?	135
7 The Russian Navy – future prospects	153
8 Future defence engagement with Russia	193
Conclusion	209
Bibliography and suggested reading	219
Index	221

Figures

0.1 The authors on board HMS *Invincible* with Soviet destroyer *Bezuprechny* in the background. July 1990. *page* vi
2.1 Memo from Piskunov about rescheduling volleyball game. 12
3.1 First Deputy Commander-in-Chief of the Russian Federation Navy Admiral Igor Kasatonov is greeted on arrival at the Northwood Command Centre by Commander-in-Chief Fleet Admiral Sir Hugo White. At the time he was courted by the Royal Navy as the successor to Admiral Gromov but that did not come to pass. 29 March 1995. 36
3.2 Pre-exercise planning on board HMS *Gloucester* during RUKUS 96. From left to right: Commander T. Cunningham (CO HMS *Gloucester*), Vice Admiral J. Brigstocke (Flag Officer Surface Flotilla), Rear Admiral V. Bessonov (Head Tactics Kuznetsov Naval Academy), Captain 1 Rank N. Zharinov (Chief of Staff Kola Flotilla) and Commander L. Geanuleas (CO USS *Samuel B. Roberts*). 37
3.3 RUKUS 98 took place at the Kuznetsov Naval Academy St Petersburg. The concluding Memorandum of Understanding to improve organisation and purposefulness of future RUKUSes. Signatories were (left to right) Rear Admiral J. Stark USN, Vice Admiral V. V. Patrushev and Commodore A. Chilton. As it happened, this was the last RUKUS for some time. 42
3.4 Admiral Sir Jock Slater (First Sea Lord) and Admiral Vladimir Kuroyedov (Commander-in-Chief Russian Federation Navy) sign the Memorandum of Understanding on Naval Cooperation in the Main Naval Staff in Moscow. Captain G. McCready (NA Moscow) and Captain 1 Rank V. Ye Andreyenkov (Assistant to C-in-C RFN) in attendance. September 1998. 44

Figures

3.5 Flag Officer Royal Yachts Rear Admiral R. Woodard (third from left) entertained St Petersburg dignitaries aboard HMY *Britannia* during the State Visit. Among the guests was the Deputy Mayor Vladimir Putin (fifth from left). Robert Avery (second from right) was the interpreter. Destroyer *Bespokoiny* is in the background. October 1994. 48

3.6 HM Yacht *Britannia* berths at the English Embankment in St Petersburg at the start of the State Visit of HM Queen Elizabeth to Russia. She was not embarked at this point, having flown to Moscow but would entertain President Yeltsin on board at the end of the visit. 15 October 1994. 49

3.7 HM Yacht *Britannia* alongside during the Royal Visit to St Petersburg. October 1994. 49

3.8 Destroyer *Bespokoiny* viewed across from HMS *Glasgow* during the Royal Visit to St Petersburg. October 1994. 50

3.9 HM Yacht *Britannia* alongside at St Petersburg during Royal Visit, Destroyer *Bespokoiny* in the background. October 1994. 50

3.10 Beat Retreat by HM Royal Marines on English Embankment St Petersburg. Viewed from HM Yacht *Britannia* during the state visit by HM Queen Elizabeth. October 1994. 51

3.11 Admirals Igor Kasatonov – First Deputy Commander-in-Chief Russian Federation Navy (right) – and Admiral Yegorov – Commander Baltic Fleet – engage Vice Admiral John Brigstocke (Flag Officer Surface Flotilla) in conversation during the Victory Day Commemorations in St Petersburg marking the fiftieth anniversary of the end of World War II. May 1995. 52

3.12 Lt Cdr David Fields (Assistant Naval Attache) and Commander Baltic Fleet, Admiral Vladimir Yegorov, on board HMS *Somerset*, St Petersburg. June 1998. 53

3.13 'I greet you, Comrade Northern Fleet Sailors!' After addressing this – in immaculate Russian – to the Guard of Honour drawn up on the flight deck of the *Udaloy*-class large anti-submarine *Admiral Levchenko*, HRH Prince Michael of Kent spent over an hour touring her and meeting the ship's company. Trafalgar 200 Review in Spithead, July 2005. 55

3.14 From HMS *Battleaxe*: close pass by large anti-submarine ship *Admiral Panteleyev* during officer-of-the-watch manoeuvres off Baltiysk. July 1992. 56

xii *Figures*

3.15 HMS *Herald* berths in St Petersburg wearing the flag of the UK Hydrographer of the Navy Rear Admiral J. Myres, welcomed by the Admiralty Band conducted by Captain 2 Rank A Karabanov. October 1991. 71
3.16 National Hydrographers Vice Admiral Anatoly Komaritsyn and Rear Admiral Nigel Essenhigh inside the Kremlin. September 1995. 74
3.17 The National Hydrographers Vice Admiral Anatoly Komaritsyn and Rear Admiral Nigel Essenhigh sign the Memorandum of Understanding on Hydrographic Cooperation in St Petersburg. September 1995. 75
4.1 Yevgeni uniform museum photo. 82
4.2 Captain Jonathan Holloway receives the Order of Friendship from President Vladimir Putin for his part in the rescue of the crew of submersible *Priz*. The ceremony took place in No. 10 Downing Street – Prime Minister Tony Blair looks on. October 2005. 86
4.3 Commodore Roger Lane-Nott (Deputy Flag Officer Submarines) at Severomorsk. HMS *Opossum* and *Kilo*-class diesel submarine in the background. August 1993. 100
4.4 Royal Navy submariners from HMS *Opossum* enjoy Russian naval hospitality in the wardroom of the *Kilo*-class host submarine. Severomorsk. August 1993. 101
4.5 HMS *Portland* and RFS *Admiral Chabanenko* sail into Norfolk, Virginia, to participate in exercise FRUKUS 2007. 101
5.1 Officers from the French ship *De Grasse*, Russian ship *Yaroslav Mudriy*, HMS *York*, USS *Normandy* and US Naval Forces Europe-Africa, walk in formation during a wreath-laying ceremony held at the Piskariovskoye Memorial Cemetery during Exercise FRUKUS 2012. 104
6.1 Old adversaries meet at the Catherine Palace reception marking the three-hundredth anniversary of the Russian Navy: From left to right: Admiral Vladimir Mikhailin (Commander Baltic Fleet 1967–75, Deputy Commander Warsaw Pact Navies 1978–83), Admiral Sir Jock Slater (First Sea Lord), Admiral Nikolai Khovrin (Commander Black Sea Fleet 1974–83), Admiral Nikolai Amel'ko (Commander Pacific Fleet 1962–69, Deputy C-in-C Soviet Navy 1969–78, Deputy Chief of Soviet General Staff, 1979–87), Admiral of the Fleet Aleksei Sorokin (last chief zampolit of the Soviet Navy 1981–91), Robert Avery (Interpreter). July 1996. 146

Figures

6.2	Rear Admiral John Lippiett (Flag Officer Sea Training) and Admiral Vladimir Yegorov (Commander Baltic Fleet) on board destroyer *Bespokoiny* during her visit to Plymouth. July 1998.	147
6.3	Rear Admiral John Lippiett (Flag Officer Sea Training) and Admiral Vladimir Yegorov (Commander Baltic Fleet) on board HMS Norfolk during the visit of destroyer *Bespokoiny* to Plymouth. July 1998.	148
6.4	Admiral Sir Hugo White – Commander-in-Chief Fleet – welcomes Commander-in-Chief Russian Federation Navy Admiral Feliks Gromov to the Northwood Command Centre. This was a historic occasion – Admiral Gromov was the first Russian admiral to go 'down the Hole' into the command bunker. May 1993.	149
8.1	Admiral Sir Jock Slater, First Sea Lord, greets Admiral Igor Kasatonov, First Deputy Commander-in-Chief Russian Federation Navy, in the Mall House Flat, 5 March 1996. Kasatonov had just handed over a letter from C-in-C RFN Admiral Feliks Gromov, thanking the Royal Navy for airlifting a sailor suffering from appendicitis from a Victor III SSN off Scotland earlier that month.	204

Tables

2.1	Warship visits RN-Soviet Navy 1945–88	*page* 8
5.1	Warship visits RN–RFN 1989–2014	110
5.2	RN–RFN Flag/Delegation Visits 1988–2014	117
5.3	RUKUS/FRUKUS 1988–2014	129
7.1	Submarine deliveries 2011–24 (December 2024)	159
7.2	Submarines under construction at Sevmash, Severodvinsk (December 2024)	161
7.3	Submarines under construction at Admiralty, St Petersburg (October 2024)	162
7.4	Upgraded legacy sub-surface units (February 2024)	162
7.5	Surface ship deliveries 2011–24 (February 2024)	164
7.6	Amphibious vessels under construction at Yantar, Kaliningrad (February 2024)	167
7.7	Universal Landing ships under construction at Zaliv, Crimea (February 2024)	168
7.8	Frigates under construction at Severnaya Verf', St Petersburg (September 2024)	170
7.9	Upgraded legacy surface units (February 2024)	171
7.10	Corvettes under construction at Severnaya Verf', St Petersburg (June 2024)	172
7.11	Corvettes under construction at Zelenodol'sk, nr Kazan (December 2024)	172
7.12	Corvettes laid down and launched at Morye, Crimea (fitted out at Pella) (February 2024)	173
7.13	Corvettes under construction at Pella, St Petersburg (February 2024)	173
7.14	Corvettes under construction at Zaliv, Crimea (August 2024)	173
7.15	Corvettes under construction at Amur, Far East (February 2024)	174
7.16	Minesweepers under construction at Srednye Nevsky, St Petersburg (August 2024)	174
7.17	Logistic support ships under construction (February 2024)	176

7.18	Icebreakers under construction at Baltzavod, St Petersburg (February 2024)	179
7.19	Icebreakers under construction at Zvezda, Far East (February 2024)	179
7.20	Ice-class patrol ships under construction at Admiralty, St Petersburg (December 2024)	180
7.21	Icebreakers under construction at Almaz, St Petersburg (February 2024)	180

Testimonies

Vice Admiral Sir Tim McClement KCB OBE – During his thirty-five-year naval career, Sir Tim commanded two submarines, two frigates, a frigate squadron and a UK Task Group on a global deployment. His last appointment was Deputy Commander-in-Chief Fleet before retiring in 2007.

Vice Admiral Charles Style CBE – Charles served for thirty-four years in the Royal Navy, retiring in 2008. Out of eleven jobs at sea, his six commands included two frigates, an aircraft carrier and a group deployment as Commander UK Maritime Force.

Captain Christopher Page – Chris's last appointment was to NATO as the Deputy Military Delegate to the Western European Union. He then served eleven years on the Naval Staff as the Head of the Naval Historical Branch. In the early 1990s, he was the Royal Navy's organiser for the RUKUS talks.

Captain Jonathan Holloway – Jon retired from the Royal Navy in 2015, with his last appointment being Captain of the Sea Cadet Corps. He was the UK Naval Attache in Moscow from 2003 to 2005.

Colonel Charlie Wilson RM – Charlie is a retired Royal Marines Lieutenant Colonel. While serving, he undertook two visits to the Russian Naval Infantry at the St Petersburg Staff College and one to the Ukrainian Naval Infantry.

First-hand accounts

1. The Russians and the Gulf – Vice Admiral Charles Style CBE
2. A short history of the Adderbury talks 1988–94 – Captain Chris Page RN
3. RFS *Neustrashimy* – Exercise Cooperative Venture 94 – Captain David Fields RN
4. Joint declaration of RUKUS 1995
5. RUKUS 1997 – interpreter's observations – Mr Robert Avery OBE
6. Memorandum of Understanding 1998 – interpreter's observations – Mr Robert Avery OBE
7. Royal Marines – Russian Naval Infantry interaction – Colonel Charlie Wilson RM
8. Meeting a Cold War adversary – this time with vodka – Vice Admiral Sir Tim McClement KCB OBE
9. Operation to rescue submersible *Priz* AS 28 – August 2005 – Captain Jon Holloway RN
10. Visit to the UK of Admiral of the Fleet Masorin, C-in-C RFN – interpreter's observations – Mr Robert Avery OBE

About the authors

Robert Avery studied Russian at Oxford and Moscow State University and taught Russian to Service personnel – predominantly Royal Navy – from 1978 until his retirement in 2017. After eight years as lecturer/tutor at BRNC Dartmouth, he went on to become Principal at Defence School of Languages Beaconsfield in 1988 (B2 Civil Servant) and subsequently at Defence Centre for Languages & Culture at Defence Academy Shrivenham. Over 1989–2007 he acted as interpreter for nearly seventy warship and Flag visits between the RN and the Russian Navy as well as the annual RUKUS tripartite (Russian/UK/US) talks/exercises. This work provided ample opportunities for observing at close quarters how the Russian Navy did business and what constitutes its culture.

David Fields' naval career included a wide range of executive, management and diplomatic roles within the military and across government, including command of the frigate HMS *Westminster*. He qualified as a Russian interpreter in 1990 and was posted to Moscow in 1997–99 as the Assistant Naval Attaché. During this period, he helped to develop the Memorandum of Understanding between the two navies on naval cooperation and organised several high-profile visits. He returned to Russia as the Naval Attaché in 2013–15, covering the start of the Ukraine crisis in 2014. From 2016, he worked in the UK MoD assisting in the development of the UK MoD's Russia policy before retiring in 2017. Since then he has been a regular contributor to a variety of organisations, including US European Command, on Russian defence procurement.

Foreword

Between 1988 and 2014, the Royal Navy, first with the Soviet Navy and then the Russian Federation Navy, developed a close working relationship, even signing a Memorandum of Understanding in 1998, which aimed to strengthen naval cooperation. *The Royal and Russian Navies: Cooperation, Competition and Confrontation* examines this unique period of history and the lessons that were learned by both sides about how their respective navies operated, as well as the conclusions drawn by Russia about the application of its maritime power to protect its national interests globally. Considering the ongoing conflict in Ukraine and the deep divisions between the Euro-Atlantic community and Russia, this book is timely in helping us not only to understand the Russians more advantageously but also how the UK's relationship and that of its allies might develop with Russia in the post-Ukraine conflict period.

As a submariner, the first two decades of my career were dominated by operations at the cutting edge of confronting the Soviet Navy's formidable naval forces. Throughout this period, in the Atlantic, the Cold War was being conducted on a daily basis. By 1974, four years after I joined the Royal Navy, the Soviet Navy was estimated to have had some three hundred submarines of various classes in service and more than two hundred major surface warships. The fluctuations in political tensions between the West and the Soviet Union, were frequently played out globally in the maritime environment through their respective military blocs, namely NATO and the Warsaw Pact. I was taught about the Soviet Union, the threat it posed to world peace, the tactics and procedures of its naval forces and how best to adapt our own methods of operation to combat them. I spent a long time with Soviet submarines on sonar screens contemplating what the real capability of the opposition was and how they might fight. In August 1991, when in command of the frigate HMS *London* and four months before the final demise of the Soviet Union, I took the ship north to take part in events in Murmansk and Arkhangelsk marking the fiftieth anniversary of the first Arctic Convoy to the USSR – Operation Dervish. I have also been fortunate to take part in the sixtieth and seventieth anniversaries of this historical operation which was so critical to the successful outcome of World War II. I started to get a measure of the personality and professionalism of my new colleagues. Prior to 1991, I gave little thought to meeting Russians or visiting their ships and submarines but in the subsequent years my interactions with them were many and varied. As First Sea Lord, I established a positive working relationship in 2012 with my opposite number, Admiral Viktor Viktorovich Chirkov, who, like many in the Russian Navy, displayed warm hospitality, friendship, a liking of whisky and a genuine respect for the Royal Navy. We had a mutual desire to deepen the already well-established bilateral cooperation programme between our two navies, which reflected the political desire at the time to reset the relationship with Russia. The second two decades of my career highlighted to me that, prior to 1991, I had been taught through a lens aimed at the Soviet Bloc rather than one focused on Russia and its people.

That is why this book is so important. While it is right that our aim is to defend and deter against the threat and challenges that Russia poses today, and will continue to pose, we also need to interpret our adversaries better and be prepared to re-engage in military-to-military dialogue as and when political circumstances allow in the aftermath of current tensions. David Fields and Robert Avery are uniquely qualified to better our understanding of the Russians and the Russian Federation Navy, as well as Russia's ambitions to become a maritime power. David was one of my Naval Assistants when I was First Sea Lord. With his depth of experience of Russia and the Russians, I appointed him as Naval Attache to Moscow in 2013, to draw on that experience as we sought then to strengthen the bilateral naval relationship. The annexation of Crimea in March 2014 put an end to that effort. Returning from Moscow in 2015, David was appointed to the UK Ministry of Defence (MoD) and worked in the policy team that authored the MoD's first Russia strategy published in 2017. Robert, who was my interpreter for the sixtieth Op Dervish anniversary in 2001, was the Principal Lecturer at the Defence School of Languages and educated all our Naval Attaches to Moscow from 1978 to 2017. He also has a deep passion for naval matters and an in-depth knowledge of the Soviet and Russian Federation Navy and its people. He was awarded the OBE for his pivotal contribution in the success of the bilateral cooperation programmes between the Royal Navy and Russian Navy.

Both David and Robert use their insight, and lived experience, in a way that brings colour and a human perspective to the Russians and their way of doing business, drawing on sources that have not hitherto been published. These insights are punctuated by personal stories from those who also had experience of dealing with the Russians. These observations, together with many photographs from the 1988 to 2014 era, underline the close relationship and respect between the two navies, underpinned by a long history and the bond which exists between sailors operating in a common hostile environment – the sea.

The authors, however, remain clear-eyed about the threat and challenges that Russia presents in the global commons, especially the maritime environment, as it seeks to confront and compete with the West. Moscow has an ambitious strategy, in which the sea and its navy plays a vital role. The world's oceans are a key arena in which the UK and its allies will be defending themselves against Russia and its strengthening naval forces. We must act so as to provide a deterrent to any thoughts it might have for aggression but at the same time leave the door open for military-to-military dialogue through which meaningful cooperation might be re-established.

The period of UK–Russia naval cooperation examined in the book, provides unique lessons to help our better understanding of the Russians. As such, it is strongly recommended reading for all of us, in particular for decision and policy-makers and those serving in the military. For Royal Naval personnel and those in allied navies, now and in the future, whether it be through confrontation, competition or cooperation, the Russian Federation Navy will play a significant and challenging role in their careers.

Admiral Sir Mark Stanhope GCB OBE DL
First Sea Lord and Chief of Naval Staff (2009–13)

The views and opinions expressed in this book are those of the authors and should not be taken to represent those of His Majesty's Government, the Ministry of Defence, HM Armed Forces or any other agency.

Preface

Against the backdrop of Russia's full-scale invasion of Ukraine in 2022, it is hard to imagine that there was once any military dialogue and cooperation between the UK and Russia. Yet there was. So much so that in March 2014, the UK and Russia were due to sign a Military Technical Cooperation Agreement (MTCA) at a foreign and defence ministerial meeting in London. Although the MTCA was modest in its aspirations, it reflected the progress in defence cooperation, following the end of the Cold War, between the respective armed forces and demonstrated the political will for it to continue. However, the MTCA was not signed and instead President Putin, on 18 March 2014, approved the formal annexation of Crimea to the Russian Federation. The UK–Russia military cooperation relationship effectively ended. Tit-for-tat expulsions of each other's Defence Attaches in May 2024 have brought that relationship to a new low. For the first time since 1941, there are now no in-country military representatives at a time when the risks of miscalculation and misunderstanding between the UK and Russia are extremely high.

The latest rupture in the political, diplomatic, economic and military relationship between Russia, the UK and the West is severe and is set to last for the foreseeable future. This breakdown in relations has arguably concluded a process that began when Putin came to power in 1999, a year which coincided with NATO's bombing campaign against Serbia and the alliance's first wave of expansion to the east, incorporating countries of the former Soviet Bloc – the Czech Republic, Hungary and Poland. Subsequent rounds of NATO expansion exacerbated Russia's frustration at the lack of a post-Cold War settlement that addressed its security concerns[1] and left the key policy clash unresolved. In essence, this can be described as Russia's desire to break Western hegemony, led by the US, and to demonstrate that it is a great power reshaping a new, multi-polar world order, challenging the West's Rules-Based International Order (RBIO) and liberal democratic values. For sure, there have been moments of cooperation and constructive dialogue following the collapse of the USSR in 1991, but for the most part, despite a few ups, the trajectory in the Russia–West relationship has been on a downward trend since 1999, with Russia's annexation of Crimea marking the start of the latest 'turn for the worse'. Indeed the period reflects the 'rollercoaster' nature of the historical relationship between Russia and the West – one that has veered between cooperation, competition and confrontation in its attempt to navigate mutual distrust, paranoia, clash of values and great power competition.

While all branches of the UK armed forces, including arms' control teams and the Russian Resettlement Programme (RRP),[2] were involved to varying degrees in dialogue and cooperation with the Russian military from the early 1990s to 2014, this book focuses on the relationship between the Royal Navy (RN) and Russian Federation Navy (RFN). It was within this relationship that perhaps some of the most in-depth interaction with the Russian armed forces was achieved, with one of the key reasons being a shared history. Examples included the founding of the Russian Navy by Peter the Great, who learned his trade in the UK and the Netherlands; a period in the nineteenth century when half the officers' list of the Russian Imperial Navy were British; and the RN's support on the Arctic Convoys to the northern ports of the USSR during World War II. Indeed, at one time Catherine the Great's navy was commanded by Admiral Samuel Greig from Scotland and it is no accident that the Russian Navy's flag, the St Andrew's flag, with the naval motto – 'God and the St Andrew's flag are with us!' – is based on the national flag of Scotland. The historical linkages between the two navies underpinned many of the good personal relationships established during bilateral naval visits and engagements in the post-Soviet period. However, history was not the only reason that these bonds formed between the two navies. Both sides had a common enemy which they frequently referred to – the sea. On an almost daily basis throughout the Cold War the RN was competing with or confronting the rapidly growing Soviet Navy and today is still interacting in one way or another at sea with the RFN, unilaterally, or as part of NATO.

The aim of the book, therefore, is to review the 1988–2014 period in the UK–Russia relationship and specifically the interaction between the two navies, as well as discuss the period of little or no military dialogue after the annexation of Crimea in 2014 up to the present day. Russians' long memories and constant referral to history mean it is important to have an understanding, in the maritime context, of the RFN's history and this will be examined first. It shows that Russia has always had global maritime aspirations since its founding, and that aim has not diminished, despite the political and economic upheavals Russia has endured over the last 325 years. Context to the bilateral naval relationship of 1988–2014 will also be provided through a brief overview of the limited naval cooperation that existed between the two navies before this latest era of engagement. Three distinct periods in the naval relationship, set against their respective political contexts, will then be discussed culminating in the collapse of cooperation in March 2014 and the present deep freeze in the UK–Russia relationship.

Naval cooperation and dialogue after the Cold War also presents an opportunity to examine the lessons learned by both sides about each other, including the RN and allied navies' inadvertent contribution to the development of Russian naval policy. The twenty-five years of engagement opened a unique window into Russian naval culture and thinking, with many of the traits observed then still prevalent today. On the one hand, an autocratic top-down approach and very slow bureaucratic decision-making, coupled with natural Russian paranoia, secrecy and brutal violence. On the other hand, a warmth and generosity of spirit of the Russians, accompanied by good humour and often unlimited vodka, which oiled the cogs of diplomacy, broke down barriers and 'got business done'. Given the many often distorted views given by each side about the other in the current crisis, a human dimension to the RFN and the Russians, good and bad, is provided through the personal anecdotes from those who engaged closely with the personnel of the RFN and from the authors themselves. These lessons and lived experience help provide a better and necessary understanding of the strategic culture of both the RFN and Russia and why its navy, and indeed the country, often operates in a manner alien or unintelligible to a Western mindset but which, nevertheless, has a logic of its own.

Defence engagement between the UK and Russia predominantly takes place in the maritime, air, space and cyber environments across three key strands of engagement, namely Defend, Deter and Dialogue. For the foreseeable future and in an era of global confrontation and competition with Russia, the focus for the UK, and other NATO allies, will be on Defend and Deter and much of that effort will be at sea and long term. Post Ukraine, there will be a danger of focusing the aperture of 'collective defence' back into Europe but in most scenarios, confrontation and competition with Russia will play out in the global commons and not in the European land environment, where the tripwires are much better defined on both sides. Indeed, the UK's 'crown jewels' to defend are all maritime by nature: the Continuous at Sea (nuclear) Deterrent (CASD), its at-sea Critical National Infrastructure (CNI), in particular subsea cables, and a key tool of military power projection and contribution to NATO, the two aircraft carriers. These 'crown jewels' are key targets for Russia and the RN plays a leading role, together with the RAF, in the defence of all three.

The 1988–2014 period of dialogue and cooperation taught us much about the navy we now need to defend against and deter, about its ambition and the way in which it operates. Peter the Great's guiding principle after he founded the Russian Navy in 1696 was that 'any power with only an army has but one arm, whilst the power with a navy has both arms'.[3] A nation's navy is a symbol of power and a projection of that power worldwide to protect and promote its national interests. Both the UK and Russia, through their respective navies, aspire to be global maritime powers. Both have developed and are developing maritime capabilities to achieve their aims, above and below water, with Russia's advanced capabilities to hold the UK's CNI at risk, of particular note. There is a tendency to focus on this acute threat to the UK homeland from Russia, often characterised as a regional power, while the rise of China in the Indo-Pacific region is seen as posing 'the greatest challenge to the UK's overseas interests and economic security'.[4] The UK's military doctrine states that the Russian Federation is viewed by NATO as the most direct threat to peace and stability in the Euro-Atlantic area.[5] While that may be the case, when compared to China, it also infers that Russia, its navy and its interests are confined to the Euro-Atlantic region. They are not and nor does Russia perceive them to be. Through geography alone, Russia stretches from the Atlantic to the High North to the Pacific. As well as the Northern and Pacific Fleets, it also maintains fleets and bases in the Baltic, the Black Sea, the Caspian Sea and the Mediterranean Sea, although the future of the base in Tartus, Syria is unclear following Bashar al-Assad's fall in December 2024. It also has agreements with many nations to use their port facilities to support its naval operations worldwide. The RFN is, therefore, an ubiquitous, global presence and Russia is building a navy, albeit in the face of significant challenges, that seeks to compete in the global commons, in order to meet Russia's geo-strategic and geo-economic ambitions.

The book will therefore consider the type of navy that Russia is seeking to procure and operate as it pursues its global maritime ambition, while highlighting some of the constraints and weaknesses it faces in achieving its aims. We also need to be mindful that the RFN has not been fully committed to the Ukraine campaign and has continued operating Russia's sea-based strategic nuclear forces and conducting other maritime operations and defence diplomacy activities worldwide. This means it has continued and will continue to pose a persistent challenge at sea to the UK and the West, despite the losses it has suffered in the Black Sea during the Ukraine war. This has included high levels of expenditure of a key maritime capability, *Kalibr* land-attack cruise missiles (LACM), which have caused so much destruction in Ukraine's cities and towns. The Ukraine conflict is also driving Russia's maritime innovation and procurement, especially in the field of sea-based drones where Ukraine has demonstrated its proficiency to Russia's cost.

The RN will also likely lead on the third strand of defence engagement with Russia – Dialogue. Conflicts and wars do end – what then? Whatever longer term strategy emerges towards Russia from the Euro-Atlantic community after the Ukraine conflict, military dialogue and re-engagement will be factors to consider, no matter how implausible that seems at present. For sure, it seems highly unlikely in the near to medium term given the depth of political rupture between Russia and the West and the devastation, death and destruction caused to Ukraine by Russia's invasion. But it does need to be thought about. Policy- and decision-makers, civilian and military, need to be as well prepared and informed as they can be for whenever that moment arises and this book contributes to that process. Drawing on what was achieved from 1988 to 2014 between the RN and RFN, the book will provide suggestions and thoughts that aim to act as a guide on any future defence dialogue, and even cooperation with Russia, as and when the political relationship allows. It will also argue that the maritime environment provides a potential pathway towards and a model for broader political coexistence between Russia and the UK and its allies, which all sides have ultimately failed to achieve for many decades, or even longer.

No matter how long it might take to re-establish military dialogue and cooperation with Russia post Ukraine, the 1988–2014 period of engagement provided the most unique first-hand insight to the RFN, and other elements of the Russian armed forces, since the 1917 October Revolution. It also provided a better understanding of the Russians and their world view, however much we might have disagreed, and do disagree, with many elements of it. The lessons learned from this period also have longevity. Russian culture and thinking is conservative and seldom changes, especially in the military. Their belief and views about the West's determination to constrain or destroy Russia are likely to remain prevalent long after the conclusion of the Ukraine conflict.

The perspective on the RFN presented in this book and the lessons learned will help those serving in the RN and other navies to develop a better understanding of their fellow mariners in the RFN. This is important because one thing is certain. For those serving in their respective navies today, and in the long term, whether it be through cooperation, competition or confrontation, Russia's navy will play an important and challenging role.

Notes

1 M. E. Sarotte, *Not One Inch: America, Russia and the Making of the Post-Cold War Stalemate*. Yale, CT: Yale University Press, 2021.

2 UK Arms Control teams were run by the JACIG established in 1990. The RRP retrained thousands of retired Russian officers at centres around Russia, to ensure a smooth transition from military to civilian life.
3 Peter the Great, *Kniga Ustav morskoi* (Naval Regulations) 1720. Foreword written by Peter himself, p. 1.
4 'Chief of Defence Intelligence RUSI Webinar May 2023', *Ministry of Defence London*, 30 May 2023, www.gov.uk/government/news/chief-of-defence-intelligence-rusi-webinar-may-2023 (accessed 2 June 2023).
5 'Joint Doctrine Publication 0-01 UK Defence Doctrine – 6th Edition', *Ministry of Defence London*, November 2022, p. 4.

Acknowledgements

This book represents the outcome of a conversation we began in 2018 based on the observation of the constantly deteriorating relationship between the Euro-Atlantic community and Russia, following the latter's annexation of Crimea in 2014. This discord was exacerbated in March 2018 by the events in Salisbury, UK and the attempted murder of the former Russian military intelligence officer Sergei Skripal and his daughter, Yulia with Novichok and the death of Dawn Sturgess. This led to British accusations of Russian state involvement and the expulsion of diplomats and intelligence officers from a number of Western Allies' countries.

Against the background of this worsening relationship between Russia and the West, it was becoming very clear that the achievements of what had once been a cooperative, although not without its problems, military-to-military relationship between the UK and Russia was being forgotten. History has taught us, however, that at some stage dialogue, political and military, will need to be re-established, no matter how implausible that might appear in 2024. Thus, the book, based on our and others' lived experiences of dealing with the Russians and the Russian Navy, aims to capture the lessons of what was achieved in the successful bilateral naval relationship between 1988 and 2014 and to offer recommendations about how one day we might re-engage with the Russian military. The book also underlines the importance of the sea in the UK–Russia relationship and how Moscow is pursuing an ambitious maritime strategy that will persistently challenge not just the Royal Navy but all navies in the Euro-Atlantic community and worldwide, and against which we will, for now, need to defend and deter.

A large number of individuals have contributed and influenced the thinking within the book, its content and structure. In particular, we owe a deep debt of gratitude to Dr Andrew Monaghan whose wise counsel, support and encouragement has frequently kept us on the straight and narrow. So too, to Captain Jon Holloway, who not only provided us with excellent material from his time in Moscow but also his first-hand account of the rescue of the Russian submersible, *Priz*, in 2005. We are also grateful to him for taking the time to read an early draft of the book, and also to our other reviewers who provided thoughtful and supportive comments namely, Dr Steven Main, George Ellis and Antony Wells. A special thanks also to Admiral Sir Jock and Lady Annie Slater for additional background material on Admiral Samuel Greig and to Vice Admiral Sir Tim McClement, Vice Admiral Charles Style, Colonel Charlie Wilson and Captain Chris Page for their personal accounts of engaging with personnel from the Russian Navy and Russian Naval Infantry. Additionally, we would like to thank Admiral Sir Jonathon Band, Vice Admiral Sir Tony Johnstone-Burt, Dr Richard Connolly, Rear Admiral Tim Lowe and Commodore Jim Perks for their invaluable insights and Lieutenant Colonel David Mason for his early support in the project. We are also extremely grateful to Admiral Sir Mark Stanhope, for his strong backing of the book and for providing the Foreword. We would also like to thank Manchester University Press for their support for the project and to the three anonymous reviewers for their very useful comments.

There are also two other groups of people to thank, without whom there would have been nothing to write about. The Naval and Assistant Naval Attaches, supported by their families during sometimes difficult times in Moscow, who worked tirelessly to facilitate cooperation between the two navies. Also we should recognise the contribution of all the 'luvvie' Royal Naval Russian interpreters, who enhanced the personal relationships between the personnel of the two navies and enabled them to communicate. Their contribution to the success of the cooperation programme between the Royal Navy and Russian Navy is immeasurable.

The paperback edition of this book was made possible with the generous support of The Gosling Foundation.

Abbreviations

ACNS	Assistant Chief of Naval Staff
AFB	Air Force Base
AMEC	Arctic Military Environmental Cooperation Agreement
ANA	Assistant Naval Attache
ASW	Anti-submarine warfare
AUKUS	Australia–UK–US Security Pact
BALTFL(O)T	Baltic Fleet (of Russian Navy)
BALTOPS	Baltic Operations (exercise)
BLKFL(O)T	Black Sea Fleet (of Russian Navy)
BRIXMIS	British Commanders'-in-Chief Mission to Soviet Forces in GDR
C1R	Captain First Rank (= RN Captain)
C2	Command and Control
C2R	Captain Second Rank (= RN Commander)
C3R	Captain Third Rank (= RN Lt Commander)
CASD	Continuous At-Sea Deterrent (nuclear)
CBM	Confidence-Building Measure(s)
C-in-C	Commander-in-Chief
CINCEASTLANT	Commander-in-Chief East Atlantic
CINCLANTFLT	Commander-in-Chief Atlantic Fleet
CINCNAVHOME	Commander-in-Chief Naval Home Command
CNI	Critical National Infrastructure
CNS	Chief of Naval Staff
COMUKMARFOR	Commander UK Maritime Forces
COS	Chief of Staff
CTG	Commander Task Group
DCLC	Defence Centre for Languages and Culture (at Shrivenham since 2014)
DES	Defence Engagement School
DISTEX	Disaster-relief exercise

DSL	Defence School of Languages (at Beaconsfield 1985–2014)
EXTAC	Maritime Manoeuvring and Tactical Procedures (manual)
FIS	Foundation for International Security
FLYCO	Flying Control Position
FOC	Full Operating Capability
FOF1	Flag Officer First Flotilla
FOF2	Flag Officer Second Flotilla
FOSF	Flag Officer Surface Flotilla
FOST	Fleet Operational (before May 2020: Flag Officer) Sea Training
FPB	Fast patrol boat
FPDA	Five-Power Defence Agreement (Australia–NZ–Singapore–Malaysia–UK)
FPV	First-Person View drone (with real-time camera)
FROD	Functionally-related observable difference(s) (in arms control)
FRUKUS	France–Russia–UK–US cooperation (succeeded RUKUS 2002)
FSB	Federal Security Service
G8GPP	G8 Global Partnership Programme
GPV	State Armament Programme
GRU	Main Intelligence Directorate of the General Staff
GUGI	Main Directorate of Deep-Sea Research
GUMVS	Main Directorate for International Military Cooperation
GUNIO	(Russian) Main Directorate for Navigation and Oceanography
HUMINT	Human Intelligence(-gathering)
ICBM	Inter-continental ballistic missile
IMDS	International Maritime Defence Show
INCSEA	Incidents at Sea Agreement
IOC	Initial Operating Capability
IR	Integrated (Defence and Security) Review (2021)
JACIG	Joint Arms Control Implementation Group
KGB	Committee for State Security
KNA	Kuznetsov Naval Academy St Petersburg
LACM	Land-attack cruise missile
MFA	Ministry of Foreign Affairs
MIC	Military-Industrial Complex
MPA	Maritime Patrol Aircraft (anti-submarine)

MOU	Memorandum of Understanding
MTCA	Military Technical Cooperation Agreement
MWC	Maritime Warfare Centre
NA	Naval Attache
NDMC	(Russian) National Defence Management Centre
NORFL(O)T	Northern Fleet (of Russian Navy)
NSR	Northern Sea Route
NSRS	NATO Submarine Rescue System
OOW	Officer of the Watch
OPCON	Operational Control
OSCE	Organisation for Security and Co-operation in Europe
OSK	United Shipbuilding Corporation
PACFL(O)T	Pacific Fleet (of Russian Navy)
PFP	Partnership for Peace
PKM	Kalashnikov machine-gun (modernised)
RAS	Replenishment at Sea
RASH	Radar-Absorbent SHeet(ing)
RBIO	Rules-Based International Order
RBU	Anti-submarine rocket launcher (Russian)
RFN	Russian Federation Navy
RFS	Russian Federation Ship
RM	Royal Marines
RN	Royal Navy
RNI	Russian Naval Infantry
ROE	Rules of Engagement
ROV	Remotely Operated Vehicle
RPG	Rocket-Propelled Grenade (launcher)
RUKUS	Russia–UK–US cooperation agreement
SACEUR	Supreme Allied Commander Europe (NATO)
SACLANT	Supreme Allied Commander Atlantic (NATO)
SAR	Search and Rescue
SAREX	Search and Rescue Exercise
SIGINT	Signals Intelligence
SLOC	Sea Line(s) of Communication
SN	Soviet Navy
SNAF	Soviet Naval Air Force
SNAPS	Satellite Navigation Position System
SOXMIS	Soviet Exercise Mission (observers) in West Germany
SPNI	Saint Petersburg Naval Institute
SPNI	Saint Petersburg Naval Institute (College)
SSBN	Nuclear-powered ballistic-missile-armed submarine

SSGN	Nuclear-powered cruise-missile-armed submarine
SSK	Diesel-electric-powered submarine
SSN	Nuclear-powered torpedo-armed submarine
TNW	Tactical Nuclear Weapon
UAV	Uncrewed Aerial Vehicle
UKHO	United Kingdom Hydrographic Office
UKSRS	United Kingdom Submarine Rescue System
USV	Uncrewed Surface Vehicle
UUV	Uncrewed Underwater Vehicle
WO(CY)	Warrant Officer (Communications Yeoman)

1

A concise history of the Russian Navy

Russian naval history has been punctuated with sharp rises and declines in Russian naval power driven by both political and military upheavals. As a land-locked state with no coastline, Russia had no sea-going navy before 1696, except for access to the White Sea in the far north. To create his navy almost from scratch, Peter the Great took as models the two leading sea powers of the age – England and Holland. Being a hands-on operator, he spent four and a half months in Dutch shipyards in 1697 using the thinly veiled alias of carpenter Pyotr Mikhailov, followed by three months in England, mainly at Deptford, London. At the start of 1698, he gained practical experience of how sea-going ships were built, preferring the more process-based and mathematical approach of the English builders to the more ad hoc approach of the Dutch. He established a relationship with William of Orange, who was also King William III of England, and attended a naval review at Spithead. The Tsar appreciated the British first and foremost as seafarers, as encapsulated in a statement recorded by the British engineer John Perry that 'he [Peter] thinks it a much happier life to be an Admiral in England, than Czar in Russia'. As well as practically destroying the house of his host, the diarist John Evelyn, during a party resulting in the then huge repair bill of £350 9s 6d (about £45,000 in 2024), he began recruiting British and Dutch shipbuilders and sailors to create Russia's fleet.[1] By 1703, the Navy numbered about twenty-eight thousand men, forty-nine ships and some eight hundred lesser craft. This force was crucial to defeating the Swedes in the Baltic and securing a toe-hold on the Baltic coast, where Peter founded St Petersburg – his 'window into Europe'.

The British naval link continued after Peter's death – the Russian victory over the Turkish fleet at Chesme in 1770 owed much to the British contribution from Rear Admiral John Elphinstone and Captains Dugdale and Mackenzie. At the Battle of Hogland (1788) in which the Swedes were defeated, the Russian fleet was commanded by the Scottish Admiral Samuel Greig (at that time a Commodore) with nine of the seventeen Russian ships of the line commanded by British captains.[2] It has been claimed that at one time in Catherine the Great's reign (1762–96), over half the entire list of officers in the Russian Navy were British.[3] In the Napoleonic Wars, there was considerable cooperation between Nelson and the Russian Navy under Admiral Fyodor Ushakov in the Mediterranean. At the Battle of Navarino in 1827, a combined British-French-Russian squadron under the command of Vice Admiral Sir Edward Codrington defeated a Turkish force, a battle crucial to securing the independence of Greece from the Ottoman Empire.

The nineteenth century saw the transition from the age of sail to the age of steam. However, Russia's slow technical and economic development in the first half of the nineteenth century caused the country to fall behind other world powers in the field of steamship construction. At the outbreak of the Crimean War in 1853, steamships were few and sailing ships predominated. The Battle of Sinope, won by Pavel Nakhimov, is remembered in history as the last significant naval battle involving sailing ships, but also saw the first use of shell-firing guns by any navy, which allowed the Russians to set the anchored Turkish fleet alight.

Russian naval advances in the nineteenth century, however, were brought to an end at the beginning of the twentieth century by the battle of Tsushima Straits in the Russo–Japanese war of 1904–5. The Russian Pacific Fleet was unprepared for the might of the Japanese Navy. To reinforce the Pacific Fleet, a decision was made to send a sizeable contingent of the Baltic Fleet around Africa and through the Indian Ocean. By the time the fleet neared Japan its ships and men were weary and worn out from the 220-day transit. The Japanese Navy secured a swift victory. In 1913, plans were made to rebuild the navy that was lost at Tsushima but the programme was barely beginning when a key political upheaval thwarted progress[4] – the October 1917 Russian Revolution.

When the Bolsheviks finally established control over Russia after the Russian Civil War, its naval forces were in disarray and a significant portion that had survived Tsushima and World War I left the country carrying refugees to various Western countries. Under Stalin, ambitious plans for massive industrialisation were undertaken and these plans included the recapitalisation of shipyards in Leningrad and Nikolayev (now Mykolayiv in Ukraine) and the construction of an entirely new shipyard in Severodvinsk on the White Sea.[5] Designs were drawn up for new ships and submarines but again barely had the construction of a new navy begun when, in 1939, World War II broke out. The Molotov-Ribbentrop pact of 1939 gave the USSR two years' 'breathing space' before Germany launched its surprise attack on the USSR in 1941. This marked the start of the USSR's Great Patriotic War, a cataclysmic event which continues to resonate deeply within Russian politics and society. Germany's land campaign was supported by its navy which effectively bottled in the Baltic Fleet once it withdrew to bases in and near

Leningrad. The Soviet Northern Fleet which was just being developed in the 1930s was also forced into a defensive posture and the Black Sea Fleet was significantly diminished with the capture of Sevastopol.

With Germany defeated and the wartime alliance between the West and the Soviet Union now entering the Cold War, both sides began to develop new naval programmes. The acquisition of German technology, documentation and scientists allowed both the USSR and the West to advance their naval capabilities. The war had shown the utility of longer range weapons such as the German V-1 flying bomb cruise missiles and the V-2 ballistic missiles and these became the starting points for the development of whole families of ground and sea-based launched weapons. When cruise and ballistic missiles were added to submarines, the capability to hold an adversary at risk or the ability to launch a surprise attack was greatly increased. By the 1960s, under the visionary leadership of Admiral Gorshkov and through his personal connections with the leadership of the Communist Party and government, the USSR had built and was continuing to construct an impressive Navy.[6]

Gorshkov's programme of rebuilding the Soviet Navy was the start of the journey to the type of navy envisaged in 2030 and beyond, with the focus on defence against a threat to Russia. Gorshkov designed a fleet to do this through a powerful combination of submarines, surface ships and naval aviation to destroy, in particular, US aircraft carrier groups at range. As a proponent of submarines and small missile-armed combatants, Gorshkov considered that submarines were the prime reason for the Navy's importance, and surface combatants and aircraft were constructed to protect the submarine force.[7]

A land power, which relied on its army to defend it, the Soviet Union had viewed the Navy as little more than a coastal force, an adjunct of the army incapable of projecting significant naval power on the high seas.[8] Gorshkov, although still mindful of the Navy's role of supporting the army in a conventional war, also recognised the supremacy of US naval power and its ability to project that power at range against the Soviet Union and more broadly threaten its interests globally. Gorshkov said, 'in their aggressive plans, the transoceanic imperialists are giving a leading role to their navies. For this reason, we too have to create a fleet capable of reliably protecting our motherland and guaranteeing its state interests on the seas and oceans.'[9] By 1974 the Soviet Navy had 245 active nuclear-powered and diesel-electric submarines and 222 major surface warships and in addition there were sixty-one nuclear-powered ballistic-missile submarines. In response to the mention of the huge numbers of hastily built platforms with a tone that questioned their quality, a Soviet naval officer reportedly said 'quantity has a quality of its own'.

But yet again, just when this apparently impressive-sized Navy appeared to be at its zenith, another calamity beset the country – the collapse of the Soviet Union. It showed a system that was rotten to the core and broke. The Navy was not immune and – as they and we were to find out – quantity certainly did not have a quality of its own. It was obvious in the early 1990s that much of Gorshkov's once-impressive Navy was inoperative, obsolete or in need of more attention than the results would merit. In the course of about ten years from 1995 to 2005, the Russian naval leadership had to make painful decisions and the choices were stark: try to save most and lose all or try to maintain the most capable and invest in the future. Unsurprisingly, they chose the latter. The fallow years of the 1990s and early 2000s were used to design and develop new more modern and capable platforms and systems, which enabled the Navy to take the lion's share of the well-funded Russian defence modernisation programme from 2010 to 2020. But as history has shown, political upheavals frequently thwart the progress of building a Russian Navy, and events since 2014 have certainly had an impact on ship building and, to a lesser extent, submarine building. However, as discussed later, the impact is in no way as catastrophic as that experienced by the Russian Navy after the 1917 October Revolution and the outbreak of World War II.

Notes

1 L. Hughes, *Peter the Great: A Biography*. Yale, CT, Yale University Press, 2002, pp. 50–51.
2 B. Ranft and G. Till, *The Sea in Soviet Strategy*. London, Macmillan, 1983, p. 8.
3 Fred T. Jane, *The Imperial Russian Navy*. London, Thacker & Co, 1904, p. 78.
4 'The Russian Navy: A Historic Transition', Office of Naval Intelligence, December 2015, https://apps.dtic.mil/sti/pdfs/AD1011686.pdf (accessed 12 February 2023).
5 *Ibid.*, p. XV.
6 *Ibid.*, p. xvii.
7 Bruce Watson, *Red Navy at Sea Soviet Naval Operations on the High Seas 1956–1980*. Boulder, CO, Westview Press, 1982, p. 3.
8 *Ibid.*, p. 2.
9 *Ibid.*, p. 5.

2

Pre-1988 UK–Russia naval relations

Russians enjoy and study history and are generally well informed in this regard – so we should be too. As well as understanding the history of Russia's navies, it is important to be aware of the history of maritime relations between the UK and Russia, to fully grasp the significance of the 1988–2014 period. Apart from minor engagements during the 1807–12 period of Russia's alliance with Napoleon, the Crimean War (1853–56), with naval actions in the Baltic and the Pacific, and the Allied intervention in Russia following the 1917 October Revolution (1919–20), with landings in North Russia and hostilities in the Baltic, mark the only two significant naval conflicts between Russia and Britain. In 1907, the Triple Entente between Great Britain, France and Russia was signed to counter the growing threat of Germany, Italy and Austria-Hungary – just fifty-one years after the end of the Crimean War: a good illustration of how former enemies can become allies in the face of a perceived greater threat from outside. In a remarkable piece of naval diplomacy on the eve of World War I in June 1914, Britain sent the First Battle-Cruiser Squadron on a courtesy visit to Kronstadt. Under the command of the charismatic Rear Admiral David Beatty, HM Ships *Lion*, *Princess Royal*, *Queen Mary* and *New Zealand* represented the technological cutting edge of the Royal Navy and must have created a powerful impression on the hosts. On completion of an extravagant stay, the ships – three of them the largest in the world – put to sea for tactical exercises with Tsar Nicholas II embarked as an observer.[1]

Between 1920 and 1941 there was no naval cooperation between the two navies, although surprisingly the Soviet battleship *Marat* attended King George VI's Coronation Review at Spithead in 1937. However, World War II saw resumed cooperation between the two navies against the common Nazi enemy, which included the loan of HMS *Royal Sovereign*, a *Resolution*-class battleship to the Soviet Navy, which served in the Northern Fleet as *Arkhangelsk* in 1944–48.

But it was the Arctic Convoys where the real cooperation happened. In July 1941 exchange naval missions, including British teams in Polyarny and

Arkhangelsk, were set up to agree boundaries between operational zones, and the establishment of logistic support and convoy protection. The first convoy of material for Russia, Operation Dervish, left Liverpool on 12 August 1941, safely reaching Arkhangelsk on 31 August. By 1945, around 1,400 merchant ships had made the perilous journey to ports in northern Russia during forty-two convoys. More than three thousand sailors, Royal Navy and merchant seamen, sacrificed their lives delivering more than four million tonnes of supplies: tanks, fighters, trucks, fuel, ammunition and food. Some eighty-five merchant ships never made it and nor did sixteen Royal Navy warships, which provided escort for them in the face of attacks from the German surface fleet, U-boats and Luftwaffe.[2]

The bonds formed between those who took part in the convoys, a voyage described by Winston Churchill, the Prime Minister, as the 'worst journey in the world', and the Russians were immensely strong and deeply personal, as witnessed by many at the various commemoration events over the last eighty years. However, it was only at the end of 2012, that the sacrifice and contribution of the convoy veterans was formally acknowledged by the UK with the award of the Arctic Star to those personnel who had served in the air forces, naval forces and merchant navy in support of the convoys. The institution of the medal, along with the Bomber Command Clasp, was the end result of a sixteen-year-long campaign by Commander Eddie Grenfell, Lieutenant Commander Dick Dykes and merchant navy veteran Jock Dempster, who stressed that service in the Arctic Convoys north of the Arctic Circle was entirely different from that in the Atlantic, for which the Atlantic Star had been awarded.

The institution of the Arctic Star paved the way for the unusual step of enabling Russia in 2013 to award its own recognition for the living survivors of the Arctic Convoys, the Ushakov Medal. The medal is named after Russia's most acclaimed Navy Commander Fyodor Ushakov, and is a State Military Award of the Russian Federation that was originally established in 1944, especially for those who demonstrated courage and prowess in sea warfare. During his visit to Downing Street in June 2013, President Putin awarded the first medals and several hundred have been awarded since.[3]

In 2012 the Russian government funded the replacement of HMS *Belfast*'s[4] two masts which had become dangerously corroded. The new masts were constructed at the St Petersburg Severnaya Verf shipyard and floated by barge to London where they were fitted by a team of Russian engineers and inaugurated by HRH Prince Philip.

After the end of the Arctic convoys and World War II in 1945, HMS *Triumph*, wearing the flag of Admiral Sir Bruce Fraser, and HMS *Rapid* visited Leningrad for ten days in July 1946. Fraser met the Baltic Fleet Commander, Admiral Tributs, and travelled on to Moscow for talks with the People's Commissar for the Navy, Admiral of the Fleet Kuznetsov. This was the first visit of a RN ship to Leningrad since before the 1917 October Revolution.

In the ensuing years, relations between East and West froze into the Cold War and for over forty years the relationship between Royal and Soviet Navies was one of confrontation but not combat. However, this was not a total deep freeze and sporadic goodwill ship visits did take place, albeit only nine visits in forty-three years.

The cruiser *Sverdlov* attended the Coronation Review in June 1953. The ship returned to Portsmouth in October 1955, wearing the flag of Baltic Fleet Commander Admiral Golovko, with the cruiser *Aleksandr Suvorov* plus destroyers *Smetlivy*, *Smotryashchy*, *Sovershenny* and *Sposobny*, coinciding with a reciprocal visit to Leningrad by the aircraft carrier HMS *Triumph* (C-in-C Home Fleet Admiral Sir Michael Denny embarked) plus five ships (minelayer *Apollo*, destroyers *Decoy*, *Diana*, *Chevron and Chieftain*). These visits were sufficiently out-of-the-ordinary to attract extensive coverage in the UK press. Less brimming with goodwill was the visit of *Sverdlov*'s sister ship, *Ordzhonikidze*, with Khrushchev and his premier Bulganin embarked, to Portsmouth in 1956. During this visit, the diver Cdr Lionel 'Buster' Crabb, recruited by MI6 to investigate the cruiser, disappeared and was never found. A headless corpse was discovered fourteen months later but could not be formally identified as Crabb. Nevertheless, goodwill visits continued intermittently, with HMS *Devonshire* visiting Odessa and the *Kashin*-class *Obraztsovy* calling into Portsmouth in 1976, before the Soviet invasion of Afghanistan in December 1979 put paid to navy-to-navy relations for over a decade.

With the elevation of Mikhail Gorbachev to the post of General Secretary of the Communist Party of the Soviet Union in 1985 and the advent of his reform programme under the keyword 'perestroika' ('reconstruction'), a slow thaw in East–West relations began and this began to affect the RN–RFN relationship. HMS *Bristol* visited Leningrad in 1989 and the *Sovremenny*-class destroyer *Bezuprechny* visited Portsmouth in July 1990, the first port call to the UK by a Soviet warship for fourteen years. Other more informal encounters were also taking place in the late 1980s such as that of HMS *Andromeda* with the *Udaloy*-class *Admiral Zakharov* in the Middle East, recounted below by Vice Admiral Charles Style CBE, HMS *Andromeda*'s then Commanding Officer. A highlight of interaction at sea in that period occurred in July 1985. HMS *Newcastle* was trailing the air-capable cruiser *Kiev* in the Barents Sea when a *Yak-38* strike fighter aircraft

Table 2.1 Warship visits RN–Soviet Navy 1945–88

RN ship (CO)	Place/event	Date	Ship (CO)	Place/event	Date
HMS *Triumph* and HMS *Rapid*	Leningrad (Flag: Admiral Sir Bruce Fraser) First RN ship to visit Leningrad since 1917	Jul 1946 (ten days)			
			Sverdlov (C1R Olimpii Ivanovich Rudakov)	Spithead – Coronation Naval Review	15 Jun 1953
			Sverdlov, Aleksandr Suvorov, Smetlivy, Smotryashchy, Sovershenny, Sposobny (Flag: Admiral Arsenyi Grigor'ievich Golovko – Commander Baltic Fleet)	Portsmouth	12–17 Oct 1955
HMS *Triumph*, HMS *Apollo*, HMS *Decoy*, HMS *Diana*, HMS *Chevron*, HMS *Chieftain*	Leningrad (Flag: Admiral Sir Michael Denny, Commander-in-Chief Home Fleet)	22 Oct 1955			
			Ordzhonikidze	Portsmouth (Flag: RAdm Vasily Fyodorovich Kotov – First Deputy Commander Baltic Fleet) Khrushchev and Bulganin embarked; Crabb incident	18–27 Apr 1956

HMS *Devonshire* and RFA *Oleander*	Leningrad (Flag: Admiral Sir John Byng Frewen – Commander-in-Chief Home Fleet)		Oct 1966
		Obraztsovy (Flag: Mikhail Vasil'ievich Mikhailin – Commander Baltic Fleet CO C2R Vladimir Ivanovich Vlasov)	Portsmouth	6–10 June 1967
HMS *Devonshire*	Odessa Last RN ship to visit USSR before Soviet invasion of Afghanistan 1979		May 1976
		Obraztsovy	Portsmouth Last Soviet warship to visit UK before Soviet invasion of Afghanistan 1979	May 1976

(NATO: Forger) crashed into the sea within a few hundred yards of *Kiev* as it attempted to land on the carrier. A sea boat from *Newcastle* was quickly on the scene to rescue the pilot who had ejected and to help him into a rescue strop lowered from a Soviet helicopter. Some years later, in June 1994, the Commandant of the Kaliningrad Higher Naval School, Rear Admiral Gennady Yasnitsky, personally thanked Vice Admiral Michael Boyce (then FOSF) for the RN's assistance that day. He had been the Commanding Officer of *Kiev* at the time. This episode illustrates the long memories Russians have and their gratitude in rescuing someone from the common enemy – the sea.[5]

The Russians and the Gulf – Vice Admiral Charles Style

HMS *Andromeda*, a steam-driven *Leander*-class frigate under my command, was deployed in 1988 to the Gulf. It was – joy of joys – a solo trip. Clearing the Strait of Gibraltar, some of us assembled on deck for 'sundowners': a drink as the light faded. As the ship rose and fell to a receding swell, the twinkling Spanish lights to port, and the red – turning grey – illumination of the Moroccan ridges to starboard, provided one of those sights seafarers never forget. We were bound for Suez; a distance of 2,500 miles before we turned south for the tropics.

Reaching Port Said in the evening, we entered the canal. Operated by a concessionary company whose shareholders were mainly British and French until Nasser nationalised it in 1956, this waterway shortened the maritime route between London and Bombay by about 4,500 miles. At a temporary night anchorage, about two thirds of the way down in the Bitter Lakes, our pilot – a shifty and taciturn fellow – demanded I sign authorisation for an additional payment, and refused to take us further if I did not. We were in a hurry following unplanned repairs before departure, and could not afford a delay. I signed the form which he shoved in my direction, adding the words 'under duress' beneath my signature, and reported this extortion to the Naval Attache. The pilot did his job up to a point, but earned a black mark in the embassy and did not receive his extra payment.

We were soon out into the Red Sea, made our way southwards across waters now once again the scene of confrontation, then through the Bab-El-Mendeb strait between Yemen to port and Djibouti and Eritrea to starboard before turning north-east. The sea was glassy, the tropical heat sweltering, although the head wind on the bridge wing made this an attractive place to relax.

Soon we were joined by escorts of flying fish bursting like silver darts from the bow waves and fanning out over a hundred yards or more; their evolution had provided them with fins designed to act as wings, and taught them how to harness 'ground effect' to skim the water. It took Soviet and American (with post-war German) know-how to convert understanding of the effect into usable technology which in the Soviet Union was first exploited in the form of the famous 'Caspian Sea Monster'.

In the open sea we passed Ra's al-Hadd, the eastern point of Arabia, and turned north west up the Gulf of Oman towards the Strait of Hormuz through which passed ships entitled to British protection in and out of the Gulf. The Iranians, the northern gate-keepers – as they saw it – of this most vital of choke points, were prone to threatening tankers carrying oil from the northern Gulf.

I already knew of course that it was not only Britain who provided such a service to merchant ships in the Gulf. Our first encounter was not Iranian. As we approached the narrowest part of the Strait, a Soviet warship of the *Udaloy* class – the *Admiral Zakharov* of seven thousand tons and thus two and a half times our displacement – hovered at the edge of the inbound lane. By VHF radio we were invited – or perhaps it sounded more like instructed – to turn away; main armament guns were trained on us. The Captain may well have known I was new in command, and on the young side. I felt sure he was testing my mettle. I replied we were about our lawful business, and would not deviate from the lane within which we had right of passage. He slowly moved aside.

Then one day, while alongside in Abu Dhabi, we heard that *Admiral Zakharov* was about to enter harbour and would berth immediately astern of us. At the time, the start of the demolition of the Berlin Wall was a year away; elections in Eastern European countries (previously under communist regimes) followed. Then in late 1991 the Soviet Union started to dissolve into its component republics. The strategic atmosphere in 1988, however, remained much as it had been throughout the Cold War: tense, edgy, but easing under the influence of Gorbachev.

It was therefore most unusual and probably unprecedented to discover that we were about to share a jetty – tail to head – with a major Soviet ship of war, though one of HM Ships had encountered one in a Gulf port the year before. We got ready to gather what intelligence we could. This was a class of ship in which Britain still had a live intelligence interest.

From *Andromeda* we noticed their idiosyncratic uniforms, and the armed sentries at the bottom of the gangway. And much more besides. The question was 'what next?' A volleyball contest was arranged for 28 January 1989. By letter I offered to call on the Captain onboard *Zakharov*; back came a warm reply by return.

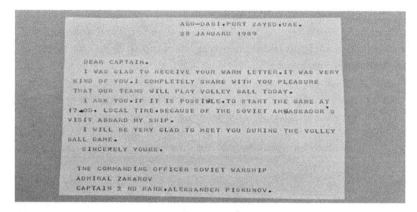

Figure 2.1 Memo from Piskunov about rescheduling volleyball game. © VAdm Charles Style.

We met ashore when watching the game together; *Andromeda* was roundly defeated. He then invited me to visit his ship.

This was certainly still in the unusual category; I genned up as fully as I could before walking up the jetty and stepping onto the gangway. Our naval upbringing and exercises had been all about potential war with the Soviet Union; certain documents in my safe likewise. At the head of the gangway, I was met by Captain First Rank Piskunov, my Soviet opposite number, and immediately taken on a tour of the ship. I noticed the radars and missile launchers and other fittings – all massive and painted in layers of dark dull grey paint – which we had come to recognise, and which we had been trained to counter. My overall impression was of weight, might, a dour dark atmosphere below decks, and perhaps some overpainting of corrosion.

In the Captain's cabin I spent a couple of hours chatting via an interpreter (no doubt the political officer), and comparing notes on our missions which were similar. I suggested we set up a communications link by which means we could deconflict our operations. This we subsequently did to good effect.

Captain Piskunov plied me with vodka in the hope of getting me plastered. In this he failed. However, my remark to him about this ploy – we were getting along well – led to a story about a similar rendezvous he remembered with an American ship. In this case the Captain had to be carried by Soviet sailors back to his gangway; or so he said. He laughed; if only I could remember how I reacted.

He accepted my suggestion of a return visit. I had made him a present of a bottle of whisky; this time the currency was vodka – naturally. So long did he stay that a platoon of armed Soviets marched to the bottom of our gangway and demanded to see him; they probably thought he'd been done in or whisked away. We appeared on deck in the sultry afternoon heat; he waved them off, and we went back to swapping stories.

As he was leaving, I suggested a race between our two ships once we were both at sea again; he agreed. We provided a rendezvous, and the rules. '3, 2, 1, go.' I knew of course that the outcome was a foregone conclusion: the same as the volleyball. His acceleration, accompanied by the growl of his powerful gas turbines, was something to behold. He won easily. With a wave, we went our separate ways. Thereafter we exchanged information by radio, and deconflicted easily.

Our daily moves were entirely driven by my wish to know the position of ships entitled to our protection on which we had reasonable intelligence, and to show up in order to provide reassurance. This was particularly important in the southern Gulf, and especially in the Strait. I always enjoyed fast and exact approaches to those enormous ships, often on a tight turn to positions close abeam, and persuaded myself they would give a reassuring impression. I was invited onboard one or two. Though in proportion at a distance, their size and tonnage were an eye opener. Their apparently low freeboard was in reality very high indeed. At normal speed, their stopping distances were measured in miles: as many as five when fully laden.

The formal practice of convoying entitled ships had been discontinued; our charges were therefore dispersed. The only case of directly threatening behaviour by the Iranians in the strait arose – inevitably – when we were some way away. Of course we turned towards the incident at our full thirty knots; a swarm of fast craft were menacing a tanker. The alarmed master of the tanker then reported that he was being boarded by – he thought – members of the Iranian Revolutionary Guard Corps. *Andromeda* would not get there in time. There was only one option; we 'scrambled' the Lynx helicopter which mounted a machine gun in one door. This form of urgent helicopter deployment meant that usual checks were dispensed with in the interests of speed. In moments my First Lieutenant (second-in-command) Steve Bramley and Flight Commander Des Tweedy appeared; I briefed them in a few sentences. I liked both; I trusted the former who was level-headed, and the latter because he was known as one of the very best helicopter pilots in the Service. I had several opportunities to see the latter launching and recovering in extreme conditions: the stuff of other stories.

Accordingly, I delegated full independent decision on action once they were up with the tanker, knowing that we would lose contact with the Lynx when at range and low. They were airborne in record time: a quarter of an hour from memory. I did not know, but later heard, that – on the way to the flight deck – Des poked his head into the wardroom, and enthusiastically told those present that 'the Captain says I can engage'. That was roughly it; but there were of course certain well rehearsed provisos! Onboard we went to action stations.

I subsequently heard that Steve and Des came upon a threatening scene indeed. However, almost immediately the Iranians departed from the tanker, and the small craft dispersed. I would like to think the helicopter's presence, and perhaps the implied proximity of *Andromeda* herself, may have had a positive effect. Who knows?

In December, the time came to head out of the Gulf for our Christmas stand-off in Mombasa. Before departure, I approached our Russian friend's anchorage where there were by now also two support ships. I stopped close abeam and sent over gifts by seaboat. A bottle of vodka, a friendly message and a whole lot of Soviet propaganda material came back. We waved our caps to each other as *Andromeda* departed. We never met again; I did, however, follow Captain Piskunov's successful career. It would be a pleasure to 'shoot the breeze' (in other words, reminisce) with him: an unlikely rendezvous, I suppose, in current dangerous times.

Five years later, in December 1993, I had a second brush with an *Udaloy* – the *Admiral Vinogradov* – when Britain was one of thirty-five members of a coalition opposing Iraq following its invasion of Kuwait. Our role was familiar, but this time I was commanding HMS *Campbeltown*. She was much younger, and more capable than dear old *Andromeda*. She was also one of a number of ships which had for the first time embarked women as members of her company; normal now, contentious then as entrenched all-male attitudes had to adjust, as did the 10 per cent of her company who were female. It was a rough path to tread at the time.

Basic exercises with *Vinogradov* were arranged. She was commanded by Captain Second Rank Sergei Tegentsev. The ship's grainy one-page pamphlet, gestetner printed in blue ink, contained these words. 'The vessel's crew represents 25 nationalities of the USSR. The age of the commissioned staff representing career officers – graduates from various military schools and academies averages 25. Eighty per cent of them are married. All warrant officers have completed special and technical secondary educational institutions Their average age is 23. Forty per cent of them are married. Men and petty officers are 18–21 years old. Three percent of them are married.'

The atmosphere in which we met this ship and her people was relaxed and open. The Captain was another jolly fellow, as were the two senior members of his team who came with him to visit *Campbeltown* at sea.

We also cross-decked our helicopters; this gave me the opportunity to fly in the Russian KA-27. The pilot was in full control, and flew the machine in a remarkably casual way while – I am fairly certain – smoking a cigarette. It had plenty of power, but the stick movements were heavy and rather extreme; even 'mushy', to use a non-technical phrase. I enjoyed the experience, while sizing up the door releases just in case!

On *Campbeltown*'s flight deck, Spetsnaz put on a show of hand-to-hand combat. They appeared to be enjoying themselves; we certainly were. I would not, however, have wanted to meet them on a dark night.

In retrospect, these were years of rapprochement which the Russians seemed to welcome as much as we did. Gorbachev brought his country into the 'family of nations'. Now we are in the middle of an international maelstrom while Putin misreads the tortured history of his own country. Dangerous and sad.

One makes unlikely friends at sea. All seafarers share a bond arising from the 'dangers of the sea' (our common enemy), humanity and sympathy between those who sail upon it, and the global obligation to mutual support between ships in the event of emergencies. War at sea can place obvious limitations; certain breaches by our enemy in World War II – at sea as well as elsewhere – were nonetheless abominable. Early rules were placed in a more formalised setting by the Geneva Convention in 1949. Captain Piskunov and the Captain of *Vinogradov* and I hit it off. It is the nature of our profession that, had the Cold War turned hot, *Andromeda* might just as well have found themselves in action against one or both. This would not have been an amusing prospect for *Andromeda*.

February 2024

From this tour d'horizon of Anglo-Russian naval relations two key points stand out. Firstly, there have been only two significant episodes of armed conflict between the two fleets, namely the Crimean War and the Intervention. There have been periods of mutual suspicion and confrontation, most notably the Cold War, but the general tenor of the relationship has been neutral or positive. This was frequently pointed out by the Russians during the various visits encapsulated by the phrase that 'we never saw you (RN) as enemies, only as adversaries'. Secondly, following a political rupture in relations between Russia and the UK, the RN has often been used to foster re-engagement in the military sphere. Ships' visits send strong diplomatic signals, the shared 'brotherhood' and dangers of operating at sea and the long enduring history between the two navies makes it easier in many ways for the RN to engage, compared to other branches of the armed forces.

Compared to the levels of cooperative naval interaction from 1945 to 1988, the period that then occurred to 2014 was a historically unique period of constructive cooperation between the two navies, both in length and depth. There were fifty-six ship visits, overwhelmingly as part of the UK–Russia bilateral programme and increasingly culminating in joint exercises at sea; fifty-eight visits involving flag officers, two of which involved heads of state using warships as diplomatic platforms, most notably the Royal Visit of HM Queen Elizabeth II to Russia embarked in HMY *Britannia* in October 1994 and three involving other members of the Royal Family. There were also several rounds of staff talks in London and Moscow, usually coinciding with the annual obligated discussions concerning the Prevention of Incidents at Sea agreement (INCSEA) signed in 1986. This period of interaction between the two navies provides a foundation on which to rebuild defence dialogue and will be discussed in more depth later when examining ways of how the UK might one day re-establish defence engagement with Russia after the Ukraine conflict.

Notes

1. S. Roskill, *Admiral of the Fleet Earl Beatty. The Last Naval Hero: An Intimate Biography*. London: William Collins, 1980, pp. 73–76.
2. 'Arctic Convoys', Institute of Contemporary British History, 2001.
3. 'President Putin Hands Top Bravery Honours to Arctic Convoy Veterans', *British Embassy Moscow*, 19 June 2013, www.gov.uk/government/news/president-putin-hands-top-bravery-honours-to-arctic-convoy-veterans (accessed 10 June 2023).
4. HMS *Belfast*, a Town-class cruiser commissioned in 1939, played a key role during the Arctic Convoys. The ship is now a museum moored on the River Thames near Tower Bridge, London.
5. Witnessed by Robert Avery as interpreter, conversation between Rear Admiral Gennady Pavlovich Yasnitsky and Vice Admiral Michael Boyce, Kaliningrad, June 1994.

3

1988–99 From confrontation to cooperation

Confidence-building measures (CBM)

It is easy to forget, thirty-five years on, what an extraordinary event the fall of the Berlin Wall in 1989 represented and the indelible memory early interaction between previous naval adversaries had on those who experienced it. The previous forty years had been one based on the fear of an escalation to 'hot' war between the Soviet Union and the West. The period was punctuated with major events such as the Cuban Missile Crisis, and from a maritime perspective littered with potentially serious incidents between NATO warships and those of the Soviet Navy and its Warsaw Pact allies, not least the 1970 collision between HMS *Ark Royal* and a *Kotlin*-class destroyer. Trust and confidence were in short supply, as indeed they will be post the current political crisis between Russia and the West.

A model for rebuilding the relationship after a serious political rupture, will possibly be through a series of CBM. These could, for example, include high-level talks, synchronised with working-level talks and visits in order to establish a minimal level of trust, avoid miscalculations and misunderstandings and improve understanding of Russian military capabilities and, importantly, intent so as to avoid future strategic surprises. This initial stage might then lead to more practical cooperation and interoperability at sea culminating in joint operations, primarily in constabulary maritime tasks such as counter-piracy or embargo operations.

INCSEA and Adderbury talks

This was the model that emerged towards the end of the 1980s and into the 1990s within a maritime context. In 1986, London and Moscow signed the INCSEA agreement, which remains in force today and was amended by a Protocol in 2021.[1] The US signed its INCSEA in 1972 and several other countries have also adopted their own bilateral INCSEAs. The agreements were made because it was recognised by the USSR and other countries that operations at sea in close proximity could have serious and unpredictable consequences and INCSEA represented diplomatic and practical steps to develop mechanisms to prevent them from occurring, or at least to mitigate the consequences if and when they did happen.

Referencing relevant provisions of the International Maritime Regulations and the International Code of Signals, the agreement includes specific instructions for keeping a safe distance from naval vessels of the other party and agreed measures to ensure caution in terms of speed of manoeuvres when in the vicinity of vessels of the other party. They further contain provisions on when and how to communicate each party's intentions and clear commitments to avoid undertaking actions that could cause embarrassment or danger to the naval forces of the other side. Negotiations and the obligated annual face-to-face review of incidents required by INCSEA, enabled interaction and dialogue between the parties even during the Cold War. Similarly when the political relationship was difficult between Russia and the UK prior to 2014, this was also the case.

Adderbury talks

The Adderbury talks were initiated by the Foundation for International Security FIS (UK), in collaboration with the American Committee for US-Soviet relations, which arranged a consultation in Moscow on common security in April 1988. The meeting was attended by senior academic experts and officials from the US, Europe and the Soviet Union. The result of this meeting was that Soviet participants felt that a dialogue on naval matters would be helpful in developing realistic CBMs, to further relations between the West and the USSR. In July 1988, the Director of FIS, Stan Windass, with the support of well-known naval historians Professors Geoff Till and Eric Grove, who were regular attendees at subsequent events, and the then Head of RN Defence Studies, Captain Wilson, convened the first set of talks at Stan Windass's house in Adderbury, Oxfordshire. The USSR's delegation of three, included Admiral Nikolai Amel'ko, after whom a new *Admiral Gorshkov*-class frigate was named in 2019. Amel'ko, a charismatic, engaging man, had been Commander of the Pacific Fleet in the 1960s and a former Deputy Chief of the General Staff. He was a key figure throughout the early Adderbury[2] and Russia–UK–US (RUKUS) programme of talks, encouraged more dialogue and cooperation, and frequently attended events around UK ship or Flag visits to St Petersburg.

The annual talks gained momentum and rotated mainly between the UK and US but Moscow also played its part in hosting, including a visit for the delegations to Sevastopol to go onboard the *Kara*-class cruiser, *Kerch*. Themes that emerged from the Soviet side, and which to a large extent remain key concerns in current Russian naval policy, were the land attack capabilities of Western carrier forces, with the additional threat of submarine-launched cruise missiles. This fear of sudden attack from the sea led to Soviet suggestions of including naval forces in arms reduction talks, so that neither side would have the capacity for a pre-emptive strike.

The third set of Adderbury talks at the end of 1989 made a significant shift from the previous talks in that they included serving Flag Officers and staff officers from all three countries, and most notably from the UK the then First Sea Lord, Admiral Sir Julian Oswald. Both authors were also present at these talks acting as interpreters throughout. The talks took place just a week after the fall of the Berlin Wall, adding a very historic atmosphere to the proceedings. The theme of the discussions centred around respective new naval strategies, which had been considered hostile towards each other in the past, and a desire to keep 'dialling down' the rhetoric. The USSR and US representatives emphasised that the Pacific was vital to both countries, and that more cooperation was required to fight the narcotic trade, piracy and to prevent ballistic missile proliferation. It is interesting to note that despite the fall of the Berlin Wall a week before, there was no sense of the impending calamity for the USSR as a superpower. The Soviet side's consistent theme was the defensive nature of its naval policy and its fleet, citing the fear of the combined might of Western maritime power. Most notable during these discussions was the Soviet delegation's claim that the possibility of using their submarines against Western Sea Lines of Communication (SLOCs) was practically non-existent. This was important because there had always been an assumption that this is exactly what the role of Soviet submarines would be used for, much like it had been for the German Navy in World Wars I and II.

A short history of the outcomes of each set of Adderbury and early RUKUS talks written in 1994 by Captain Chris Page, then Head of RN Defence Studies, is included here.

A short history of the Adderbury talks 1988–94

The Foundation for International Security, in collaboration with the American Committee for US–Soviet Relations, initiated a consultation on common security in April 1988. The meeting, held in Moscow, was attended by senior academic experts and officials from the USA, Europe and the Soviet Union. The result of this meeting was that Soviet participants felt that a dialogue on naval matters would be helpful in developing realistic confidence-building measures, to further relations between the West and the USSR.

Adderbury, 30/31 July 1988 – East–West conversations on naval strategy and arms control

The first in the series of the 'Adderbury' talks was held on 30–31 July 1988. This was held in an academic environment under the auspices of the Foundation for International Security, with representatives from the UK, USSR, and the USA. The proceedings were conducted on an 'off the record' basis. Western and Soviet naval strategies were described and discussed.

The Soviets expressed great concern over the land attack capabilities of Western carrier forces, with an additional threat from submarine launched cruise missiles. The subject of tactical nuclear weapons was also raised. One of the Soviets felt that all should be banned. However, others decided that they needed a nuclear capability, for example using Air Launched Cruise Missiles of the SNAF to counter the carrier threat.

The Americans emphasised the importance of Atlantic communications to defend Europe, thus the new Soviet bomber posed a particular threat. Discussion of nuclear weapons indicated that the West considered the most threatening Soviet weapons at sea to be long-range air-to-surface missiles. There was also an expression of a common interest in removing TNWs at sea.

Verification based on functionally related observable differences (FRODs) was suggested by one Soviet participant. There seemed to be a genuine willingness to exchange more details of equipment.

A possible link between asymmetrical arms reductions in land systems and naval forces was discussed, but it was agreed that the two should be pursued in parallel. Further to this, there was a suggestion that both sides should adopt a defensive strategy.

In conclusion, it was agreed that naval arms reductions would be difficult, the best initial course being to enhance confidence-building measures. Agreement was reached on the usefulness of the INCSEA forum in promoting confidence. Further to this there was a willingness by the Soviets to conduct exploratory talks involving highly placed officials.

Moscow, 20/21 February 1989 – consulations on limitations of naval activities and confidence-building measures at sea

This was a follow-up meeting, under joint auspices of FIS and the Soviet Committee for European Security and Cooperation. Again there were a number of academic representatives from the US, UK and the USSR.

The Soviet participants emphasised some important developments since the last meeting, e.g. implementation of the Intermediate Nuclear Forces treaty, withdrawal from Afghanistan and the impending visit of Gorbachev to the UK. They went on to identify problem areas, expressing concern over the US argument that it should be the preponderant naval power. The Soviets also were fearful of the possibility of a sudden attack from the sea. Soviet proposals included reducing forces so that neither side would have the capacity for a pre-emptive strike. In effect the Soviets were willing to trade their capability to interdict the SLOCs for a removal of the strike fleet threat to shore targets and also SSBNs.

The Soviets recognised the naval component as part of the strategic balance. They also considered the elimination of the entire nuclear arsenal, excepting Submarine Launched Ballistic Missiles, as attractive, because the selective use of such weapons could only lead to all out nuclear war.

The idea of using the INCSEA agreement as a foundation for expansion of ideas was reiterated. There was also agreement to an exchange of data on force levels, ship building programmes and the withdrawal of ships from operational use.

A significant event was the visit by the Western group to the city of Sevastopol, and to a *Kara*-class cruiser *Kerch*.

Adderbury, 17–20 November 1989 – FIS Weekend Conference with Soviet Participation on Maritime Strategy and Arms Control Issues

Those present included two serving Soviet Flag Officers, a former Deputy C-in-C of the Soviet Navy, a former Supreme Allied Commander Atlantic and a former US C-in-C Pacific. The British group included both serving officers, with a brief attendance by the First Sea Lord, and academic experts. The main objective was to improve further communication between the parties, which was seen as a precondition for progress in the maritime control area. It had been found that the dissimilar concepts of strategy, with two sets of weapons and differing operations, produced misperceptions.

The Soviets addressed the subject of their own naval strategy, claiming it was essentially defensive in nature, and that they had never even practised a major submarine effort against Western SLOCs. Informal geographical lines of concern were revealed, i.e. ship movements in certain areas caused concern to Moscow. In general a reduction in shipbuilding plans had been introduced, but effects would not be noticed for a year or two.

There was a contradiction in the opinions expressed previously concerning nuclear war, mention was made of the possibility of a short war in Europe leading to tactical and strategic nuclear exchanges. This was surprising to the Soviets considering their claim of no first nuclear use.

For the first time the Pacific was discussed. Both sides emphasised that the Pacific was often ignored but it was vital to both superpowers, therefore more cooperation was required especially to fight narcotics, piracy and to prevent ballistic missile proliferation.

The US described a more flexible maritime strategy with less emphasis on aggressive rhetoric which had previously worried the Soviets. The Soviets were concerned about the ambiguity of the new strategy but welcomed the less aggressive tone.

Following the meeting, the Soviets visited the frigate HMS *Avenger*, in a reciprocal exercise in openness following on from the *Kerch* visit.

Brown University, Providence, RI, 31 October–3 November 1990 – UK/USA/USSR Conference on Naval Strategy and Defence

The fourth in the series of talks was held under the auspices of the Center for Foreign Policy Development and the Institute for International Studies of the University, on behalf of the Center for Naval Warfare Studies of the US Naval War College. This was the first occasion in which serving officers, five Captains, of the USN participated.

The new structure of US forces was described, with 'Maritime Strategy' changing to 'Naval Policy' and orientated to regional contingencies. There would also be a reduction of about 25 per cent, with force structures based on intentions as opposed to capabilities. The USN was developing new thinking with the emphasis on regional threats rather than ideological differences, corresponding reductions in ASW and submarines were declared.

The Soviets were still concerned over SLOCs, fearing the combined might of the Western maritime power. This showed the degree of misunderstanding between the two sides. The defensive nature of the Soviet fleet was re-emphasised, with the claim that the possibility of using subs against the SLOCs was practically non-existent. The Soviets also outlined their budgeting and procurement system.

The increasing emphasis on the Mediterranean was considered. The Soviets understood the need for a carrier in the area, and felt that all navies could coexist there. Some even envisaged cooperation between them. In conclusion the participants decided that such a gathering could be used as the basis for more talks.

Brown University, Providence, RI, 9–12 November 1991 – UK/USA/USSR Conference on Naval Strategy and Defence

The US Naval War College again organised this meeting, which included serving Flag Officers of all three navies. The agenda was structured around naval roles, strategies and programmes. However, the conference was overshadowed by the prospect of further change in the Soviet Union.

1988–99 From confrontation to cooperation 23

The role of the SN was presented, with an acceptance of the change from confronting western navies to concentrating forces in home waters. A re-evaluation of naval missions and balance of maritime strategic forces was underway. It was pointed out that the SN was taking serious measures to reduce numbers because of changed threat perceptions.

The Soviet defence budget was explained, with great difficulties foreseen due to the transition to the market economy. This would increase prices, and combined with budget cuts, would reduce the construction programme. The future will be more geared towards smaller ships for operation in home waters. When considering personnel it was estimated that personnel costs would double necessitating a reduction in numbers.

Budgetary pressures on Western nations will reduce force numbers by about 30 per cent. Maritime strategy is being redefined. The Gulf experience has placed emphasis on presence in the Pacific, Persian Gulf, the Mediterranean and the Atlantic. The US was concerned about regional powers, with the emphasis of US policy moving to operations in littoral areas.

The Soviet Navy was keen to advance multi-national naval cooperation, claiming that they would have been willing to participate in Desert Storm. The conference concluded that more cooperation and dialogue were required, with the possibility of bilateral exercises in the future.

Moscow, 22–26 June 1992 – US/UK/ Russian naval strategy talks

These were more formalised talks, organised by the Russian MFA, each team led by a serving officer of two star rank. The primary theme was initiatives to enhance cooperation and understanding.

The Russians presented their current strategy and thinking. They emphasised the desire to continue as a significant sea power and also revealed that there was now a separate naval strategy. Concern was expressed about conflicts between themselves and former USSR republics, with difficulties over the allocation of ships to Ukraine, Georgia and Azerbaijan. The Russians were keen for the West not to get involved.

The Russian budget was addressed, revealing considerable planned reductions in force levels. The building programme had been curtailed because of financial constraints and also difficulties with non-Russian yards.

Concerning cooperation, the area of submarine safety was raised as an area for dialogue. Multi-national naval cooperation, with the possible establishment of a Pacific and an Atlantic force, under the control of the UN, with the question of compatibility seen as the most difficult obstacle to this.

The Americans emphasised the fundamental change of strategy from blue-water operations targeted against the USSR to littoral operations on a worldwide basis. Budget reductions were also outlined with a general feeling that force levels should not be cut further in the interests of global stability.

There was strong agreement on the continuation of such dialogue as a forum for the exploration of ideas on an informal basis. The idea of a seminar game on co-operation was also raised.

UK, 3–7 May 1993 –RN/USN/RFN Meeting on Maritime Issues

This conference marked a significant departure from the traditional format seen previously. There were three distinct phases including discussions, gaming, and viewing of training demonstrations. The delegations included a mix of naval officers, civil servants and academics.

The talks, held at RNC Greenwich, remained informal and non-attributable and covered aspects of maritime co-operation. A number of case studies were presented and used to highlight previous areas of co-operation and the differing command and control structures employed. Further presentations considered technical, political, and financial factors affecting humanitarian operations.

The meeting then moved on to the RN Maritime Tactical School for a trilateral humanitarian aid game known as 'Triple Trust'. This was based upon a generic UN embargo exercise which allowed comparisons between the three countries' concepts of operations, command and control, and the management of a ROE system. The game demonstrated that difficulties in co-operation could arise very quickly, highlighting a lack of understanding between the West and Russia of each other's capabilities and practices.

The final phase saw the delegates embarked in HMS *York* and RFA *Black Rover*, where they viewed a simulated UN 'blockade type' operation, involving the insertion of a boarding party using helicopters, with RFA *Black Rover* as an uncooperative merchantman. Finally the delegates witnessed HMS *Argyll* in a disaster relief exercise (DISTEX) in Plymouth, Devon.[3]

Discussions continued throughout the week on the future of the talks. There was agreement that the talks had been a success but there would be a move away from the issues previously covered in order to avoid duplication of the bilateral staff talks between Russia and the USA. The next meeting would pursue the trilateral gaming scenario, utilising the facilities of the USNWC.

Newport, 1–6 May 1994 –tripartite maritime cooperation talks between the RFN/RN/USN

It was the turn of the US Naval War College for the latest round of trilateral naval discussions, with representation at flag level from all three countries. The meeting was based around a game scenario involving a trilateral naval force operating in support of a UNSC Resolution. The task was to evacuate civilian and military personnel from a potentially hostile location with the possibility of engagement by rogue elements of one of the hostile nations.

The objectives of the game were to advance mutual understanding in co-operative security and standard procedures of force employment. The problem of interoperability was also investigated.

A number of issues were raised as a result of the game. There were significant differences in the application of the ROE, therefore it was felt that more discussion would be required to develop common ROE. There was also a requirement for the standardisation of terminology and prior translation of tactical publications.

Following on from the game, there were a number of planned visits. There was a briefing on current USN operations at the command centre of CINCLANTFLT. There was also a visit to the USS *Kearsarge*, a new amphibious ship. The submariners also welcomed the opportunity to view nuclear hunter-killer submarines. An additional tour was arranged to Langley AFB.

Russia–UK–US (RUKUS)

This account by Captain Page shows the evolution of informal CBM discussions into the more formalised structure of what became RUKUS from 1992. The 1993 RUKUS talks were of particular importance as they included a phase of training at sea, which had not been done before.

What was becoming clear from the ambitious 1993 RUKUS and the subsequent ones in 1994 (US) and 1995 (Russia), which did not have sea phases but concentrated on the gaming of scenarios started in 1993, were four key things.

- *Communications*, not least the language barrier requiring interpreters, and the lack of a common set of translated operations' procedures plus the need for equipment and secure telephones. Around this time, the RN had about forty qualified Russian interpreters, led by one of the authors, Mr Robert Avery from the Defence School of Languages, who was awarded an OBE for his significant contribution to the success of this period of cooperation with the RFN. The importance of interpreters and the role played by them in helping those interacting with the Russians understand Russian culture, in particular military culture, was a key lesson and will be an important enabler for any future defence engagement.

- Russian unfamiliarity with *Rules of Engagement (ROE)*. This recurring theme led to the Russians finally admitting that they did not have an ROE process in the Western sense, indeed they had no Russian term for ROE. The former Communist system had generated a top-down command and control approach with instructions issued to unit commanders from the central HQs, which were not questioned. The art of delegating authority within a set of ROE guidelines was anathema. It could be argued in light of Russia's conduct of operations in Ukraine, often with senior commanders having to go forward to implement plans, that the development of ROE still remains restricted.
- It also emerged from conversations that the Russians took some time to come to terms with the broader *utility of warships*. It appeared from these early talks that, from a Russian perspective, warships existed to fight wars and defend the Motherland – the 'war' in 'warship'. A warship engaging in embargo or humanitarian operations was counter-intuitive. That changed and developed over time as exemplified in Russia's Naval Policy 2017 (discussed in Chapter 7), which outlines the attributes that its maritime forces aim to possess, e.g. power projection, presence, coercion, leverage. These have been amply demonstrated during operations in Syria and Ukraine, for example, through long-range land-attack missile strikes, as well as counter-piracy operations off the Horn of Africa and an increased emphasis on defence diplomacy ship visits.[4]
- The simulated UN blockade-enforcement exercise and the DISTEX revealed differing conceptual approaches to *manpower allocation* between the Royal and Russian Navies. The Russians expressed surprise that the RN boarding party in the former was comprised of members of the ship's company from different departments rather than a dedicated unit – usually of naval infantry – embarked specifically for such a task, which would be the case in the Russian Navy. Similarly, they were surprised that DISTEX was for training a whole ship's company rather than a sub-unit especially configured for the purpose. This conceptual difference would recur time and time again, with the RN emphasis on breadth of training as opposed to Russian emphasis on what they perceived as depth of capability. At first the Russians were dubious about the RN approach, regarding it as amateurish and possibly being put on as a piece of theatre to deceive them. As time went on, however, they could see that a fully professional navy without conscripts can train to this standard and provide a built-in breadth of capability within a single ship, instantly available to react to any crisis or challenge. A similar contrast later became evident to

the organisation of damage control within a ship. This theme will be returned to in Chapter 6.

During these early Adderbury and RUKUS exchanges, Russia was also taking part in multi-national exercises and in particular joined NATO's Partnership for Peace programme (PfP)[5] programme in June 1994, initiated by NATO to create a pathway for those former Soviet states who wished to become full members of NATO. In October 1994, the Russian Navy took part for the first time in a PfP exercise (Cooperative Venture 94) with RFS *Neustrashimy*. The ship had already taken part in BALTOPS 93 and 94 and therefore was no stranger to operating with NATO ships but it found PfP far more challenging since the exercise required more interaction with the other ships. The author David Fields acted as the UK interpreter and observer onboard for the duration of the exercise. The material state of the five-year-old ship stood out as extremely poor. Cockroaches in the accommodation and rats elsewhere were seen. Everything was filthy and standards of hygiene in the galley and the heads (toilets) were atrocious, bordering on unsafe. The boilers onboard had broken down prior to arrival in Norway at the start of the exercise. No attempt had been made to fix them and therefore there was only cold water and no showers throughout the entire week-long exercise.[6]

Some of the key points witnessed during this PfP exercise also reflected what was being seen around the tables and tactical floors of the Adderbury/ RUKUS events. A very autocratic top-down command structure leading to slow decision-making on even the most basic of serials. For example, the embarked Admiral took charge from the bridge of basic flying operations and indeed was consulted on most issues; there was only one competent English speaker on board and there was a lack of common tactical communication procedures. Another theme from the RFS *Neustrashimy* visit and which was becoming more obvious and continued right throughout this period of interaction, was the RFN's esteem it held for the RN, and its aspiration to emulate it.

RFS *Neustrashimy* – Exercise Cooperative Venture 94

(Observations by Lt Cdr D. Fields, October 1994)

1. The key players – The participating Russian ships originally consisted of two Krivaks. However, on the Thursday prior to the exercise it was reported to me that the RFS *Neustrashimy* had replaced one of the Krivaks. When I arrived onboard I mentioned that it was bad luck to be called up for an exercise at such short notice. The reply from an

Officer was one of surprise and the comment that they had always been planning to come. The ship itself has already taken part in BALTOPS 93 and 94 and is therefore not a complete stranger to operating with NATO ships. However, it is worth noting that the Officers onboard felt that they had achieved far more in Cooperative Venture than Baitops. This was as a result of more interaction with the other ships, overnight manoeuvring and communications exercises which were not so evident during Baitops. The Captain, Captain Second Rank (RN Commander) Igor Ryzhkov, has been in command for almost two years and clearly knows his business.

2. There was also a large staff onboard from Moscow and the ship's base port Baltiysk which was headed by Rear Admiral Kazakov, who had been present at the original briefings at Northwood. Rear Admiral Kudryavtsev, a former FPB Squadron Commander in the Baltic, was the CTG of the two Russian ships in the exercise. Judging by the copious amount of note taking their aims were obviously to acquire as much experience and learn as much as possible from the exercise.

3. Their attitude towards me was at first suspicious and I was interviewed by their best English speaker as to which Intelligence Service I was working for. He was surprised to find out that in fact I was only on loan from the RN Gunnery School and had no prior briefings. Although this was less than an ideal situation it subsequently helped me as their attitude towards me was more relaxed after this interview. During my discussions with this Officer he was telling me that in the planned reorganisation of their Service they want to try and do it along the lines of the Royal Navy for whom they have the greatest respect and consider it to be the best. I naturally agreed!

4. Harbour phase – The need for interpreters during the pre-sail briefs was clearly borne out by the lack of English speaking officers on the Russian ships. As Rear Admiral Kazakov's Chief of Staff said to me, the reason so few of them speak English is that they thought they would never have to use it because they had not envisaged the possibility of ever working together. This need for Interpreters obviously carries on into the social side of these harbour phases and helps to break down the old misconceptions we have of each other and to enjoy each other's company. The hospitality and warm generous nature of the Russians surprised and still surprises many people when first meeting them. One telling comment from a Russian during one of these social events was that they never perceived us as enemies, only adversaries.

5. When in harbour the ship's company is paid in American dollars but they did not have enough onboard. Coupled with this was the Russian

Embassy's inability to provide Kroner to the ship during their time in Krisstiansand. This resulted in very few runs ashore and the ship's chandler not being paid on leaving. Arrangements were made to pay all bills when the ship arrived in Stavangar.

6. Living conditions – For a ship which is only some five years old living conditions and levels of hygiene onboard were basic. The cabins had cockroaches, the heads were a First Lieutenant's nightmare and the food, although edible, was basic. Both Admirals and the Captain, although they had their own cabins, ate in the Wardroom with the rest of the Officers. The boilers onboard had broken down prior to arrival in Norway and no attempt had been made to fix them. Therefore there was cold water throughout and no showers.

7. The standard of cleanliness on two decks was poor and there was quite a stale pungent smell from various sources. The ratings heads consisted of rudimentary metal troughs which were filthy. The dining hall was grimy with damaged furniture and servery. Although I did not personally see the galley, a tour from HNS *Newcastle* did and reported that if I had seen it I would never have eaten onboard. I was not allowed to see the food storage areas – my guide was too embarrassed.

8. The Russians evidently know their ships are not in a good state but with the lack of shore support and funds it is little wonder that the state of repair and living conditions of their ships is so poor. The ships always look immaculate on the outside but just beneath the surface all is not so well. This is quite an accurate reflection on their society as a whole now and during the last sixty or seventy years.

9. The dissemination of information to the ship's company is certainly not via Daily Orders, Shortcasts and Longcasts but by an initial pipe at the beginning of the day with supplementary pipes as required. The Admiral's staff had made up a very detailed WPP based on the exercise WPP which was kept on the Bridge.

10. The ratings were scruffy in their appearance, lacked motivation and had a glazed almost lifeless expression in their eyes. There were only 170 ships' Officers and Ratings onboard supplemented with approximately fifteen Staff Officers.

11. Leaving harbour – All four gas turbines were running with the Olympus equivalents being engaged (the ship is also fitted with five diesel generators). The engines were in Bridge control but in normal cruising are in SCC control. The Captain appeared to be doing everything himself with little input from his Navigator or Executive Officer. He kept the con throughout even during the pilotage out of harbour and indeed during the initial sets of OOW manoeuvres. At sea the Captain was on the Bridge

the entire time being relieved only by the Admiral for a few hours at night and meal times.
12. Decision-making – From the moment of leaving harbour it became abundantly clear throughout the remainder of the exercise that the art of delegation in the Russian Navy is still in its infancy and the decision-making organisation is incredibly top heavy and cumbersome. What for us would be decisions on very routine matters taken at OOW or PWO level were consistently referred to the CTG or his staff who referred to him anyway! The sight of an Admiral taking charge of flying operations in the Flyco was somewhat alien. Any changes in the published programme caused great debate and there was a certain lack of flexibility in adjusting the plan. The following incident is a useful example of this point and is just one of many! *Newcastle*'s Lynx was due to arrive at 1100 for rapid-roping demonstration. At 1010 an order was received by the *Neustrashimy* to launch her Helix for a SAREX. However, the decision had just been taken to stow the helo ready for the arrival of *Newcastle*'s Lynx. The Helix was still on deck and could have been airborne within twenty minutes and therefore clear by 1100. Because the scramble of the Helix was relatively unexpected the Admiral had again to be consulted for a decision. This took ten to fifteen minutes and by that time to launch the Helix for the SAREX before the Lynx arrived fitted into the 'all too difficult box'. They are clearly not of a reactive nature, probably as a direct result of the regime they have been living under for so long when all the thinking has been done for them.
13. OOW manoeuvres/comms – This was comprehensively debriefed in Stavangar but there are one or two things worthy of note. Firstly the WO(CY) who spoke a bit of English was on the Bridge the entire exercise with no sign of anyone else being trained up and with help only from either myself or one of two Officers, whose English was adequate but limited. Although the Russian Navy has a similar publication to EXTAC 768 the WO(CY) considered it in no way as comprehensive as the EXTAC. They do not possess the same level of complex OOW manoeuvres and screening exercises and serials involving, for example, rotating a screen caused some confusion. I was surprised that they did not have similar manoeuvres but having glanced at their Bridge Watchkeeping guide I noticed the manoeuvring exercise chapter was quite basic.
14. Ceremonial between ships is carried out in the same way as the Royal Navy even between a Russian and a Lithuanian!
15. The communications outfit on *Neustrashimy* was in the opinion of their Communications Officer worse than the Krivak's. Apart from SATCOMS they had only 3HF, 5UHF and 2VHF sets. This is obviously quite a significant limitation.

16. RAS approaches – During the two-hour serial the ship only achieved one RAS approach. There was no distance off tables and the whole evolution was done by the eye of the Captain. There were no RAS SSD and the Captain gave the Executive Officer detailed instructions on how to conduct the transfer, which one would have expected him to know. All four gas turbines were running and it was the Olympus equivalents which were used for the approach at a speed of twenty-two knots. At approximately 1.5 cables, speed was reduced and as the bow drew level with the stern of RFA *Olna* the ship's speed was sixteen knots. At this time speed was further reduced to the RAS speed of twelve knots but the ship was astern of station. The breakaway was achieved by simply reducing speed and slipping astern.
17. FLYEX – The pilot had four thousand hours experience of flying a HELIX and therefore I considered it reasonably safe to get airborne, which was an interesting experience. The FLYCO, situated overlooking the Flight Deck, maintained close liaison with the Bridge and was responsible for the control of the aircraft as tasked by the Ops Room. A problem arose concerning the ship's course and speed with regard to suitability for flying, and it was the Admiral who eventually sorted out the problem. Not all the flight deck crew had ear defenders and one strange sight was of a crew member wiping the helicopter's windscreen with a box of tissues in one hand and the rotors fully engaged. The pilot preferred the ship to be going into wind for take offs and landings and was not able to operate in a cross deck wind, the HELIX being unable to swivel. Indeed the helicopter was very limited in its positioning of landing as there were no extendable lashings, only chain lashings, which meant the aircraft had to be landed very precisely on the spot. The chain lashings were not tensioned until the rotors had come to a complete stop because excessive vibration as the rotors slowed was liable to snap the securing chains. The Helo has a data link capability and carries only ASW weapons which can be loaded directly onto the helo via a hatch in the Flight deck. Crossdeck Ops were successfully carried out with the USS *Connolly*, SPS *Santa Maria*.
18. Navigation/stability – Visibility from the bridge was very poor with small heated windows and a bulkhead dissecting the Bridge with the International Rule of the Road written on it. The Navigation was carried out in the charthouse at the back of the bridge with Decca and Snaps which were fairly agricultural but worked. There was a chart table on the bridge but this was being used by the staff for planning purposes. I was questioned about the stability of our ships, a problem which still exists with Russian ships due to their top weight. NEUSTRASHIMY despite having stabilisers was rolling about eight degrees in what was only a gentle swell (approx. 2M).

19. Operations Room – The action information system called TRON was not running during the exercise. There was a radar watchman on duty providing a service to the OOW. When the Ops Room is fully operational the Executive Officer is in overall charge with the heads of various sections such as Missile, and ASW closed up at their respective consoles. Ops room manning is very officer orientated. Judging by the key to the symbology shown on the display the system can handle a reasonable amount of information. Injections are made by light pen, but although the displays look modern they still have quite an agricultural feel about them. There are two large computers feeding into a large SNAPS fitted chart table which displays the surface and sub-surface picture.

    Vertical Perspex plotting displays are still evident as a back-up for the display of the air picture. The Executive Officer has his own computer display and a form of OPCON which he can use to shore stations or with ships of the group. The Captain is always on the bridge when the Ops Room is fully closed up. Voice pipe comms are still used from the Ops Room to the Bridge but at least they never break down!

20. Weapons fit – The ship is currently not fitted with SSN25 but this is due to take place during her first refit in about three years' time. The ship is fitted with four (two on each side) – ten barrelled seduction and infrared chaff launchers. In addition she also has two (one on each side) sixteen barrelled confusion chaff launchers. The ship is fitted with a lowerable transducer from the port side which is used purely for anti terrorist purposes when at anchor. The ship was RASH fitted but to date the effectiveness of it had not been properly trialled. The remainder of the ship's weapon fit was as stated in Jane's.

21. The ship successfully conducted a gunnery shoot firing fifteen rounds. However, the Gunnery Officer was concerned that the ship was not going fast enough and said that twelve knots was the best speed for stabilising the gun. A safety trace of fifteen degrees either side of the line of fire out to double the range of the predicted point of impact is cleared for all types of firings. A formal brief was not given for this serial or indeed for any of the other serials.

22. Standards of living – During many conversations with the officers I was asked the standard questions about how much I earned, did I have my own house, how many cars was I allowed to own, and was the food better in Royal Navy ships! An experienced pilot whose rank equated to an RN Commander is earning $230 per month. Prices are steadily rising but the pay is not keeping in step. Married quarters for a young Lieutenant in Baltiysk consists of a 20 m(sq) room on a floor where there are eight other families. The families have two kitchens between them and three

bathrooms. Unfortunately, I never did find out what living conditions were like for the sailors but it cannot have been better. Despite all this the Russian is still a generous man with what little he has and there always seems to be an adequate supply of vodka! Nevertheless as is well known morale is not high and they know better than anyone that there is a long way for them to go.

23. Russian interpreters – The value of Russian interpreters for such exercises as Cooperative Venture and visits by ships both to this country and to Russia cannot be over emphasised. The advantages of being able to communicate with each other, which in turn increases understanding between our two countries, are obvious. Unfortunately there appears to be no central budget on which interpreters are able to draw to pay for travel expenses particularly when it is to support a ship visit. With a major exercise such as this it was a little different with the cost of travel being borne by CINCEASTLANT. However, it is for consideration that provision is made for easy access to a budget by interpreters to assist in travelling expenses. This would also avoid wasting valuable time in circular discussions and arguments as to which authority will pay for Interpreters to go where their assistance is required.

This early operational exposure and the RUKUS talks in 1995 led to an overwhelming sense that more practical experience of co-operation was required and the joint declaration of RUKUS 1995 reflected that.[7] It concluded that it is 'appropriate to develop the theoretical conclusions arrived at in the consultations within the practical setting of actual joint exercises between the ships, aircraft and naval infantry units of the three countries'.[8] It was time to put words into action.

Joint declaration

By the Heads of Delegation of the Navies of the Russian Federation, USA and Great Britain on the results of consultations concerning cooperation between three navies.

St. Petersburg   22 April 1995

The Heads of Delegation of the Navies of Russia, Great Britain and the USA taking part in the 'RUKUS-95' consultations on naval questions and the associated wargame which took place in the Kuznetsov Naval Academy 17–22 April 1995, agree on the following points:

- The consultations on questions of naval cooperation promote the development of mutual understanding and trust between the navies of our three nations, enable us effectively to exchange opinions on the use of naval forces and to address questions of cooperation when carrying out possible joint operations agreed upon at an international level.
- These consultations on questions of naval cooperation should take place once a year, with the venue rotating in sequence between the three host countries (UK, USA and Russia). The next consultations take place in the UK in 1996.
- The following personnel should be included in the delegations (based on the experience of the last three meetings): staff officers, officers from naval training establishments and those directly from operational service. Such delegation composition enables a deeper and detailed analysis of the questions being addressed.
- We consider it appropriate to develop the theoretical conclusions arrived at in the consultations within the practical set of actual joint exercises between the ships/aircraft/naval infantry units of our three countries.
- These exercises should be carried out as passage exercises (passexes) between our ships/aircraft when encountering each other at sea as convenient, as well as during official visits and routine port calls between three navies, organisational procedures for cooperation should be refined and worked up in joint training exercises together.
- To these exercises should be invited – on a mutual basis – staff officers, officers from naval training establishments and commanding officers of squadrons (divisions/brigades) and of warships.

Result of these conclusions on naval cooperation should be reported to High Commands of the armed forces of our three nations. Organisational questions concerning naval cooperation are most efficiently resolved through the channels of naval attaches in Moscow, Washington and London, conducting business directly with the Headquarters of our three navies.

The UK took up the challenge as host country of RUKUS 1996 to organise the most comprehensive RUKUS event to that date. The event focused on preparing for and conducting a sea phase that involved HMS *Gloucester* (Type 42 destroyer), USS *Samuel B. Roberts* (*Perry* class), RFS *Admiral Levchenko* (*Udaloy*-class) and RFA *Black Rover* (tanker). The scenario was a UN embargo operation to locate a suspected nuclear device being smuggled by a merchant vessel simulated by RFA *Black Rover*, with boardings conducted by both Royal Marines via helicopter insertion and Russian Naval Infantry. There would be a prize for the team that found the nuclear device first.

Discussions and planning took place at the Royal Naval College (RNC) Greenwich on 28 April 1996 for two days. What became abundantly clear during this phase, and had already been evident in other interactions, was the thorough and meticulous approach to planning that the Russians adopted. The graphics they produced for each serial, which included, for example, timings of when manoeuvres would take place, how the formation of the ships would look on completion were works of art, the likes of which no one in the Royal or US Navies had ever seen before. There also seemed to be little acknowledgement that things could change either because of meteorological conditions or other shipping in the area – it was as if the planners were turning a blind eye to this and that once the orders had been given and the 'work of art' approved by the senior officer, then only he could change it. There was little evidence of a mission-command approach and flexibility in fulfilling tasks without higher, often much higher, approval. Throughout the subsequent years of cooperation this top-down approach of command did not seem to change significantly, and arguably has been a fundamental weakness in the conduct of Russia's 'special military operation' in Ukraine.

Following a tactical wargame at the RN Martime Warfare Centre (MWC) on 1 May and a press conference the following day, the ships sailed on 2 May from Portsmouth to Plymouth to conduct the exercise. Serials included Officer of the Watch manoeuvres (tactical manoeuvres between ships in close proximity), communication exercises and the boarding operation/competition. The Russian Naval Infantry won this competition but not without some controversy. Both boarding teams had been directed not to search the Master's cabin. However, the Russians, assuming perhaps this was a deception and without the constraints or understanding of ROE, set about tearing the Master's cabin apart and damaging it. It was a reflection, albeit a minor example, of the natural Russian lack of restraint in the use of force, underpinned by suspicions of the motives of others.

RUKUS 96 was a highly complex event, which also involved Admiral of the Fleet Sir Julian Oswald GCB (former First Sea Lord) and Admiral Igor Kasatonov (RFN First Deputy Commander 1992–97) speaking together at RUSI. The exercise proved that the three countries could operate together with sufficient detailed planning and the availability of interpreters but that any further complexity was going to take some time, if such exercises or joint operations were to be done with any great confidence. The 1997 (US) and 1998 (Russia) RUKUS returned to the shore phases format, focusing on ROE development and joint operation procedures. Drawing on the lessons from the sea phases in the previous years, the table-top exercises expanded to a trilateral combined HQ, conducting operational planning and execution, and the employment of naval infantry forces with limited joint service involvement.

Figure 3.1 First Deputy Commander-in-Chief of the Russian Federation Navy Admiral Igor Kasatonov is greeted on arrival at the Northwood Command Centre by Commander-in-Chief Fleet Admiral Sir Hugo White. At the time he was courted by the Royal Navy as the successor to Admiral Gromov but that did not come to pass. 29 March 1995. © Crown Copyright.

What made Adderbury/RUKUS 1988–99 a success?

This eleven-year naval interaction between the USSR/Russia, the UK and the USA, which was set to expand in 2002 with the addition of the French Navy, was considered a success. In the first instance, and unlike the present political climate between the West and Russia, there existed *fora* in which the Soviet military already conducted mil-mil dialogue with Western militaries, e.g. BRIXMIS and SOXMIS in Germany.[9] Also agreements had been negotiated face to face such as INCSEA and signed by the US (1972) and UK (1986), which necessitated discussion and interaction. CBMs in other organisations existed such as Open Skies and the NATO Permanent Joint Council in 1997, replaced by the NATO–Russia Council in 2002. Thus, there was nothing out of the ordinary about conducting military dialogue even when tensions were running high in the Cold War or in its immediate aftermath. The initial informal nature of the early Adderbury talks also kept the interaction between USSR and US/UK under the political radar and, in any event, coincided with President Gorbachev's era of 'Glasnost' ('Openness'). Other reasons for success included:

- Continuity – Small delegations, originally eight to ten members, with a fairly regular cast of participants, especially from the RFN, encouraged familiarity and openness and the growth of trust.

Figure 3.2 Pre-exercise planning on board HMS *Gloucester* during RUKUS 96. From left to right: Commander T. Cunningham (CO HMS *Gloucester*), Vice Admiral J. Brigstocke (Flag Officer Surface Flotilla), Rear Admiral V. Bessonov (Head Tactics Kuznetsov Naval Academy), Captain 1 Rank N. Zharinov (Chief of Staff Kola Flotilla) and Commander L. Geanuleas (CO USS *Samuel B. Roberts*). © Crown Copyright.

- Informality – Meetings spread over three to five days provided considerable downtime in the evenings over dinner and drinks. Some of the best ideas were the result of this informal, off-the-record interaction, such as the RUKUS 1995 Memorandum of Understanding (put together on the last day).
- Three-way interaction – Unlike bilateral ship visits involving two navies, RUKUS involved a regular three-way, later four-way (with France) interaction, with the RN often acting as the cultural bridge between the Americans (Anglo-Saxons) and the Russians (Europeans). This created a unique chemistry not found in bilateral talks or ship visits.
- Consistent two- to three-star engagement – Delegations soon became routinely headed by Rear (RN/USN) and Vice (RFN) Admirals from central staffs, giving weight to the proceedings and indicating the importance given to RUKUS by the member nations.
- Highest-level interest – Very senior players showed consistent interest and became involved: Admiral N. N. Amel'ko (ex Deputy Chief General Staff), Admiral I. V. Kasatonov (Deputy Cdr Russian Navy), Admiral of the Fleet Sir Julian Oswald (First Sea Lord), Admiral Sir James Eberle

(former CINC-Naval Home Commander) and Admiral W. MacDonald (former Supreme Allied Commander Atlantic, SACLANT, NATO) all made guest appearances, as did HRH Prince Michael of Kent. RUKUS was perceived to be significant and the place to be seen.

- Warship participation – Involvement of warships in the sea phase of later RUKUSes gave the process weight and clear outcomes for real cooperation at sea; the combination of presentations followed by a war game which was then put into practice with real ships made RUKUS unique.
- Interpreters – Above all other interactions, RUKUS underlined the importance of good interpreter support to facilitate effective communication. Language could be a stumbling block even with strong interpreter cover when concepts in the RN and USN had no equivalents in the RFN, most significantly the concept of ROE. Interpreters then had to agree how to bridge the resulting conceptual and terminological gaps. The underinvestment in recent years to grow Russian speakers in the RN and more broadly across UK MoD will need to be addressed, to enable future defence engagement to be more effective.
- Rotation of venues – The rotation of venues between the three and later four participant countries, provided fascinating and valuable insights into each other's naval cultures.
- Trust – The length, twenty-six years with some breaks, of the (F)RUKUS relationship fostered genuine trust and mutual professional respect between those directly involved but also frequent exasperation.
- Robustness – The fact that the process endured as long as it did is a testament to its robustness and perceived value to all participants. It weathered the international political squalls of Kosovo (1999) and Georgia (2008), each leading to a two-year break in the process. The annexation of Crimea by Russia in 2014, delivered the coup de grace to a project invested with much hope for a more cooperative world.
- The sea – A sense of the unifying bond of the brotherhood of the sea, a hostile environment to both sides, and professional respect between navies helped foster open, respectful and warm discussions from the outset.

Compared to what had existed pre-1988, these multilateral *fora* and bilateral interactions, which will be discussed next, represented a step change in defence dialogue between the UK and Russia. However, these successes were hard fought for against deeply ingrained cultures of both sides, driven largely by distrust of each other and our motives. An unspoken but nevertheless prevalent political background to the naval interactions was a sense from the West that it had 'won' the Cold War and the Russians had 'lost'. This played into the Russian mindset of victimhood, resentment and inferiority. Certainly the state of the ships and equipment the Russians possessed compared to Western technology appeared to lag by some way – and they knew it. Negotiations over visits, programmes and subjects to be discussed were tortuous and difficult. Just about everything proposed to the Russian naval staff had first to work through its own laboured bureaucracy and approved at a higher level, before then meeting the obstacle of the dead hand of the even more suspicious External Relations Department of the Russian Ministry of Defence (GUMVS) for further approval, as well as the Ministry of Foreign Affairs. It took more open minded Russian naval staff members to break these domestic deadlocks, or sometimes to take risk, often resulting in last-minute agreements, much to the frustration of the Western culture of more detailed and timely forward planning. The highly suspicious Russian military intelligence organisation (GRU) also had a major presence either as part of the delegations or through their in-country attaches. They exerted pressure on other members of the Russian delegations, even those who were very senior, making those delegates less willing to 'stick their necks out' and be more forward-leaning in developing closer ties. These themes ran as a constant thread through all interactions with the Russian military, not just navy-to-navy, until the political rupture in 2014. They will present an even greater challenge and potential obstacle to the re-establishment of defence dialogue after the war in Ukraine. A good example of the type of Russian individuals that were involved and the tensions that existed between them, is contained in the observations of RUKUS 1997 by the author, Robert Avery. The report also highlights the important role that interpreters play, not just for interpreting at meetings but also in the margins and at social events where insight to the RFN can be gleaned from conversations over dinner or drinks in an informal setting.

RUKUS 1997

US Naval War College, Newport, Rhode Island

Interpreter's observations

The Russian delegation contained six officers who had previously attended a RUKUS: Patrushev, Bessonov, Kupreyenkov, Avilov and Dragunov – all 1996 attendees except for Kupreyenkov (1993) and Bessonov (1995 and 1996).

The Kuznetsov Academy element was strong, with Bessonov (Head of Tactics) and his deputy Novikov; the Main Naval Staff was represented by Patrushev (Deputy Chief), Avilov (Head of Pacific Desk Ops Directorate), Kupreyenkov (responsible for war games and exercises and the MNS interface with the Academy), Dragunov (Legal Dept) and Aleksandrov (International Liaison). Kupreyenkov is the Main Naval Staff officer tasked with running RUKUS 98 in St Petersburg with Novikov as the main point of contact for RUKUS 98 at the Kuznetsov Academy. Lt Col Andrei Akulov did not come as interpreter, having apparently incurred Patrushev's displeasure last year for being unreliable and unkempt. His place was taken by Aleksei Sorokin from the Russian Embassy in Washington who told me he had not undergone diplomatic training but had entered the diplomatic service as a language specialist after two years in language school in Moscow studying interpreting (he was taught by, among others, Pyotr Palazchenko – Gorbachev's interpreter). The Embassy presence – Sorokin – and the probably GRU Aleksandrov seemed to weigh on Patrushev, as did that of Krutskikh from the MFA. My impression was that he was greatly constrained by their presence, the interpreter shadowing him constantly to the exclusion of others. For the second year running, no representative of the General Staff was in the delegation (a task undertaken for some years by Capt 2 Rank Borisov).

Patrushev's somewhat tense demeanour may not be unconnected with turbulence within the Russian Flag List. Admiral Khmel'nov was sacked barely a month ago over corruption charges, depriving the Main Naval Staff of its chief. Khmel'nov has not been formally replaced and his duties are being temporarily discharged by Vice Admiral Il'yin, Patrushev's immediate superior, so the stress of extra workloads and uncertainty as to future appointments around and above him may be telling on Patrushev. Concerning the Flag plot, I was told by Dragunov that C-in-C Gromov was going to retire at sixty (in August) and become Yeltsin's consultant on CIS naval affairs, parallel to Shaposhnikov's role as CIS aviation adviser to the president. First Deputy C-in-C Kasatonov has already been appointed Deputy Minister of defence for Education (vospitaniye) but the appointment has not yet been promulgated because of the upheaval over Khmel'nov. This same story was told to me by Bessonov, Novikov and Dragunov separately. They perceived it to be good news for the navy in the corridors of power, since no naval officer has held this kind of ministerial post since the Soviet era. However, Kasatonov's brief would be personnel and welfare across *all* the armed forces, so his ability to influence purely naval matters might actually be weakened. Dragonov said that Kasatonov might be replaced by Yeryomin (currently head of Kuznetsov Academy) or not replaced at all, the post lapsing. He said that Yerofeyev – Northern Fleet Commander – was out of the running because of age (fifty-seven) and other reasons. He is also expected to retire soon. Gurinov was suggested as another possible successor but because of age and the fact he was dismissed as Pacific Fleet Commander over the Vladivostok explosion (1995) this seems hardly plausible. Black Sea Fleet Commander Kravchenko would not succeed Gromov because continuity was now essential there and he was perceived to be doing a good job after Baltin's outbursts (who is now retired). Dragunov's view was that Admiral Kuroyedov – currently Pacific Fleet Commander – was most likely to relieve Gromov as C-in-C. Given Dragunov's many contacts within the Main Naval Staff and his usual reliability, it is worth giving some credence to this theory. A huge shake-up is clearly imminent.

At the Kuznetsov Academy, Vice Admiral Zakorin is still First Deputy Commandant (to Admiral Yeryomin) and Vice Admiral Prusakov still Deputy Commandant. (Major-?) General Sviridov was still there in July 1997 (source: Bessonov) in an unidentified post but took part in the Tercentenary March Past in St Petersburg in July 1997 marching directly behind Yeryomin, so he may be a Deputy Commandant (for Aviation?).

Vice Admiral Viktor Patrushev

Deputy Chief Main Naval Staff (since 07/95). Northern Fleet submariner who handles INCSEA/bilateral talks with a whole series of Western navies. Highly thoughtful, reflective, incisive and cultivated man (who infrequently quotes from Russian literature – often from less famous authors like Saltykov-Shchedrin). Tendency towards introversion accentuated by presence of Zaikin, Krutskikh and Sorokin on this occasion; he became more expansive at the dinner on the last night. Confided in me last year that the Main Naval Staff was 'Suvorov's slippery parquet floor' for the uninitiated – like him. He had *never* set foot in the MNS before being appointed its Deputy Chief.

Captain 1 Rank Vladimir Kupreyenkov

MNS point of contact with the Kuznetsov Naval Academy with special responsibility for war-gaming and exercises. Apparently gruff unsmiling official exterior conceals a man of great good humour, warmth, dynamism and subtlety (he frequently quotes from the poetry of Pushkin). Regarded the RUKUS 97 war game as shallow and the directing staff as unprofessional. He is a driving force behind RUKUS 98 and considerable powers have been delegated to him over organising it. A key figure in the success of future RUKUSes.

Captain 1 Rank Viktor Zaikin

NA Washington and clearly GRU with all the standard ingredients: excellent English, a good line in cynical mocking and sarcasm and generally exercising baleful control over the whole delegation. He ordered them to leave the officers' club as a delegation and imposed a curfew on them going ashore after Rear Admiral Stark's dinner on the last night. Best given a wide berth.

Mr Krutskikh

MFA representative. 'Consultant on Technical Matters'. Involved in Arms Control Negotiations. Excellent English. Very friendly with Zaikin and Aleksandrov. Switched to 'transmit' most of the time (driving Russian naval officers to distraction at meals) although his point about demonstrating the value of RUKUS to the Ministry of defence and the General Staff is well made. Infuriated Americans by ordering largest and most expensive dishes at all meals ashore and encouraging his fellow delegates to do the same. Also rubbished (quite unjustifiably) the Russian translations of the Game Book, ROE and Glossary of Terms, further annoying his hosts.

Robert Avery, Defence School of Languages,
Beaconsfield, 19 May 1997

Figure 3.3 RUKUS 98 took place at the Kuznetsov Naval Academy St Petersburg. The concluding Memorandum of Understanding to improve organisation and purposefulness of future RUKUSes. Signatories were (left to right) Rear Admiral J. Stark USN, Vice Admiral V. V. Patrushev and Commodore A. Chilton. As it happened, this was the last RUKUS for some time. © Author – Robert Avery.

Bilateral relationship

The Adderbury/RUKUS framework, combined with annual INCSEA and Naval Staff talks, laid the foundations for the RN and RFN bi-lateral relationship which sought to discuss and develop methods for more practical cooperation between naval units at sea. Both sides soon discovered that, while there was a shared maritime history since the time of Peter the Great, approaches to operating at sea, the role of warships, as well as the contribution of naval power in respective military doctrines, were quite different. Thus, the 1990s could be described as a 'voyage of discovery' of each other's people, ships and submarines.

This voyage reached an important milestone in September 1998 at the Russian Main Naval Staff, Moscow with a Memorandum of Understanding (MoU) on Naval Cooperation between the RN and RFN, signed by Admiral Sir Jock Slater, then First Sea Lord, and Admiral Kuroyedov, C-in-C RFN. Historical connections oiled the cogs of this event. The evening before the official MoU signing ceremony, a formal dinner took place at the UK Naval Attache's flat, to which all the key participants were invited. Both authors were present at this event and Robert Avery's notes and observations are captured in the text box below. The Russians were already aware and impressed that Admiral Slater was the great nephew of the former First Sea Lord Admiral of the Fleet Andrew Browne Cunningham, First Viscount Cunningham of Hyndhope. That fact, however, was eclipsed when Admiral Slater introduced his wife, Lady Slater, to Admiral Kuroyedov explaining that she was the great-great-great-great granddaughter of none other than Admiral Samuel Greig, who had commanded Catherine the Great's Imperial Navy in the eighteenth century. There was a short stunned silence followed by several vodka toasts to the close historical links between the two navies and Kuroyedov's musing about how his intelligence people had failed to inform him of this fact. Indeed, Lady Slater's programme the next day was changed to include her in the MoU signing ceremony at the Main Naval Staff, where there was a portrait of Admiral Greig or Samuil Karlovich Greig, as he was known in Russia. These historical linkages and history should not be underestimated or forgotten when dealing with the Russians. History, shared or otherwise, was, throughout the whole 1988–2014 period, an important enabler to dialogue and cooperation, and the Russians frequently demonstrated a better grasp of our history than we did.

The MoU laid the basis for all future naval cooperation, codifying activity to date and acting as a 'legal' document to which both sides could return or adapt, as the political circumstances dictated. This was particularly

Figure 3.4 Admiral Sir Jock Slater (First Sea Lord) and Admiral Vladimir Kuroyedov (Commander-in-Chief Russian Federation Navy) sign the Memorandum of Understanding on Naval Cooperation in the Main Naval Staff in Moscow. Captain G. McCready (NA Moscow) and Captain 1 Rank V. Ye Andreyenkov (Assistant to C-in-C RFN) in attendance. September 1998.
© Author – Robert Avery.

important in the period from 2000 to 2014, which will be discussed later, when there were several upticks in activity and improvement in the military relationship, frequently suspended by political disagreements. The MoU provided and should provide a mechanism through which naval dialogue was and could be re-established in the future.

Meeting of Admiral Sir Jock Slater and Admiral Vladimir Ivanovich Kuroyedov to sign Memorandum of Understanding on Naval Cooperation, Moscow, 25–26 September 1998

Interpreter's observations

1. Admiral Kuroyedov

Although he seemed very slightly apprehensive during the first minutes of NA's supper party (it is an unfamiliar social vehicle in Russia for military contacts), he was quickly put at ease by 1SL and by Admiral Yegorov's joviality and familiarity with the English way (e.g. dinner party at Admiral Lippiett's in July). He showed a good sense of humour; Yegorov's presence helped him to get into his stride but also to relax. I cannot imagine Gromov being quite so at ease in this situation.

His comprehension of English is not at all bad and he ventured some phrases in English. He had inspected the Kronstadt Naval Cadet School (Kadetsky korpus) for eight- to fifteen-year-olds and quizzed them in English; when they could no longer answer/understand in English, he told the teacher to increase and intensify their English studies 'as every naval officer should know several languages'. He much respected 1SL's address in Russian for this reason. Yegorov was an avuncular but unobtrusive presence who greatly assisted as a catalyst to conversation.

Kuroyedov did not discuss his predecessor, even when 1SL broached the subject on at least three occasions. Gromov is not mentioned in the military press and no eulogies accompanied his retirement. Kuroyedov never really served under Gromov directly (i.e. on his staff) so was probably not that close to him. (Contrast his attitude to Yegorov.) He is also clearly anxious to show he is his own man.

He has, like many Russians, a great respect for history and 1SL's direct connections to Admirals Greig and Cunningham meant much to him. He referred to this historical continuity in both his speech at the supper and his opening address at the press conference. Naval history is a three-hundred-year link binding Russian to the Western tradition (England, Scotland, Holland). The Soviet period (like the Mongol occupation some seven hundred years before) broke Russia's European links and emphasised her isolation, 'Asian-ness' and even backwardness.

It is of supreme importance to many Russians that they are being accepted *back* into the European fold (and thereby the respectable world community). This is one of the few ways that many educated, cultured and intelligent Russians can interpret the woes brought upon them by the collapse of the Soviet Union as a transient evil yet also the prerequisite to 'retuning' to a European 'wavelength'. Prestige based on inspiring fear abroad by force (yet based on dubious legality) is thus replaced on respect from European equals who have not lost the thread of historical continuity. Hence the significance of Kuroyedov's comments: 1SL's historical connections make him the living embodiment of a naval tradition Russia has temporarily lost touch with but is desperate to rejoin. This struck a deep chord in Kuroyedov. NB: also his other historical references e.g. the importance of the MOU being signed in the office once occupied by Kuznetsov and Gorshkov; the new 'tradition' of missile cruiser *Varyag* visiting the Korean port each year to pay respects to the 1904 *Varyag* sunk there against enormous odds by the Japanese (but refusing to surrender).

2. Importance of Yegorov

His value as a bridge to Kuroyedov for the RN cannot be overemphasised. His prestige is enormous and his counsel almost certainly sought by Kuroyedov and Kravchenko. He was an important social catalyst during the visit. He stated with feeling how memorable and wonderful his UK visit had been, saying the impressions become more intense as the actual events recede in time.

He is the only Russian admiral who happily uses the UK interpreter without a Russian interpreter to cross-check. It is perhaps significant that Kuroyedov was also happy to do so at supper.

3. Absence of Kasatonov

I am not clear as to whether the Deputy C-in-C was unable to attend or simply excluded. The latter seems likelier: he was the only senior admiral missing from the C-in-C/fleet commanders press conference at the end of August. This was confirmed by his use of Rear Admiral Avdeichik to pass a book to 1SL as a gift – not Kuroyedov or Yegorov. Avdeichik was Head of the Northern Fleet Command Post when Kasatonov was First Deputy Commander Northern Fleet, so he appears to have been deemed by Kasatonov as a more suitable go-between to 1SL than Kuroyedov... Perhaps this confirms the eclipse of Kasatonov. His relegation to the background would imply that we should not be surprised by his early departure from the High Command, perhaps at his own request.

4. Absence of Kravchenko

Although it was in one way a pity that he did not attend (he has never met a British admiral before and his comments as Black Sea Fleet Commander were often pointedly anti-NATO), his absence probably assisted the social dynamic (he may well have been ill at ease). His absence may be explained by the Russian practice that either a commander *or* his chief of staff should always be 'minding the shop'.

5. 'Purple' thinking

Yegorov attributed the 'blueprint' for the new unified Kaliningrad (and Kamchatka) command structure directly to Kuroyedov; he said Kuroyedov had elaborated much of the detail when Chief of Staff of the Baltic Fleet. Kuroyedov was a clear advocate of 'purple' thinking, stating that duplicated structures were a 'profligacy' Russia could no longer afford; a useful indication of his long-term thinking.

6. Importance of Bespokoiny and 12th Surface Ship Division

This unit was judged the best formation in the Russian Navy two years running (1996 and 1997). The destroyer *Nastoichivy* is 'best ship' but both Yegorov and Kuroyedov place weight on letting her close rival *Bespokoiny* carry out defence diplomacy in view of her guard ship role to HMY *Britannia* – again the force of history. *Bespokoiny* has a presidential honour-scroll for her royal duties. UK suggestions to continue the 'F6–Twelfth Division' link are therefore most welcome to the Russian Navy.

7. Proposals

Kuroyedov and Yegorov would like an RN ship in the Navy Day review at Baltiysk in 1999. (Sunday 25 July is the likely date.) This is a rare – perhaps unprecedented – honour for a NATO warship.

They would also like *Bespokoiny* to come to Plymouth Navy Days and be the exercise partner. (*Sovremenny* DDG; the only rival is sister *Nastoichivy*.)

The West Pacific Seapower Symposium would see a Russian proposal to end all intelligence gathering in littoral waters (Kuroyedov stated this at the call).

8. Conclusion

Exceptionally good meeting: good human dynamics, considerable frankness ('It's difficult persuading politicians of the naval case when the government changes every three months!' – Kuroyedov) and genuine warmth and mutual respect.

The signing of the MOU is a highly symbolic and concrete affirmation of common European traditions and continuity between two major navies. It places an unambiguous line under nearly seventy-five years of historical discontinuity and fracture as embodied by the Soviet era and anchors the Russian Navy to external cooperation – whatever the internal political vicissitudes within Russia.

Robert Avery, Defence School of Languages, Beaconsfield, 29 September 1998

This ten-year activity and interaction between the two navies, capped by the signing of the MoU in 1998, was remarkable and exceeded any period in history. The number of ship visits, twenty-five between 1988 and 1999, and the forty meetings involving Flag Officers in the same period shown in Tables 5.1 and 5.2 respectively, bear witness to this. Moreover, there were Royal visits, most notably by HMY *Britannia* in 1994 to St Petersburg, with HM the Queen and HRH the Duke of Edinburgh embarked, hosting President Yeltsin and others. One of the other guests present was a grey, dour, nondescript Deputy Mayor of St Petersburg who attended a lunch, hosted by Flag Officer Royal Yachts, and who said very little – Vladimir Vladimirovich Putin. The visit also included, by kind permission of HM the Queen, a pirate party onboard the Royal Yacht for children from a local orphanage – a demonstration of the breadth and scope a ship visit, Royal or otherwise, can provide in building bonds and relationships.

The 1995 RUKUS declaration, which had encouraged more joint exercises between ships, aircraft and naval infantry units of the three countries, as well as the involvement of naval training establishments and commanding officers of squadrons (divisions/brigades), acted as the catalyst to bilateral activity. For example, links were established between the Maritime Warfare Centre, HMS *Dryad* and the Kuznetsov Naval Academy (KNA), St Petersburg and also the two navies' junior officer basic training establishments – the Saint Petersburg Naval Institute (SPNI) (formerly known as the M. V. Frunze Higher Naval School) and Britannia Royal Naval College (BRNC).[10] These early links played an important role in the early 2000s after the first political rupture with Russia generated by Kosovo 1999 and will be discussed later.

Figure 3.5 Flag Officer Royal Yachts Rear Admiral R. Woodard (third from left) entertained St Petersburg dignitaries aboard HMY *Britannia* during the State Visit. Among the guests was the Deputy Mayor Vladimir Putin (fifth from left). Robert Avery (second from right) was the interpreter. Destroyer *Bespokoiny* is in the background. October 1994. © Crown Copyright.

1988–99 From confrontation to cooperation 49

Figure 3.6 HM Yacht *Britannia* berths at the English Embankment in St Petersburg at the start of the State Visit of HM Queen Elizabeth to Russia. She was not embarked at this point, having flown to Moscow but would entertain President Yeltsin on board at the end of the visit. 15 October 1994. © Author – Robert Avery.

Figure 3.7 HM Yacht *Britannia* alongside during the Royal Visit to St Petersburg. October 1994. © Author – Robert Avery.

Figure 3.8 Destroyer *Bespokoiny* viewed across from HMS *Glasgow* during the Royal Visit to St Petersburg. October 1994. © Author – Robert Avery.

Figure 3.9 HM Yacht *Britannia* alongside at St Petersburg during Royal Visit, Destroyer *Bespokoiny* in the background. October 1994. © Author – Robert Avery.

Figure 3.10 Beat Retreat by HM Royal Marines on English Embankment St Petersburg. Viewed from HM Yacht *Britannia* during the state visit by HM Queen Elizabeth. October 1994. © Author – Robert Avery.

Links between commanders of ship squadrons settled on the RFN's main surface ship squadron in Baltiysk, the Twelfth Division of Surface Ships and the RN's Sixth Frigate Squadron in Devonport. This was driven in large part by geography, with the Northern Fleet considered too far, and the frequency of operational exercises in the Baltic Sea involving Russia, with diplomatic visits to St Petersburg often followed by sea exercises afterwards with ships of the Twelfth Division. The aspiration was for some sort of formal twinning relationship that would, in time, lead to a cross-pollination of lessons and ideas from exercises that would develop future maritime operating procedures between the two navies. The process had to start with the establishment of a personal relationship between a senior RN officer and his Russian opposite number. That happened in May 1998 during a visit to St Petersburg by HMS *Somerset*. This visit was in many ways the culmination of ten years worth of visits. It saw the formalisation of bilateral activity and various linkages and preceded the signing of the MoU in September that year. It also included the visit of Rear Admiral Peter Franklyn, Flag Officer Surface Flotilla and HRH Prince Andrew.

The successful twinning of the Twelfth Division and Sixth Frigate Squadron was driven in large part by the charismatic and forward leaning commanders of their respective squadrons – Captain First Rank Oleg Demyanchenko[11] and Captain Adrian Nance. A meeting of minds and mutual aspirations for the relationship quickly led to a warm and cordial professional meeting. The nature of this first meeting laid the foundation for future interaction between the squadrons and their people, including the establishment of a sports competition for the Baltic Cup (a repurposed RN trophy) between visiting RN ships and their RFN hosts. The twinning of the squadrons also assisted better interoperability between RFN and RN ships in the Baltic, often linked to participation in the annual NATO BALTOPS/PfP exercise that the RFN was taking part in at that time. Captain Demyanchenko set a positive tone for the relationship with commanders of the Sixth Frigate Squadron after Captain Nance and enthusiastically supported closer cooperation. However, it did at times feel that he was doing this against the grain of some in Main Naval Staff and other security agencies but he nevertheless had the courage to persevere.[12]

The overall success of this 1998 visit, indeed many of the interactions with the RFN in St Petersburg and Baltiysk, must rest with the then Commander of the Twice Red Banner Baltic Fleet,[13] Admiral Vladimir Yegorov. He spent his career in the Baltic Fleet and became the commander in 1991. On retirement, Yegorov was elected Governor of the Kaliningrad Oblast in November 2000. A personable, softly spoken man, he supported and promoted better relationships between the two navies and encouraged more cooperation at sea, despite no doubt some resistance from some of the more hawkish and suspicious members of the Main Naval Staff. He was inquisitive, open-minded and extremely knowledgeable and always displayed great

Figure 3.11 Admirals Igor Kasatonov – First Deputy Commander-in-Chief Russian Federation Navy (right) – and Admiral Yegorov – Commander Baltic Fleet – engage Vice Admiral John Brigstocke (Flag Officer Surface Flotilla) in conversation during the Victory Day Commemorations in St Petersburg marking the fiftieth anniversary of the end of World War II. May 1995. © Author – Robert Avery.

Figure 3.12 Lt Cdr David Fields (Assistant Naval Attache) and Commander Baltic Fleet, Admiral Vladimir Yegorov, on board HMS *Somerset*, St Petersburg. June 1998. © Author – Robert Avery.

warmth and affection towards the Royal Navy. He died in June 2022 at the age of eighty-three.

Ship visits

While the 1998 visit to St Petersburg was unusual in its scale, it nevertheless contained many elements of other visits that took place over this twenty-six-year period, and which were spread across the four main fleets – Northern, Baltic, Pacific and Black Sea (see Table 5.1). Preparation and planning for the visits was frequently tortuous and bureaucratic, subject to the Russian culture of confirming plans at the last minute, not keeping everyone informed of any changes, and always referring any perceived difficult requests for specific events during a visit back up the change of command for approval. For a Royal Naval culture that prides itself on forward planning down to the last meticulous detail this was anathema and a constant source of frustration and a test certainly of senior officers' patience. But somehow the visits happened and largely to a plan and left a lasting impression on those who experienced them. Some of the most memorable moments included embarked Royal Marines Bands' playing of the flight decks of British frigates, sailing up the River Neva, past the Admiralty shipyard, which constructs the very capable diesel-electric Kilo-class submarines, with the smell and hubbub of St Petersburg in the background and the golden dome of St Isaac's Cathedral glistening in the distance and with the spire of the Peter and Paul Fortress on the other bank similarly standing out. The berth of choice for RN platforms was often alongside the aptly named *Angliyskaya naberezhnaya – the English Embankment*. The Embankment was built between 1763 and 1767 and was named after the former British Embassy and the English church that was located at building No 56. It was from the English Embankment that at two am on 25 October 1917, the gunshot from the cruiser *Aurora* sent the signal to storm the Winter Palace marking the start of the Russian Revolution. (Between 1918 and 1994 it was named *naberezhnaya Krasnogo Flota – Red Navy Embankment*, reverting to its original name on 8 September 1994 in honour of the forthcoming visit by HM Queen Elizabeth in the following month.)

While the focus of the early visits was very much centred on a typical defence diplomacy agenda, e.g. meetings between visiting Flag Officers, official receptions, ships' tours, city visits and sports events for personnel from the ships, as well as the ships being open to the Russian public, these soon developed to include a practical element at sea. These elements, planned in harbour during the visit, focused on exercises such as communications, Officer-of-the-Watch (OOW) manoeuvres, Replenishment at Sea approaches and helicopter cross-decking operations, replicating or enhancing what was already being developed through the RUKUS process. Visits were often timed to coincide with key historical events, the chief amongst these being the anniversaries of the first Arctic Convoy, Operation Dervish, to Arkhangelsk in August 1941. The UK was represented at the fiftieth, sixtieth and seventieth anniversaries by Admiral Sir Mark Stanhope first in 1991, when he was in command of HMS *London* and then in 2011 at the seventieth anniversary as the First Sea Lord. Of note, the visit in 1991 was the first foreign warship of any nation to visit the Soviet Union after the August Coup the week before, a failed attempt by hardliners of the Soviet Union's Communist Party to forcibly seize control of the country from Mikhail Gorbachev.

Table 5.1 shows that there were fewer RFN ship visits to the UK than those by the UK to Russia. Two of the most notable were RFS *Neutsrashimy*'s visit to London in 2003 in support of President Putin's state visit and two years later in 2005, RFS *Admiral Levchenko* took part in the two-hundredth anniversary of the Battle of Trafalgar at the Trafalgar 200 naval review off Portsmouth. HRH Prince Michael of Kent went on board and surprised the Guard of Honour by addressing them in Russian in the correct ceremonial manner.

While this may seem to indicate less enthusiasm from a Russian perspective for developing a bilateral relationship through ship visits, it was in fact

Figure 3.13 'I greet you, Comrade Northern Fleet Sailors!' After addressing this – in immaculate Russian – to the Guard of Honour drawn up on the flight deck of the *Udaloy*-class large anti-submarine *Admiral Levchenko*, HRH Prince Michael of Kent spent over an hour touring her and meeting the ship's company. Trafalgar 200 Review in Spithead, July 2005. © Author – Robert Avery.

more to do with the availability of platforms, and ones which were serviceable and able to deploy. The 1990s and early 2000s coincided with the RFN making difficult choices over which platforms to continue operating while designing and developing new more modern and capable platforms and systems for the future. Manpower also needed restructuring and saw a desire to employ more contract personnel than conscripts to professionalise the RFN. Therefore, the paucity of platforms available and the demands placed on them both for national tasking and also bilateral visits to other nations meant significantly fewer RFN ships seen in UK ports. Moreover, those that did visit tended to be the same 'old warhorses' some of which remain in service.

Russian Naval Infantry and Royal Marines

The Russian Naval Infantry (RNI) is an elite element of Russia's armed forces. As such, they were heavily involved in the initial stages of Putin's 'special military operation', launched against Ukraine in February 2022 and subsequent operations. The RNI have also suffered significant casualty rates,

Figure 3.14 From HMS *Battleaxe*: close pass by large anti-submarine ship *Admiral Panteleyev* during officer-of-the-watch manoeuvres off Baltiysk. July 1992. © Author – Robert Avery.

in particular the 155th Naval Infantry Brigade of the Pacific Fleet. Given the status of the RNI and UK's own elite Royal Marines (RM), efforts were made from as early as 1992 to establish a working relationship between the two forces. There was mixed success which ultimately led to little of any real substance being achieved.

The first contact between the RNI and RM was in 1992 during HMS *Battleaxe*'s visit to Baltiysk, home of the Baltic Fleet and the 336th Guards Naval Infantry Brigade. It was unclear whether a meeting between the RNI and RM would take place but it did, thanks to Colonel Charlie Wilson, a young RM at the time, who had learned Russian at university and was now being asked to repay some of that training. Wilson's full account of that visit is included, since it captures the terror of a young Russian speaker being asked to use his language skills in what was a totally alien environment of a country, which only a few years before had been the UK and the West's sworn enemy. Wilson's account also shines a light into the culture and nature of both ordinary Russians and those in the RNI. Many of these observations, as discussed later, remain prevalent today. Subsequent interaction between the RNI and RM remained low-key and restricted to one off visits. This included a RM visit in 1998 to Baltiysk, which Wilson also captures, including the extraordinary, daring arrival of the UK delegation who crossed the Lithuanian border at night to arrive in time for the start of the visit after the flight from Moscow to Kaliningrad was diverted. This achievement set a very positive tone with the RNI hosts for the rest of the visit. The main effort in two further exchanges in 2005 and 2006, was to explore the possibility of RNI personnel taking part in the RM All Arms Commando Course at Lympstone and to attempt to involve the RNI in the amphibious element of the Partnership for Peace BALTOPS exercise. Neither ambition was achieved in part due to the gathering political headwinds and more strained strategic relationship between Russia and the UK.

Royal Marines – Russian Naval Infantry interaction: the beginning

Colonel Charlie Wilson Royal Marines

Introduction

It all began by chance in 1975. As a newly arrived undergraduate at Aberdeen University, I decided to study Russian as a component subject for the award of an MA for no other reason than wanting to know more about the nation that had produced authors, composers and playwrights with whom I had become familiar during secondary education. I also relished the challenge of adding to my small portfolio of French and German by linguistically going beyond the Latin alphabet: Cyrillic offered that challenge. Three years later, I achieved my MA, and without looking back or thinking any more about the Russian language headed south to the Commando Training Centre Royal Marines to begin my career in the Corps.

Preparation

In 1992, I had the privilege of commanding Ten Training Squadron Royal Marines, based on the shore of Poole harbour and responsible for training all levels of Royal Marines landing and small craft crews. It was a perfect afternoon, and all was well with the world and the training programme. I was therefore contemplating indulging in a little seamanship continuation training for myself by taking one of the unit's sailing dinghies for a trip around the further reaches of the harbour. However, I was prevented from leaving the office by the ringing of the phone; on picking up, I found, to my surprise, that I was being addressed personally by our Military Secretary calling from Old Admiralty Buildings in Whitehall. He was, as ever, to the point of saying 'you speak Russian, don't you'; it was more of a statement than a question. To my stuttered reply that I had last done so thirteen years previously, he replied, 'Well, there are four Russian speakers in the Corps; three are doing it properly and there's you. HMS *Battleaxe* is on her way to Baltiysk to carry out a RN visit establishing relationships with the Russian Navy as a first step towards *Glasnost*. Rear Admiral Bruce Richardson, Chief of Staff to FOSF and former Naval Attache Moscow in 1982, was leading the RN contingent. There is the possibility of liaison with the Russian Naval Infantry Brigade based there, and you will be the liaison officer, if it happens. We know no more. You fly to Kiel to meet the ship the day after tomorrow...get the books out and start revising. It's time to repay some of that investment the Queen made in you at university!'

The experience

After four days of frantic but largely unsuccessful revision, arrival in Baltiysk was a strange mixture of the normal – procedures for entering harbour, working with tugboats and coming alongside – and the anticipation of reaching a place that no one aboard the ship (except Admiral Richardson) had been to before, and was therefore unsure of what to expect. The view on entering the harbour was of many Russian naval ships of all sizes and classes rafted up on each other on the jetties (several displaying a clear air of neglect), of many trees actually in the dockyard just behind the quays creating a rural atmosphere inside this large military base, and in the middle distance a skyline punctuated by Khruschevka-style blocks of flats. The quay itself was expansive (probably reserved for large vessels or important visiting ships) but cobbled, giving it a distinctly dated feel, with grass growing between the stones. A smartly turned-out Russian naval band awaited us there, as well as a group of senior Russian naval officers (but no sign of anyone from the Naval Infantry). There was a large crowd of civilian onlookers. Ceremonial formalities having been exchanged, HMS *Battleaxe* came gently alongside to the tuneful strains of the Russian naval band and the extraordinary experience for all began. It is worth saying here with hindsight that events constituting this visit were so full-on that the visit is a blur of memory with several outstanding features, which I will attempt to describe in the hope that some understanding of this extraordinary exchange might be imparted. Throughout, I and my RN counterparts realised how privileged we were to be taking part in this encounter, all the while metaphorically pinching ourselves to prove the reality of what we were going though.

The Naval Attache Moscow accompanied the Russian naval VIP hosting group aboard to conduct the welcome formalities. This naval visit programme had been finalised well before the arrival in Baltiysk; the putative Russian Naval Infantry programme remained in the 'possibly/maybe/might be' category: nothing was arranged or certain. I therefore kept out of the way while the main visit rolled forward. Soon after the VIP party embarked, the ship was opened to visitors, and the waiting crowd filed on board. What struck us onlookers was the contrast between Russian males and females: the former were almost universally wearing cheap imitation leather jackets, peaked caps and black trousers, were mostly unshaven and shabby with bad teeth. The

Russian females, by contrast, were strikingly pretty and neatly dressed with most sporting what must have been a newly arrived shipment of leggings, a fashion item that had swept through Europe some months previously. The Russians were all as curious and excited to meet these aliens from the UK as we were to encounter them: both parties were probably equally surprised to find that human exchanges were possible with the other, consisting mostly of amusement at each other's attempts at Russian or English. Meanwhile, I stayed to one side, watching the jetty and wondering if the Russian Naval Infantry would show up and how on earth I would communicate with them if they did.

An hour and half or so after our arrival alongside, a single small open jeep-type vehicle driven by a lone Russian Naval Infantryman pulled up on the jetty. Acting on the assumption that this might be something to do with me, I donned my Lovat uniform jacket and belt and stepped off the ship to accost him. He spoke no English, but I managed to make him understand that I was the Royal Marines Captain whom the RNI Brigade might be expecting. He nodded, indicating that I should join him and we left the naval base.

The drive lasted about fifteen minutes, and what was striking outside the naval base was the rough condition of the roads, which were mostly cobbles linked by potholes. The town of Baltiysk was a mixture of old and new: Soviet style blocks of flats interspersed with old wooden houses with grass roofs. These were standing in small plots, all of which appeared to be untended sites of scientific interest. There were few cars on the road, and equally few pedestrians. Arrival at the barracks was memorable because of the relatively shabby appearance of its gate and guardroom, an impression that was reinforced once inside: the barracks was extensive by comparison with Royal Marines standards, and the barrack blocks themselves were impressively large, but looked badly in need of maintenance, as did most of the paved areas in it. The jeep drew up outside a single storey building that I realised was the Brigade headquarters of the 336th Independent Guards Naval Infantry Brigade, and I was ushered inside. Awaiting me was an officer to whom I was introduced as the Brigade Commander. He immediately invited me along a wide, dark-wood panelled corridor into his office, redolent with what I later came to recognise as a smell particular to Russian corporate buildings – a mixture of mustiness, stale pungent tobacco, drains and old cooking. This was where my experience began.

*

At this stage, I was experiencing a certain quiet panic. I had no interpreter, minimum grasp of Russian, with limited spoken and comprehension abilities in the language, not having used it for about thirteen years; I was not sure where I was nor what to expect, and had received no pre-briefing except the wonderfully general instruction to 'liaise'. In short, I was on my own and had no option but to liaise in the best way that I could while waiting to see how the visit developed. Conversation with the pleasant but clearly somewhat bemused Brigade Commander was stilted at first. I had no military vocabulary, an equally absent capability to discuss current global geo-political matters such as the thawing relationship between the West and the Russian Federation, and a cluster of recently revised Russian vocabulary and grammar whirling around in my head in no form of order, all while listening to the Brigade Commander and trying to understand what he had said to me. However, this initially embarrassing opening encounter was noticeably improved when he took a large bottle of vodka from his desk drawer, cemented squares of a Spam-like product to rye bread with what I hoped was margarine and insisted we share both products copiously. Mercifully, the vodka anaesthetised the worst effects of the Spam 'appetisers' as well as giving my limited Russian language abilities a kick start.

Formalities and far more fluent conversation were soon concluded with the Brigade Commander, whereupon he introduced me to a senior Major on his staff, Sasha, under whose care I stayed for the remainder of my visit. Sasha turned out to be a gem, and very different from many of the Russians I encountered on this visit and others later. He was relatively young, was clearly intelligent, did not smoke (!), had a smattering of English which complemented my smattering of Russian and was a charming individual who opened his home and hospitality to me unconditionally. This was all in the future, but he started with a briefing about the 336th Naval Infantry Brigade, which had history behind it: having emerged from an Army formation mobilised in The Great Patriotic War in the east of Soviet Union, it arrived in Minsk in 1945 via the battles of Stalingrad and Kursk and other campaigns. The formation was reallocated to the Soviet Naval Infantry in the late 1950s and stationed in Baltiysk from 1963 until the present. There followed a walk around the barracks, including a look into the troops' accommodation. Basic is an understatement, with each block being in poor state of repair, containing enormous dormitories in which each man seemed to have only one locker by his bed, and ablution facilities with almost no privacy. Outside, the barracks presented a curious air of old world militarism in the way it was laid out, its large obviously Eastern European style buildings, its cobbled or gravel pathways and the abundance of untended grass and seemingly unintended 'wild' areas. There was a spectacular assault and confidence course with many obstacles clearly related to those with which I was more familiar, but all appearing to be in a grave state of decay. We were to witness action on this later in the visit. I was also taken to the Brigade's equipment park where I was shown in detail over its armoured fighting vehicles, personnel carriers and tanks. What stayed in my mind from this opportunity was the basic nature of these vehicles: all cramped, with apparently rudimentary fixtures and fittings and crudely finished inside with little thought given to the comfort of those being carried in them. The counter to this impression was the heavy armament each vehicle could carry and the relative simplicity of each model: one interlocutor proudly told me they could run on the poorest quality fuel, and did not require specialist vehicle mechanics to carry out first aid repairs in the field. The second memorable impression to emerge from this visit was the sheer quantity of these vehicles: in the old adage, what they may have lacked in quality, they made up for in quantity.

At the end of the afternoon, I finally understood that Sasha would take me to his home, where unstinting kindness was shown to me. I was introduced to his wife and two young daughters. The flat had one bedroom for the girls and a curtained sleeping space for Sasha and his wife off the main living room, as well as a small kitchen area. It was surprisingly small for a senior Brigade officer, but was immaculately clean and well cared for, in contrast to much of what I had seen in the military estate that afternoon. Tea was produced with some small cakes, and conversation stumbled along, greatly enlivened and lightened when the girls asked if they could practise their English, which was done with much giggling. Gradually I became aware that preparations were being made for Sasha and me to go out, with much mention being made of a word I did not know: 'yantar'. I understood that I was to be taken somewhere, but no more than that. Outside the flat, we got into a military car of some sort and drove off into the hinterland.

After forty minutes or so on the road I still did not understand where we were going or what the oft-mentioned 'yantar' held in store. I was wondering if Sasha, despite his charm and kindness, was in fact a KGB/FSB operative and I was being taken somewhere whence I would not return, or were we embarking on a monumental night out from which I would emerge the worse for wear and a prime candidate for blackmail and turning into a Russian agent. Fortunately these fevered imaginings were soon dispelled: we turned off the main road (such as it was) and entered a lane through a forest. The car halted at the top of a slight rise where a breathtaking and unexpected view was revealed: a huge quarry was in front of us, extending deep below us into the yellow, sandy soil of the Oblast and as far as I could see to left and right. Excavation machines and diggers in the quarry had the scale of Tonka toys. The penny still had not dropped completely, but I did begin to understand that this quarry was extracting something important to the region and indeed to Russia, and was the introductory part of what I had been brought to see. Turning around, the car went back down the forest lane and continued to the outskirts of a town, which as we entered it turned out to be historic and reasonably well preserved. We passed a sign with the town's name on it: 'Yantar' again, so things were slowly becoming clear: thus far, this was not a honeytrap. Finally drawing up outside the entrance to what looked like a well preserved eighteenth-century fortress, Sasha leapt out and went into what appeared to be a ticket office. Very soon, he beckoned me to follow him and I found myself in a museum and its attached souvenir shop dedicated to... amber, or, as I now rapidly deduced the 'yantar' that had been the subject of so much earlier conversation. I also realised that Sasha had had this place opened purely for my benefit, and that I was the sole visitor. As I now discovered, amber was the prized export of the Kaliningrad Oblast, a commodity that was shipped from here all over the Federation and to customers around the world. The Oblast Russians were very proud of their heritage in this material, and I could see why: the museum had a vast array of amber of all shapes, sizes and colour variations, as well as some incredible fossilisation within it. To round off the generosity of this visit, I was invited to choose some amber merchandise from the shop to take home, which I thought was very kind. With an amber necklace and bracelet in hand, we withdrew to the car and I was taken intact, un-turned and relieved that the day had gone well, to the naval base for an eagerly anticipated return to the familiarity of HMS *Battleaxe*. It had been an extraordinary day in an environment in which I had never imagined finding myself, but realised I was very fortunate to be having this experience. I had quickly learned that the people who had been our enemies thus far in my military career, and against whom we had regularly prepared to defend NATO's northern flank, were as human as we were. The pleasure of discovering this humanity behind the forbidding façade of the recently-demised Soviet bear was genuine. As I left him, Sasha said he would see me the next day.

I was collected the following morning by the same driver as before. I had also discovered aboard the ship that the Royal Naval visit party would spend much of the next day with the Russian Naval Infantry, which was a relief to me as it meant that my weak Russian language skills would be less exposed, and I could use the immeasurably better abilities of the RN interpreters assigned to the visit to cover my linguistic embarrassment.

Thus, I arrived separately from the RN visitors, to be warmly greeted by the Brigade Commander and several of his staff – said greeting being largely built around extravagant shots of vodka. This process was repeated when the RN visitors arrived, which was followed by a repeat of the briefing I had received the previous day, delivered and received this time in convivial style. Thanks also to the presence of the RN interpreters, I was able to understand much more about the 336th Guards Independent Naval Infantry Brigade. What became much clearer to me now was their esprit de corps, born from their pride in being Naval Infantry and the fascinating history of their roots in 1942, participation in two of the defining Soviet battles of World War II, their gradual migration from the south eastern corner of the Soviet Union to its western fringe and associated sense of responsibility for protecting that flank. There was also a nice irony to understand that during the Cold War this formation had been earmarked to attack NATO's Northern flank through Norway, with full knowledge that the Royal Marines would be their adversary. This caused much good natured, if slightly competitive, banter. (In a subsequent visit, I was told that the RNI knew about the defensive positions planned for northern Norway and how to circumvent them!) I found it interesting that the RNI had the same relationship with their parent naval service as did the Royal Marines with the RN: probably best described as one of sibling rivalry.

On completion of the welcoming brief, we were poured into an antiquated bus and driven through the camp to the next item on the visit programme: range work. We decanted well behind the firing point of what seemed to be the base's main range. Like so many things I had seen thus far, it was recognisable from my own experience of similar facilities in the UK, but was very different. It had pre-dug trenches at the firing point, to enable users to practise shooting from different positions, but unlike most British ranges, had no intermediate firing points for shooting at a different ranges and targets were fixed in the butts, with no facility for 'popping up' targets at varying ranges to train users to react to 'advancing troops'. The range itself was about 600 m long, and, with long, un-mowed grass resembled a meadow. Arranged behind the firing point was a complete collection of Soviet/Russian weaponry, with which I and my peers had become familiar during our careers: Makarov pistols, the ubiquitous AK74 assault weapon, Dragunov sniper rifles, PKM general purpose machine guns (curious how similar this weapon's working parts were to our own General Purpose Machine Gun – it was familiar throughout) and intriguingly, RPG-7 anti-tank weapons. I also noticed that off to a flank were some RNI armoured personnel carriers. More prosaically, the area behind the firing point was alive with a crowd of family members of our RNI hosts, obviously invited to see the spectacle of these strange beings from the UK making fools of themselves with Russian weaponry.

Before the fun started, and somewhat unexpectedly, was the obligatory pre-shooting ritual: no, not a range safety briefing or explanation of any unusual characteristics of a weapon we were about to fire, but a round of toasts with yet more vodka, presumably to wish each round well on its way down range or to give the firers better eyesight, steadier hands and quicker reactions. Once all were well lubricated and convinced of their own superlative shooting abilities, the firing started, with the visitors divided into 'round robin' groups experiencing a generous allocation of ammunition with each weapon, and with a RNI host to help if we experienced a difficulty with the weapon. It was at this point that I experienced the most frightening moment on a range of my entire career. Family members, civilians, were wandering freely around the range and firing point watching proceedings under no form of control. I was using an AK-74, enjoying the opportunity to fire it on automatic, something that could only be done with similar weapons on certain specialist UK ranges: it was a rare treat. As I was about to loose off my second magazine, safety catch off and having taken up the first pressure on the weapon's trigger, to my horror into my line of sight came the top of a young boy's head. In a cold sweat I immediately raised the weapon's muzzle, applied the safety catch, put the weapon down and saw that he and others were unconcernedly strolling in front of and around the firing points, presumably to have a better view of the visitors. There was no range supervision to speak of, and certainly no thought about controlling the civilians for their own safety. Our Russian hosts saw what had happened, but appeared unflustered, apparently treating this as a normal occurrence. I was flabbergasted and not a little frightened by how close this had come to tragedy: such a thing, had it been able to happen in the UK, would have resulted in an instantaneous closure of the range, a board of enquiry at least and consequent disciplinary action, but the circumstances around this near-disaster would never have been never have been allowed to arise.

A much better highlight occurred a little later on the range, when we had the chance to fire the RPG 7 – no helmet, ear defenders or anything effete like that: just rest it on the shoulder, squint down the rudimentary sights and fire. All very well in theory, but extremely difficult to control with the tube resting on the protruding metal stars of my rank badges. With a deafening roar, a blinding cloud of smoke and a jump of the tube I launched the round down the range – and straight into the ground about twenty yards ahead of the firing point. This gave rise to great mirth amongst our Russian hosts and, inevitably, another round of embarrassment-relieving vodka. The demonstration was completed with heavy calibre weapons firing by the AFVs that had waited patiently to a flank: a very impressive and consistent weight of fire was delivered.

Lunch, accompanied by yet more vodka followed. We were led in due course to the assault course I had seen the previous day. What followed was an extraordinarily well choreographed display of assault course techniques by large numbers of Naval Infantrymen scaling walls, abseiling down others, negotiating high level rope courses, leaping ditches, crawling under barbed wire entanglements, all accompanied by coloured smoke, explosions and gunfire from blank ammunition. There was even a simulated parachute drop. A highlight of this display was marines leaping through or over blazing obstacles, which added to the smoke and sense of battlefield chaos. As soon as this was complete, another group emerged from their waiting area and gave an equally well choreographed unarmed combat display. Unlike the RM equivalent, where the moves are carried out by four marines and generally merge sequentially into each other, this was almost balletic, with several groups going through the same routines in synchronisation. The grand finale, however, was performed by a single marine. In the best Bond film villain style, a huge man wearing combat trousers and a green singlet approached a stack of bricks about three courses high and one thick. After a series of warm-up drills, he knelt beside the stack; pausing to gather his strength, he tensed and brought his forehead down sharply on the bricks, which, unable to stand the violence of the assault, immediately shattered to much applause from the onlookers. It would have been churlish to suggest at this point that these were specially doctored bricks. Besides, it made for a fittingly theatrical climax to a spectacular show. On reflection, this demonstration impressed by sheer numbers and the amount of simultaneous activity going on across the assault course 'stage', rather than demonstrating the physical skills and endurance of individual or small groups of marines, such as would be the aim in the UK. It was, in summary, a typically Russian approach to showing outsiders their collective strength – similar to the psychology behind the annual May Day parade.

That evening, by way of complete contrast, I was invited to Sasha's house again. On arrival, I discovered that his family's friends had contributed to a wonderful feast of Russian specialities, and I was warmly welcomed into this group. It was a splendid and very happy evening throughout which I experienced the warmth and generosity of Russian people that I would be subject to during future visits. I referred to contrast at the start of this section, and this aspect of Russia became a constant thread through all my subsequent visits. The federation is indeed a land of contrast: people endowed with great charm and warmth, yet who can be cold and distant in a formal setting, not to mention the institutional cruelty in Russia's history; wonderful culture superimposed on poverty; a collective subservience in contrast to individual character, spirit and a sense of humour not far removed from that of the British. At every turn in that country the difference presents itself. Of course this is a sweeping generalisation and Russia is not alone in presenting myriad contrasts to visitors, but it is a place where they are in evidence in every facet of daily life. As a first time visitor, such contrasts were particularly striking and are a characteristic of that fascinating nation that has stayed with me.

The visit was drawing to its close, probably to the exhausted relief of all concerned. The next morning, Sasha showed me around Baltiysk, which was a curious mixture of the very old (wooden buildings with grass roofs and semi-wild gardens) and the relatively new (unprepossessing concrete blocks of flats and office buildings), all built on the unusual feature of a long sand spit separating a large lagoon from the Baltic Sea. All was fairly tatty and run down except, notably, the town's main school, which looked well cared for. However, a pleasant and better kept part of the town was on its waterfront, marked by a statue of Peter the Great, a cobbled promenade and a fine lighthouse which I understood to have been first established in the seventeenth century when the region was Prussian. I thought that would be our final interaction, but the RNI had another surprise in store for me.

Several times during the morning frequent mention had been made of a word that even I, with my limited and rusty Russian vocabulary, understood; 'sauna'. This held all sorts of attractions, based on sauna experiences during previous winter deployments to Norway; however, most of which were not met in the event! Sasha took me in his vehicle away from the base and out into the Brigade's training area. I was beginning to have flashbacks to the Yantar experience, wondering where I was being taken, when after bouncing up a rough track, we drew up at what looked like a crumbling single story small stone barn. Sasha proudly announced that this was the sauna, and on close inspection I could see a solitary RNI marine sitting at its rear tending a fire in what appeared to be a bread oven attached to the building. There was a pond adjacent to it, which gave the spot a pleasantly rustic air. Despite its outward appearance, on entering the building it was relatively well appointed, with a few changing rooms, a communal lounge and showers. Three or four Brigade officers were already there and about to start the purification process. With little hesitation, I changed and joined in. To my surprise, despite the seemingly primitive heating system, the sauna was very hot, and for the first time I experienced birch twig beating, which certainly opened up the capillaries in the epidermis and allowed impurities to escape. The moment came to leave the heat chamber and cool off, so I confidently made off to the showers, preparing to douse myself with a cold shower. However, loud shouts of 'no' and 'does not work' followed me: I was beginning to realise this was Russian normality. Disappointed, I was led outside to one side of the sauna building where I saw what I had missed earlier: a short wooden 'jetty' projecting over the green stagnant waters of the pond about six feet above its weed-encrusted surface. With cries of joy, the Russian officers led the way, entering the water with the abandon of children leaping into a swimming pool. Dubiously, I followed suit, concerned not to imbibe any of the bilious looking water. It was refreshing enough, and I thought it wise to move away from my cavorting companions, so I decided to swim the pond's perimeter. At the furthest extremity from the entry point I became aware I was not alone: not from a Russian suddenly surfacing next to me, or any other convivial surprises, but from a light tickling sensation across one of my legs. Treading water and looking around, expecting to see that I was enmeshed in a weed bed or something similar, my curiosity turned to disgust tinged with horror: I was surrounded by a horde of furry creatures with pointed faces, projecting front teeth and long thick tails. Closing every orifice and stifling my cry of distress, I turned round and fled at a speed that would have qualified me for Olympic swimming, barely touching the rickety ladder that signalled safety. These antics gave rise to great mirth and merriment amongst my companions, which of course seemed to be the perfect reason to retire to the lounge to feast on a strange mixture of milk, pickled cucumber and vodka. My first experience of a sauna in Russia was certainly memorable and not one that I wished to repeat – but I did, unwillingly, on a second visit to Baltiysk a few years later.

The sauna experience was the last of many unexpected and mind-broadening moments that I had during those extraordinary three days with the generous and kind opposite numbers whom we had previously known would be our adversaries in any military clash in Northern Norway. Fond farewells were said with a genuine sense of sadness, and the hopes expressed that we would be able to renew our acquaintanceships under the contemporary warming relationships between the Russian Federation and NATO members. That is what happened over succeeding years. In many ways, the whole visit to the RNI in Baltiysk had been surreal, not only because of the surprise at the openness and kindness shown to me by my hosts throughout but also because I was actually in Russia, the place I had wanted to visit during my studies but that had of course been off limits then and throughout my career to date. I had had an opportunity to spend time behind the veil of secrecy and mystery that had shrouded Russia from my peers and me. While I was of course interested in our Russian hosts, as one might be in creatures from another world, the curiosity was mutual and we exchanged many thoughts and views about our earlier perceptions of each other. To the surprise of the entire visiting group, taking photographs of the equipment and people was permitted, with the gentle request not to photograph aerials or other obviously electronic installations. I left Baltiysk with the impression that the 336th Guards Infantry Brigade was a formation based on high self esteem and esprit de corps, very like my parent Service, and that it had capable, if doctrinaire, troops and significant combat support assets that were robust and simply constructed to afford maximum battlefield survivability and ease of repair. What was not in evidence was the notion of logistic second and third line support, which supports the Soviet theory of taking what is needed from the battlefield and surrounding regions. I may have misunderstood, but I believe I was told that the Brigade's main second line food supply was a large herd of cows that would be moved into rear areas as part of follow-on forces in the event of conflict. I took with me from the visit a wealth of fond and fascinated memories of a unique experience that I had been incredibly fortunate to have. However, departure from Baltiysk did not mean that Russia, in all its quirkiness and contrast, had finished with me yet.

Departure

The departure from Baltiysk, and indeed the Russian Federation, had several memorable moments in store for us as a group. The plan was for the non-ship's company visitors to fly from Kaliningrad to Moscow, spend the night there and then return to the UK the following morning. On our final evening in Baltiysk, we gathered in what we had been told was the town's best (possibly only) restaurant, to mark what we all considered had been a successful visit and a unique experience. This was when I met one of Russia's, and East Europe's, most common social customs: the shrinking menu. To almost every customer choice, the waiting staff member's response is a variant of 'I am sorry, that is not available today'. This is what happened that evening, until the final choices were some form of unidentifiable salad or a steak. Naturally, the latter was the popular choice, so the orders were submitted. Before long an unpleasantly strong smell of something rotten, emanated from the kitchen but we thought little of it, ascribing it to 'just Russia'. In due course, the waitress proudly started bringing out impressively large steaks but steaks that also emitted the earlier smell at ten times the strength: it was appallingly putrid, and the meat inedible. It was probably horse rather than beef, and obviously long past whatever sell-by date might once have been assigned to it. There was no apology, just a shrug and we reverted to the uncertain salad accompanied by yet more vodka – which in the event turned out to be a much better meal than it sounds.

The following morning we moved to Kaliningrad airport. It was a simple place with no departure lounge as such, just a small hall with doors opening onto the hard standing; we could see the aircraft a hundred yards or so away, and a jostling crowd of passengers waiting to board. There were also no boarding passes as we would recognise them, but thought nothing of it. We dutifully queued at the rear of this small throng. With no announcement the doors were opened and the Russians were off like greyhounds out of the trap. We followed more sedately, and quickly found that the only seats left would have us scattered throughout the aircraft in ones and twos. At this point, our wonderful lead interpreter, Robert Avery (who knew the Russians better than they did themselves and was a regular State Visit interpreter) pushed his way to the front of the cabin, elbowed the stewardess aside (no mean feat as she was a well-built unit) and started haranguing the Russians in their own language. I picked up some of what he said, but by no means all, although I thought I heard a reference to Prince Charles. When he had finished, the Russian passengers all sheepishly stood up and made their way to the rear of the aircraft, leaving us space at the front to sit as a group. Bemused, I asked Robert what he had said. He explained that Russians will always obey the last order given by the person with the loudest voice, which he had become because he had told them that they had been very rude to a group of visiting British VIPs and that they had better give up their seats or there would be repercussions – unspecified, but threatened. I asked him if I had heard the mention of Prince Charles correctly, to which he had the grace to look slightly embarrassed and admitted that he had used my name in vain by allocating me temporarily to the British Royal Family. Such an outrageous fabrication worked well on this occasion, and was an object lesson in understanding the workings of the Russian mind, and how to manipulate them to the benefit of the person with the loudest voice! Moscow presented a stark contrast to Baltiysk. Looking down on it from the orbiting aircraft, I was struck by its huge size and concentric, apparently endless rings of khrushchevka housing blocks. Even at this stage, the surprises were not over. Having been taken to our hotel in the city centre by British Embassy Defence Section staff, we went out to see the sights; Red Square would be our first stop. Long before we reached it, we could hear music, which could be identified as operatic singing as we approached. We found ourselves at the back of a huge crowd enjoying a concert by The Three Tenors, with St Basil's Cathedral providing the magnificent backdrop to the stage. The contrast between the cultural wonders of Pavarotti and co, with their admiring audience and the myriad Muscovite ladies of the night thronging the outer edges of the square and who were not backward about coming forward, was a wonderful summation of the surprises and contrasts that we had all experienced during this amazing visit.

The evening, and indeed the visit, was rounded off with yet another small example of Russia's contrasts. British Embassy Defence Section staff took us to dinner in a restaurant specialising in traditional Russian food, with a side order of folklore and culture. The restaurant was busy and the meal, service and ambience reflected a quantum leap from that suffered in Baltiysk, with entertainment on the restaurant's stage by 'Cossacks', folk singers and balalaika players. In the middle of this, I caught a movement out of the corner of my eye on the wall beside me which on inspection turned out to be an enormous cockroach marching placidly towards a new hiding place. Not what one would have expected in such a place, but according to our hosts it was normal enough not to warrant even a raised eyebrow.

Epilogue

After that final twist, the flight home was uneventful, although it is worth recording that we were royally looked after by the British Airways cabin crew who somehow knew who we were and what we had been doing. It took some time after returning to come down from the intensity and novelty of what we had experienced and for us to return to the normal routines of life in Britain. I was aware that I had been very fortunate to have participated in such a unique experience, and still carry with me the memories of all that Russia represented to me on that first visit and subsequent ones: the fascination of seeing behind the veil of secrecy that had hidden the real Russia for so long; great personal kindness and hospitality, mingled with a lively sense of humour, contrasting with the granite-faced hardness of officialdom and total reliance on centralised decision-making; the rural nature of Russian cottages and smallholdings in direct contrast with the severity of their neighbouring bleak accommodation blocks; ancient and modern, but modern reflecting only post-war communist morals, attitudes and culture; the unexpected openness displayed towards us, and the genuine mutual exchange of views and knowledge.

    I was fortunate enough to take part in follow-on visits in succeeding years. Each one built to some extent on the relationship started in 1991, not so much with the individuals (although there was an element of that) but with the institution. Each one, too, gave rise to different experiences and observations of the contrast and contrariness that Russia can display. Two of these stand out for me. Perhaps the most extraordinary occurred in 1998 when I was part of an RM group that visited Baltiysk and the 336th Independent Guards Naval Infantry Brigade again. Our late evening flight there from Moscow was diverted to Kaunas in Lithuania due to thick fog. While this was awkward, it was not insoluble as we had a slush fund for emergencies, so we hired the only two taxis at the airport and directed the drivers to take us to Kaliningrad. It was only after an hour or so that it dawned on us that we faced a problem: on arrival in Lithuania, our passports had been stamped, meaning that we had officially left Russia, which was not at all what was required and would make re-entry into the country, and particularly into the military restricted zone of the Kaliningrad Oblast, extremely difficult. This proved to be the case at about midnight with the duty granite faced border guard being most reluctant to listen to or understand my rudimentary explanation of why six British men with passports showing that they had left the Russian Federation were trying to enter this sensitive zone. The mist billowed, the guard dogs in their kennels howled and we waited while interminable phone calls between the guard and Moscow were made, each one taking him higher up the food chain. After about three hours approval for us to continue our journey was given, and in an instant our man became our best friend: the huge hat came off, the granite exterior dissolved into smiles that displayed poor dentistry to full effect and he produced a bottle of vodka from beneath his desk which had to be emptied before we were allowed to depart. This improvisation, and the fact that we had managed to re-enter Russia in such a way greatly impressed our RNI hosts and set the tone for the remainder of the visit.

    During my final visit to Baltiysk in 2006, again in a group of about six Royal Marines of all ranks, we had had a highly successful visit on a personal level, including drinking our FSB minder under the table at a 336th Independent Guards Naval Infantry Brigade officers' and SNCOs' ball and planting a green beret atop the statue of Peter the Great on Baltiysk waterfront, both acts being applauded by our hosts. Departing the morning after this extravaganza, we were ambushed at breakfast by the Brigade Commander and some of his senior staff officers who forced the inevitable vodka upon us, which was not overly welcome at that time of day. Imbibing continued throughout the journey to Kaliningrad airport, which turned out to be fogbound. While waiting for the visibility to improve, we were introduced to the (apparently) traditional Russian custom of wishing good luck to those departing on a long journey: the *na pasashok*, or toasting of all thirty-six moving parts of a horse so that they may continue working throughout the trip. By the time we decided the fog was not going to clear and that we would use our slush fund to leave Russia and the oblast by train, the RNI officers were almost beyond sensible thought. However, our decision brought them up with a jolt, and thereafter drinking was replaced by worried phone calls to Moscow because we had taken a unilateral decision to depart from the plan. These continued while we were seen onto the train; relief came to our hosts when it was clear that the train was about to leave with us on it and we would no longer be their responsibility, whereupon the vodka made its final appearance. As the train pulled out of the station to start its long journey to Berlin, we breathed a sigh of relief that enforced vodka drinking was no longer part of the daily schedule.

Figure 3.15 HMS *Herald* berths in St Petersburg wearing the flag of the UK Hydrographer of the Navy Rear Admiral J. Myres, welcomed by the Admiralty Band conducted by Captain 2 Rank A Karabanov. October 1991. © Author – Robert Avery.

Hydrographic department cooperation

An important area of cooperation in the maritime environment that spanned the 1988–2014 period, and indeed beyond, was between the two hydrographic departments – the UK Hydrographic Office (UKHO) and the Russian Main Directorate for Navigation and Oceanography (GUNIO). This relationship started positively but after 1995 the interaction became much reduced and did not fulfil the promise of those early days. Both the UK and Russia were quick to grasp the mutual advantages of exchanging material in order to ensure the currency of their worldwide chart coverage. Both sides have had a policy (with the US) of charting the whole 'World Ocean' (to use the Russian term) and realised that each had its strengths, e.g. regularly/recently surveyed areas, which could be beneficial to the other.

The first professional encounter was the visit to London in October 1991 of the large oceanographic ship *Ivan Kruzenshtern* with the Director of GUNIO, Vice Admiral Yuri Zheglov, and his senior team embarked. Rear Admiral John Myres, the Hydrographer of the Navy, was hosted. The visit, coming as it did two months after the August Coup against Gorbachev, had special significance and even merited an impromptu call to the ship by HRH the Duke of York. It would also be the last call of a Soviet Navy ship to the UK.

The two senior hydrographers quickly established a personal and professional rapport which set a productive tone for the visit. Myres invited the Russians to visit UKHO, Taunton where useful contacts were made and archive treasures, such as Captain Cook's charts of Australia were displayed much to the delight of the visitors. Plans for a return visit were proposed and a year later, in October 1992, HMS *Herald* visited St Petersburg with the Hydrographer of the Navy embarked. This marked the first visit to Russia by an RN hydrographic vessel since HMS *Vidal* in 1964. Another first for both navies was the Trafalgar Night dinner[14] on 21 October, with Vice Admiral Zheglov and Rear Admirals Grishanov (Leningrad Naval Base Commander) and Koval'chuk (first CO of *Kirov*) invited as guests of honour. This visit proved to be a success with the involvement of a UKHO team under the Deputy Chief Executive, Barbara Bond. Extensive professional discussions took place in the Main Chart Production Facility, which laid the groundwork for serious cooperation in the years to come. As a gesture of openness the UK delegation were presented with a set of eight charts, which were technically classified and related to ports such as Kandalaksha. A MoU was also signed marking the intention of both hydrographic departments to work closer together.

This period coincided with the start of a technological revolution with the transition from paper to electronic charts. The International Hydrographic

Organisation was then establishing the Worldwide Electronic Navigational Chart Data-Base (WEND) Committee to coordinate the digitisation process across its member-states. This major cultural shift from copper-plate skills honed over centuries to a totally new technology was exercising both hydrographic departments and each saw value in sharing experience with the other during the transition. It was clear that there were major commercial opportunities to be exploited, which was a key driver in discussions at the time and subsequent practical engagement to draw up bilateral agreements. Intensive work in this direction was conducted over the next three years.

Momentum was maintained by the visit to Portsmouth in March 1995 of the Russian hydrographic vessel *Sibiryakov* with the newly appointed Director of GUNIO Vice Admiral Anatoly Komaritsyn embarked, replacing Vice Admiral Zheglov who had died in post in 1994. He was hosted by the new Hydrographer of the Navy, Rear Admiral Nigel Essenhigh,[15] and cordial personal relations were quickly established. Admiral Essenhigh invited Komaritsyn to dinner at his house in Selsey and a call on the First Sea Lord – Admiral Sir Benjamin Bathurst – was arranged. The two new heads of hydrography found they had much in common as neither was a career hydrographer. Essenhigh was a warfare officer and Komaritsyn a submariner. They had evidently been appointed to impart dynamism to their traditionally conservative departments in implementing the shift from paper to electronic charting.

Cooperation culminated in the visit to Russia in September 1995 by Essenhigh to finalise and sign agreements with Komaritsyn. The significance of the visit was underlined by calls on the C-in-C of the RFN, Admiral Gromov, and his First Deputy Admiral Kasatonov in Moscow. There was also a visit to the Del'fin Central Research Institute, headed by Academician Oleg Bogomolov who had held his post for two decades. In subsequent discussions with Russian hydrographers, it emerged that Del'fin was not held in the highest regard by key technical staff in GUNIO, who regarded it as wasteful of resources and a drag on electronic chart development. The torch for this had been grabbed by GUNIO and cooperation with UKHO in this field strengthened their hand in this inter-departmental rivalry. However, it became apparent that investment in digital systems was far less than the Russians were claiming, as well as a lack of required expertise.

Both sides saw sharing of data and expertise as advantageous. UKHO was particularly interested in up-to-date Russian coverage of the Baltic and Black Seas as well as Northern/North-Eastern Russia. GUNIO identified assistance with digitisation and commercial opportunities to strengthen its financial autonomy in a climate of meagre state funding.

The result was the signing of a Bilateral Arrangement between UKHO and GUNIO by the two national hydrographers at the end of the visit. The

Figure 3.16 National Hydrographers Vice Admiral Anatoly Komaritsyn and Rear Admiral Nigel Essenhigh inside the Kremlin. September 1995. © Author – Robert Avery.

key plank of this arrangement was the automatic exchange of charts. Much of the negotiation quickly found common ground and differences to be resolved were mainly technical in nature, e.g. problems arising from the use of Cyrillic and Russian symbology on many Russian charts. The arrangement formalised the exchange of products, data, materials and services, and the sharing of expertise in the field of hydrography and related disciplines. It sought to enhance international maritime safety and the protection of the environment and to avoid duplication of effort between the participants.

The success of getting the agreement over the line owed much to the warm Komaritsyn-Essenhigh relationship, and underpins how important personal and mutual respect between individuals is in developing bilateral

Figure 3.17 The National Hydrographers Vice Admiral Anatoly Komaritsyn and Rear Admiral Nigel Essenhigh sign the Memorandum of Understanding on Hydrographic Cooperation in St Petersburg. September 1995.
© Author – Robert Avery.

cooperation. What had been achieved in a relatively short space of time, was not replicated in the following twenty years, nor moved forward to any great extent. Despite the agreement formalising the processes for the exchange of hydrographic products, this was never achieved at a government-to-government level, although the UKHO did on occasion purchase some Russian charts. Meetings between the UKHO and the GUNIO, bilaterally or within mult-lateral *fora* such as the International Hydrographic Organisation, were characterised as polite and based on technical discussions but achieved very little. Bilateral activity was also affected by the political relationship between Russia and the UK and the frequent ruptures thus led to fragmented interaction between the UKHO and GUNIO.

Notes

1 'UK/Russian Federation: Protocol of Amendments to Agreement Concerning Prevention of Incidents at Sea beyond the Territorial Sea 15 July 1986 (CS Russian Federation No.1/2021)', *Gov.uk*, 16 June 2021, www.gov.uk/government/publications/ukrussian-federation-protocol-of-amendments-to-agreement-concerning-prevention-of-incidents-at-sea-beyond-the-territorial-sea-15–july-1986-cs-russi (accessed 7 May 2023).

2 Amel'ko and other Soviet Naval participants visited HMS *Avenger* in Plymouth as part of the Adderbury programme in November 1989. Amel'ko insisted on shopping in Exeter after the visit. The prime aim was to source a Barbie doll for his granddaughter and cleaning products for his wife. Witnessed by Robert Avery as interpreter.
3 These exercises are designed to test a ship's capability in providing humanitarian aid to a civilian population in times of natural environmental disasters.
4 These ship visits support a nation's policy of soft power engagement with countries to enhance political, defence and trade relationships as well as building a better mutual understanding.
5 A 1994 NATO initiative aimed at creating trust between the member states of NATO and other states mostly in Europe, including post-Soviet states. More information: www.nato.int/cps/en/natohq/topics_50349.htm#:~:text=The%20Partnership%20for%20Peace%20 (accessed 15 May 2023).
6 *Neustrashimy* returned to service in April 2023 following a prolonged refit.
7 Signed by the heads of delegations: Russia – VAdm Yu Kaisin, UK – RA J. Trewby, US – RAdm J. Strasser.
8 E. Grove, *Jane's Navy International*, April 1998 (Vol. 103, No. 3). The authors of the present work have drawn extensively on Professor Grove's article summarising the achievements of the Adderbury/RUKUS process on the occasion of its tenth anniversary.
9 Created by an agreement to exchange military missions in 1946, the stated object of BRIXMIS – and the Soviet equivalent in the British Zone, SOXMIS – was 'to maintain Liaison between the Staff of the two Commanders-in-Chief and their Military Governments in the Zones'. BRIXMIS lasted until 1990.
10 The first visit from BRNC to Frunze to establish this link was in 1998 by Lieutenant Commander Tony Radakin who went on to become the Chief of Defence Staff in 2021.
11 Demyanchenko went on to command the St Petersburg Higher Naval Institute as Rear Admiral in 2003 before being sacked in 2006 over an incident which saw an officer and five cadets die in a boating accident.
12 Conversation author, David Fields, with Vice Admiral Sir Tony Johnstone-Burt KCVO, CB, OBE, DL, Master of the Household, 14 March 2024 and who had been Captain Sixth Frigate Squadron 2000–1.
13 The Order was established on 16 September 1918, during the Russian Civil War. Recipients, including military formations, were recognised for heroism, dedication and courage demonstrated on the battlefield. Only the Baltic Fleet is Twice Red Banner.
14 Trafalgar Night is celebrated every year by the RN to commemorate Admiral Lord Nelson's famous victory over the combined French and Spanish Fleets on 21 October 1805 off Cape Trafalgar.
15 Admiral Sir Nigel Essenhigh GCB was First Sea Lord 2001–2.

4

1999–2010 Back towards confrontation

The progress that appeared to have been made in building a stronger relationship between the RFN and RN from 1988 to 1998 hit a number of speed bumps in the next decade, driven by political tensions between Russia, the UK and other Western allies. These bumps included the 1999 NATO bombing campaign against Serbia, the Orange Revolution in Ukraine in 2004, the murder of Alexander Litvinenko in London in 2006, Russia's invasion of Georgia in 2008 and three rounds of NATO expansion eastwards towards Russia. Periodic pauses were implemented in the defence cooperation programme, but despite this, positive engagement was achieved, especially in submarine search and rescue. Nevertheless, it is fair to conclude that this period saw an overall steady deterioration in Russia's relationship with the West and this did have an impact on the RN–RFN relationship. The year 1999 also saw the arrival of a little known entity at the time as Russia's Prime Minister – Vladimir Vladimirovich Putin – who then became President on the eve of the new millennium.

The first impact on the naval relationship came just before the turn of 1999, in December 1998. Flushed with the success of the 1998 bilateral programme and the signing of the MoU on Naval Cooperation in September, the Assistant Naval Attache[1] (ANA) hosted members of the International Cooperation Staff of the RFN to dinner at his flat on 15 December to finalise details of the ambitious bilateral programme for 1999. That night the US and UK launched Operation Desert Fox against Iraq, a four-day campaign of strikes designed to degrade Iraq's ability to manufacture and use weapons of mass destruction. Within twenty-four hours of the Desert Fox strikes, a diplomatic note from the Russian Ministry of Defence put those bilateral plans on hold indefinitely. The only ray of light that day was a telephone call between a desk officer at the Main Naval Staff and the ANA during which the often repeated phrase over this twenty-five-year period was made – 'Politiki-Politiki' – 'politicians are politicians'. The Russian naval staff were keen to point out that this suspension in cooperation did not diminish the bilateral work of the previous ten years. They said that when the 'politiki had sorted themselves out', the MoU between the RFN and RN existed and could be used to reinstate the naval relationship, when the political circumstances permitted.

The second speed bump in furthering the bilateral naval relationship, which occurred shortly after Desert Fox, was NATO's bombing campaign from March 1999 against Serbia in relation to Kosovo. This was subjected to repeated accusations by Russia as an illegal campaign, to which other Western military interventions have since been added, namely in Iraq, Afghanistan, Libya and Syria. Despite this cooling in the relationship in 1999, there was still some naval interaction both through the RUKUS format and ship and submarine visits commemorating events such as; the sixtieth anniversary in 2001 of Operation Dervish (Arctic Convoy), the centenary of the RN submarine service in 2001, marked with a visit by a *Kilo*-class submarine to Faslane, and the sixtieth anniversary of the Battle of the Atlantic held in Liverpool in 2003. The seventieth anniversary of the latter in 2013, again in Liverpool, marked the last ship visit between the two countries, with the participation of the *Udaloy*-class destroyer *Vitse-Admiral Kulakov*.

History was also made in 2003, when HMS *St Albans* visited St Petersburg to commemorate the three-hundredth anniversary of both the Baltic Fleet and the city itself. The visit was made more poignant by the visit of HRH the Prince of Wales, who formally handed over a British Nicholson 55 yacht, *Adventure*, to the Russian Naval Academy as a gift. The yacht had come to the end of her economic life in 2002 but was rescued by the RN through the efforts of the Naval Attache at the time – now Vice Admiral Sir Simon Lister. In 2013, Adventure, crewed by twelve Russian sea cadets aged between sixteen and seventeen and their four instructors, visited Gosport and the Joint Services Adventurous Sail Training Centre.[2] It was intended that Officer Cadets from BRNC would sail with the Russian cadets from Gosport to Edinburgh but a defect with the yacht precluded this. The aim was a small step to introduce cadets at an early age to each other in an attempt to begin breaking down prejudices on both sides. Plans were drawn up for another attempt to sail together in 2014 but political events dictated otherwise.

Historical events and their anniversaries played a very large and useful part in providing the hooks for interaction between the two navies throughout the entire period of 1988–2014. This sense of a proud and often shared history, even when political tensions were running high, was particularly important. The repeated phrase during these visits, which were often connected to World War II, or the Great Patriotic War as it is known in Russia, was that 'we had fought shoulder to shoulder against a common enemy' – Мы сражались плечом к плечу против общего врага – (*My srazhalis' plechom k plechu protiv obshchevo vraga*) – namely fascism and Nazis. In this current confrontation with Russia, the UK and the West are perceived by the Russians as supporters of fascism and neo-Nazis in Ukraine, which will make what used to be a useful hook to re-engage with Russia and the Russian military, in particular, even harder.

As for the RUKUS talks, post the 1999 watershed event of NATO's actions over Kosovo, they still continued. Talks took place in 1999 at Brasenose College, Oxford, albeit at a much reduced level and with no serving personnel taking part. It was not until 2002, again hosted by the UK, that RUKUS formally took place with serving officers present and for the first time with French participation, leading to the formal transformation of RUKUS to FRUKUS in 2003. At the same time, the UK recruited a retired submariner Captain First Rank, Victor Konusov, as the permanent secretary to FRUKUS. He worked from the British Consulate in St Petersburg and contributed enormously to the success of the talks for next ten years or so providing both continuity and archiving outputs, as well as providing linkages into the RFN Main Naval Staff, the Fleet staffs and the external relations department of the Russian MoD. Konusov continued working at the Consulate until it closed in 2018 after twenty-six years in response to the ever-worsening political relationship, following the poisoning of the Skripals in Salisbury in 2018.

Submarine escape and rescue

One of the dominant themes in the 2000s, in both bilateral and multilateral relationships with Russia, was that of submarine escape and rescue and programmes that sought to assist Russia in the disposal of decommissioned nuclear submarines. The loss of the Oscar II-class submarine *Kursk* in August 2000 was the catalyst in the debate on submarine escape and rescue. Initial Russian obfuscation about the causes of the accident, including blaming the loss on a collision with a UK submarine, the refusal of help from the UK and other nations and the delays by the RFN in rescuing the trapped submariners, led to all 118 of the crew being lost. Putin's apparent indifference towards the grief of the families backfired badly. A particularly poignant visit to Russia took place only days after the incident, when HMS *Cornwall* and HMS *Newcastle* visited Vladivostok. HMS *Cornwall* was commanded by Captain (now Vice Admiral Sir) Tim McClement, a submariner, and on the day of the ship's arrival he stepped ashore into a hostile media storm on the jetty. McClement was able to assure the gathered press that the nearest UK submarine had been at least one thousand miles away but he was not believed and the questioning became more hostile. It was a personal submariner's story told by McClement that calmed the atmosphere and led to a senior Russian submariner reaching out to him after the interview that ultimately led to a memorable visit, captured in McClement's personal account below. The visit strengthened the navy-to-navy bonds, and also demonstrated the vital importance of knowledgeable interpreters, who have an in-depth understanding of both navies and their traditions. (In this case the interpreter was one of the authors, Robert Avery.)

Meeting a Cold War adversary – this time with vodka

Vladivostok, August 2000

On 12 August 2000 the Russian *Oscar*-class submarine *Kursk* sank in the Barents Sea with the loss of all 118 crew. On 22 August the Russian Press accused the UK's nuclear-powered submarine HMS *Splendid* of causing *Kursk* to sink. On 24 August I took my Frigate HMS *Cornwall* into Vladivostok for a three-day visit.

In May 2000 I was in command of HMS *Cornwall* and the lead ship of an eight-ship UK Task Group that sailed round the world; out through Suez and back through Panama. We were gone for over six months. HMS *Triumph*, a nuclear-powered submarine, joined the Group in the Pacific. Her Commanding Officer, Phil Buckley, had been on board HMS *Conqueror* with me in the Falklands Conflict in 1982. In June 1982 as we were returning to our home port in Faslane, Amanda, his then girl-friend, sent him a Familygram which said: YOUR FATHER SAID YES CHURCH BOOKED 14 NOV GET LEAVE. We all enjoyed their wedding. In 2000 we lived opposite each other in Naval Quarters near Plymouth.

Vladivostok is the base port of the Russian Pacific Fleet and was closed to all foreigners until 1990. In 2000 it was a city in decline, but nonetheless most welcoming.

I was asked to speak to thirty-five members of the Russian press; they were very hostile. In my white uniform my submarine badge shone brightly in the sunlight, which only seemed to make it worse. I fielded the questions through my interpreter. I had telephoned Flag Officer Submarines the night before we arrived to ask about the allegation that HMS *Splendid* had caused the sinking. He assured me that at the time of the accident our nearest submarine had been over one thousand miles away. The questioning was getting more and more aggressive; it didn't matter what I said, they did not believe me.

I then said that as a submariner I could empathise with the tragic loss of the families of *Kursk*'s crew; that my wife truly understood their anguish as she had had the same fears whenever I deployed in a submarine under the Arctic ice. She told me that when she heard about the *Kursk* on the BBC Evening News, she had immediately thought of Amanda and how she would be worrying about Phil and his submarine somewhere deep in the Pacific. She had grabbed a bottle of gin and gone across the road to comfort Amanda, as only another submariner's wife could. When Lynne was half way across the road Amanda's front door had opened and Amanda had come out, a bottle of gin in her hand, on her way to seek comfort from Lynne. The reaction from the hostile press was astonishing. One of them apparently asked my interpreter to repeat what I had said, and as he repeated it they all looked at my face. The reporter started clapping, then more followed and finally all of them were applauding; I had no idea why. The rest of the questions were all civil. Afterwards my interpreter explained that Russians are very family-orientated and my wife's understanding and compassion for her friend had touched their hearts; they had been applauding her. I told him it was true, that I hadn't made it up. He looked at me and said it was obviously true from my face and that anyway no one could have made that up.

The next day I received an invitation from Admiral Yevgeni Timofeevich Laputskiy, a retired submariner, who had commanded an *Akula* SSN and a *Typhoon* SSBN during the Cold War. He had seen my interview on the news the night before and wanted to meet me. He invited me and six officers to join him, his wife and children and some friends on a boat trip the next day. I accepted with pleasure. To spend a day on a boat swimming, eating and drinking with a retired Soviet submarine admiral and his family and friends, and find they are the same as us was a wonderful experience. We toasted everything with vodka; I gave him a bottle of Plymouth Gin, he called it 'English vodka' and there were more toasts until it was all gone. It was very poignant. I had joined the Navy thirty years earlier and spent the first twenty years of my naval career as a submariner playing 'cat and mouse' with the Soviets at the height of the 'Cold War'; it was good to meet the 'old enemy' face to face. Through the interpreter we discovered that he had played 'cat and mouse' too, but he had always been in the Pacific and I had always been in the Atlantic, so we had never met. We toasted that too.

In return I invited everyone to come on board HMS *Cornwall* the next day for tea in my cabin. They all came. The interpreter discovered it was the Admiral's wife's birthday so I gave her a balloon. She asked why I had a drawer full and I explained that at sea whenever one of my Ship's Company had a birthday I gave him or her a balloon. The Admiral was fascinated and we had a long chat about command and leadership at sea. The tea went cold and the 'English vodka' came out. I explained that Western submariners had considered Soviet submariners to be '7 feet tall'. The Admiral laughed: the Soviets had considered NATO submariners to be '2 metres tall'. He quoted Tom Clancy: 'American submariners may be respected, but it is the British subs that are feared.' He said after the Falklands War they feared the British the most, because our military had shown what we could do and we had Margaret Thatcher who would use us. Just before they left the Admiral asked permission

Figure 4.1 Yevgeni uniform museum photo. © VAdm Sir Tim McClement.

to address us all. Surprised, I approved and he asked us all to sit. He explained he had been on patrol in the Control Room of his *Akula* when he received the signal promoting him to Admiral. He then opened a bag and took out a faded blue and white striped uniform T-shirt and a well-worn forage cap. He told us he had been wearing them when he received the signal and that he wanted me to have them, because if I did then I too would be promoted to Admiral.

I had been told I could not refuse any gift I was given. So I accepted his treasured uniform with honour. All I could think of in return was to take my Dolphins off my uniform and pin them on his shirt. We toasted each other one more time with 'English vodka' and parted true friends.

We sailed from Vladivostok the next morning having thoroughly enjoyed the warmth and friendship of our Russian hosts.

Seven months later I wrote to Yevgeni to tell him his uniform had worked and I had been promoted Admiral. Conscious of the advice of never refusing a gift, I offered to return his uniform, or, alternatively, I would be proud to put it on a manikin in a display cabinet in the Royal Naval Submarine Museum in Gosport, next to a model of an *Akula* and one of a *Typhoon*, a card telling our story and a photograph of the two of us. He told me he would be honoured to have his uniform in our museum. It is still on display today.

Although UK and international assistance was refused by the Russians to save those trapped in the *Kursk* until it was too late, the tragic accident did lead to more discussions between the UK and Russia on Submarine Escape and Rescue, with the aspiration to develop a UK–Russia MoU on the subject. However, despite considerable efforts on the UK side and support on the Russian side from a range of important actors, including the Rubin Design Bureau, Russia's largest submarine design bureau, and some key officers in the RFN Main Naval Staff, attempts to agree the MoU ultimately came to nothing. In September 2003, a UK delegation visited St Petersburg with the aim of producing a draft MoU text. The meeting, held in the offices of Rubin, went ahead in a very positive atmosphere and there was much goodwill to achieve real progress at this working level. However, once the meeting was over the draft text disappeared into the RFN Main Naval Staff, where it languished until the next meeting in July 2004, again in St Petersburg; nor was there much momentum on the UK side in the interim and this meant that this meeting started at the point where the previous one had finished, with little or no staff work having been done.

Again, the atmospherics of the July 2004 meeting were excellent and the UK Assistant Chief of Naval Staff took part in at least one session while in St Petersburg for the RFN-hosted FRUKUS event. However, too much time was spent on social events, cultural visits and giving presentations that had relatively little relevance to the hard-nosed process of producing a text that satisfied both sides' requirements. An added problem was the difference in legal approach adopted by each side. The RFN was keen for a legally binding text that would have the status of a treaty, whereas UK MoD lawyers were insistent that it should be a MoU that would be morally but not legally binding; they were very wary of any text written in 'treaty language' that could suggest a legal obligation.

Sinking of *K-159*

Despite the lack of progress on an MoU on Submarine Escape and Rescue, one incident in August 2003, three years after the loss of *Kursk*, did signal that interaction between the RN and RFN on the subject had improved a little, when an offer to help the stricken *November*-class SSN *K-159* was made by the UK and was given serious consideration by the RFN. The *K-159* sank while under tow from the remote Gremikha naval base to the Murmansk area where it was scheduled to be dismantled. The submarine was in a very poor physical condition, especially the ballast tanks which could not be relied on to provide the required buoyancy. The RFN was therefore using pontoons secured to the submarine to provide additional buoyancy. However, the pontoons used were designed for lifting static weights from the sea bed and totally unsuited for towing operations. When the submarine hit bad weather the pontoons were torn away and the submarine sank, taking nine of the ten transit crew with it.

The UK NA, Captain Holloway, found out about the incident via the media, rather than through any communication from the RFN. He alerted the RN's Duty Fleet Controller at Northwood, who put the UK Submarine Rescue Service on alert, and then called the Foreign Liaison Office of the RFN Main Naval Staff to ask whether there was anything that the UK could do to help. Initially a holding response was received, saying that the UK offer would be passed on to the appropriate officers. When no response was received for several hours, the NA called back and was told that there would be no rescue operation as it was known that the submarine was completely flooded. Cables passing through the internal hatches meant that none of them could be shut and only one crew member had been rescued. This incident shows that although the RFN at least apparently gave the offer of assistance some thought, it was only through the proaction of the UK NA that any interaction with the RFN was generated. Sluggish responses from the Russian system, fear of those within it potentially 'sticking their necks out' without 'top cover' are always potential reasons for this phenomenon.

G8 Global Partnerships Programme and the Arctic Military Environmental Cooperation Programme (AMEC) – 2003 to 2006

The sinking of the nuclear-powered *K-159* highlighted the importance of the G8 Global Partnerships Programme (G8GPP), which was launched at the 2002 G8 Summit, of which Russia was a member, at Kananaskis, Canada. Its purpose was to reduce the risk of the proliferation of weapons of mass destruction, with particular emphasis on destroying stockpiles of chemical weapons, dismantling decommissioned nuclear submarines, safeguarding/disposing of fissile material and finding employment for former weapons scientists. The UK's contribution to this programme was $750M and these funds were stewarded by the then Department of Trade and Industry (DTI), with support from MoD and FCO; DTI employed the consultants RWE NUKEM to oversee individual projects funded through the programme.

Much of the UK's G8GPP funds were spent in Russia, with a particular focus on securing nuclear material on the Kola Peninsula where hazards included: unsafe storage of nuclear fuel removed from nuclear-powered vessels, including submarines and icebreakers; handling and storage of damaged nuclear fuel; and the defuelling and decommissioning of nuclear-powered submarines and surface vessels. While a significant number of projects were delivered directly between the DTI and the Russian nuclear agency RosAtom, in early 2003 it was decided that closer cooperation with the Russian MoD was required and negotiations began for the UK to join the Arctic Military Environmental Cooperation programme (AMEC).

AMEC had been established in 1996 as a trilateral programme between the MoDs of Russia, Norway and the USA, with the aim of reducing the environmental impact of Cold War military activities in fragile Arctic ecosystems. While, in theory, projects could have been delivered anywhere in the Arctic, in practice the main focus was on the Kola Peninsula. Following negotiations, the UK joined AMEC in late 2003 with the then Commodore Simon Lister as the UK Principal (a role that he kept on an 'ad hominem' basis throughout AMEC's active life) and the Naval Attache as the UK Steering Group Co-Chairman, responsible for the day-to-day running of the programme.

During AMEC's active life from 2003 to 2007, the UK made significant financial and/or technical contributions to a number of successful major projects, the main ones being:

- The design and construction of pontoons to allow the safe movement of decommissioned nuclear-powered submarines whose ballast tanks had deteriorated to the point where they could no longer contribute to the vessel's buoyancy. This project was given added importance following the sinking of the *K-159*.
- The safe movement of the decommissioned November-class submarine *K-291* from Gremikha to the Nerpa shipyard near Murmansk onboard a heavy-lift ship in September 2006. This was the first ever movement of a nuclear-powered vessel onboard a heavy-lift ship and a major technical achievement.
- The subsequent defuelling and dismantlement of *K-291* at Nerpa.

The UK's membership of AMEC did not always run smoothly. While the relationship with the Russian MoD was mostly cordial due to clear common interests (the UK had money to spend on projects, the Russian MoD had projects that needed to be funded), there were distinct tensions with Norway and the US, due mainly to significant differences about how projects were to be delivered. The UK wanted projects to be delivered bilaterally under the AMEC umbrella, while Norway and the US wanted all projects to be quadrilateral, with an inevitable increase in cost, time and bureaucracy. By mid-2006 both Norway and the US had said that they would reduce their participation to that of observers, while the murder of Alexander Litvinenko in November 2006 resulted in an inevitable reduction in the UK's political commitment to funding nuclear legacy projects in Russia.

Although it has never been formally disbanded, AMEC has been moribund since 2007. While the role of Steering Group Co-Chairman was time-consuming and overly bureaucratic, it did provide a useful conduit for the UK Naval Attache to engage with technical directorates of the RFN Main Naval Staff and with senior officers of the Northern Fleet.

The rescue of *AS-28 Priz*

The successful rescue operation in August 2005 of the Russian *AS-28 Priz* submersible was and could have been a game changer in submarine escape and rescue. The operation by the UK Submarine Rescue Service (James Fisher and Sons PLC) which deployed its Scorpio UUV (unmanned underwater vehicle) to Kamchatka to free the trapped submersible, illustrated how far things had moved forward on a practical level since the *Kursk* disaster in 2000. Key personnel in the two countries' rescue organisations knew and trusted each other and, at the political level, the usual urge for secrecy was overcome by the overriding need for a successful rescue, even if it meant involving Western nations. This personal account of the rescue operation by the then UK NA, Captain Holloway, shows that although there was indeed an urgency to get the rescue done, the Russian ingrained desire for secrecy and bureaucratic, stove-piped procedures, very nearly derailed the effort. In October 2005, Holloway was awarded the Order of Friendship of the Russian Federation by President Putin in No. 10 Downing Street,[3] along with others closely involved: remote vehicle operators Stuart Gold and Peter Nuttall, Squadron Leader Keith Hewitt RAF and Commander Ian Riches

Figure 4.2 Captain Jonathan Holloway receives the Order of Friendship from President Vladimir Putin for his part in the rescue of the crew of submersible *Priz*. The ceremony took place in No. 10 Downing Street – Prime Minister Tony Blair looks on. October 2005. © Crown Copyright.

RN. In the current toxic political atmosphere it is hard to imagine that such an event took place.

Operation to rescue submersible *Priz AS 28* – August 2005

Captain Jon Holloway RN – UK NA
(All times quoted are in Moscow Time GMT +4 hours)

I became aware of the problem with *AS 28* from press reports shortly after I arrived in the Embassy at 0830 on Friday 5 August 2005 and immediately rang the Fleet Headquarters at Northwood and advised the Duty Fleet Controller to alert the UK Submarine Escape and Rescue Service (UKSRS) to allow them to consider what help they would be able to provide should it become necessary. I also called the International Relations Office of the Russian Main Naval Staff to try and find out some more information (a nugatory exercise this early in the operation as they were very uncommunicative) and to tell them that the UK was actively considering what help it may be able to offer. I was promised that this information would be passed on to the appropriate senior officer; a nervous few hours then passed while we waited for news and for the UK's system to swing into action. Around midday I received a call from London – the UKSRS's Scorpio remotely operated vehicle (ROV) was available and could be flown to Kamchatka by RAF C17 to take part in the rescue operation and the process was already under way to obtain Ministerial approval to make a formal offer of help. By this time I knew that the Russian Navy had already asked the United States to investigate what help it could provide so began to prepare a diplomatic note which would be the formal offer of assistance. At 1400 I was told that the duty Minister in the UK MoD had given the go-ahead for the operation and immediately drove to the External Relations Department of the Russian MoD and handed over the diplomatic note and briefed the duty officer on exactly what help the UK could provide.

The Russian MoD responded very quickly (almost unbelievably quickly when you compare this event with the delays and obfuscation which surrounded the *Kursk* operation) and within half an hour I was speaking with Vice Admiral Avdoshin, Head of the Operations Department on the Main Naval Staff, and discussing with him the details of the UK's offer. Within two hours the offer of help had been accepted and we were doing what we could to advance the take-off time of the C17 and in the end we managed to shorten the preparation time by four hours and the plane left Prestwick Airport in Scotland at about 2300. By this time I had returned home, quickly packed a suitcase and then driven to the airport to catch the overnight Aeroflot flight to Petropavlovsk-Kamchatsky. A minor problem which had to be overcome was that all the tickets for the flight had been sold, I therefore had to use all my powers of diplomatic persuasion, combined where necessary with thinly-veiled threats (an essential negotiating technique when dealing with Russian bureaucracy) to persuade the Aeroflot duty manager that I had to get on the plane. The flight to Kamchatka was, for me, the most difficult part of the whole operation as I was out of contact and had no means of knowing how the effort to rescue the crew of *AS 28* was going and I therefore spent nine uncomfortable hours (Aeroflot had grudgingly given me an Economy ticket, having sold all the Business Class tickets to members of the media), willing the journey to be over so that we could get on with our efforts.

I arrived in Petropavlovsk-Kamchatsky at 0745 (although it was already early evening there – it is still a shock to me when I realise just how big Russia is!) and was met by a Liaison Officer from the Pacific Fleet who offered to take me to a hotel, he seemed rather surprised when I insisted on going straight to the military side of the airport where we waited nervously for the RAF plane to arrive. It landed on schedule at 0920 and over the following hours it was joined by a number of US C17s and a C5 which brought the equipment which the United States were contributing to the rescue effort. It was at this point that we ran into the one significant problem which affected the speed of the operation – in order to unload the heavier equipment we needed a device called a K-loader which allows loads to be moved horizontally out of the aircraft's hold but it transpired that the airport didn't have this type of equipment. I left the majority of the UKSRS team grappling with the problem of unloading the aircraft while I went on ahead with two of the team to start the process of preparing the chosen mother-ship to receive all the equipment; it took some time for us to talk our way past the security guard – we weren't on his list and as the mother-ship was at the civilian port it was not controlled by the Russian MoD so the fact that a rescue operation was underway cut no ice with him. Luckily for everyone we were eventually admitted and back at the airport the US C5 aircraft had a K-loader onboard and this was soon at work unloading the Scorpio ROV and its support equipment. It was a noble gesture by the US team to allow the Brits to use the K-loader first and this demonstrates the atmosphere of teamwork which pervades the submarine escape and rescue community.

By 1500 all the equipment had arrived at the commercial port where the mother-ship *KIL 27* was waiting to receive it and the process of reinforcing the ship's decks to take the loads imposed by the equipment was well underway. It took nearly four hours for us to get all the equipment onboard and secured adequately enough to allow us to sail and at 1850 (0350 local time) we left the quayside and headed at full speed for the scene of the incident. As we sailed the feverish pace of activity continued – there was still a need to continue the securing process and all Scorpio's pre-dive checks had to be completed to ensure that it would be ready to go into the water as soon as we arrived on station – this was not a simple process as the rough ride over Kamchatka's roads had resulted in a number of defects which had to be fixed. During the five-hour voyage the UKSRS team received a detailed briefing on what was known about the physical condition of *AS 28* and her crew, from this it was clear that we had to move as quickly as possible if we were to ensure their safety.

We arrived at the scene at around midnight and began the process of mooring *KIL 27* between two other ships – it is essential that the mother-ship stays in the same position at all times in order to ensure that the ROV will not be pulled off station and *KIL 27* was not fitted with a dynamic-positioning system. This process took just over an hour and by 0130 the final checks on Scorpio were complete and she entered the water and began her work. By this time the mood onboard was tense but optimistic – the team had a good understanding of the nature of the problem and were confident that Scorpio had the capability to free *AS 28*. This confidence was further enhanced when the accident site was found and soon the ROV's hydraulic cutter was carrying out the delicate job of removing the fishing nets which were wrapped around *AS 28*'s hull and fouling its propeller. At times the process seemed to be agonisingly slow but as the hours passed more and more of the netting was cut away and by 0600 there were only a few strands remaining. However, at this point the ROV developed a number of minor defects so had to be recovered for fifteen minutes while repairs were effected, luckily none of the problems were serious and work soon recommenced.

By 0700 all the netting which Scorpio could reach had been cut away but there were still a few strands which prevented her from moving and we had to make a difficult decision. *AS 28* could use her remaining air supply to blow water out of her ballast tanks which would provide positive buoyancy and possibly break the remaining strands, allowing her to rise to the surface. However, if the buoyancy was insufficient to break the strands then the submersible would still be trapped and there would be no air left for another attempt. After what seemed like an interminable delay the officer in charge of the rescue operation made his decision and ordered *AS 28*'s crew to blow the ballast tanks.

The atmosphere was extremely tense as we waited on the deck of *KIL 27* to see what would happen. Suddenly the door to Scorpio's control cabin burst open and the Russian Navy Liaison Officer ran out with a cry of 'Vsplivayet!!' – 'She's coming up!' The crew operating the ROV had seen *AS 28* move upwards as the air was injected and could no longer see her on Scorpio's cameras – she must be on her way to the surface.

Everyone rushed to the port side of the ship as we knew that *AS 28* was about 100 m off the port beam, I stood there with my camera ready to capture our expected success for posterity. Despite the fact that we were certain that the submersible was on her way to the surface the sea remained agonisingly calm and after a couple of minutes doubts began to creep in – could she still be trapped by the nets? Suddenly there was a cry of 'She's over there!' and we all ran to the starboard side where *AS 28* was floating quite happily not far off *KIL 27*'s bow – during her ascent she had obviously moved a considerable distance sideways and had surfaced on the opposite side to where we were all waiting – hence the lack of any photographs of this event!

AS 28 came to the surface at 0720 – less than forty-eight hours after we first became aware that there was a problem. The ability to deploy the UKSRS's Scorpio ROV across twelve time zones from Scotland to Kamchatka and effect a rescue in less than two days is a clear endorsement of the professionalism of all those who took part in the operation – British, Russian and American. I am very proud of the fact that I was able to play a part in this operation which shows how well the navies of the UK and Russia can work together when the need dictates and politics is not allowed to intervene.

While the *Priz* rescue generated much goodwill it did not appear to inject any great momentum into the desire for an MoU on submarine escape and rescue. The next formal meeting to discuss the MoU was held in Sevastopol in 2006, with the agreement of the Ukrainian Navy that a UK delegation could visit the RFN on Ukrainian territory, but again there appeared to be little urgency on the RFN side to move towards a formal agreement on this subject and the visit was heavy on cultural activity and very light on content. In many ways it felt like a 'thank you' for the *Priz* rescue rather than a serious attempt to move the MoU forward.

By this time the forthcoming introduction of a NATO Submarine Rescue System (NSRS) in 2008 replacing the UK's capability was reducing enthusiasm on the UK side for a bilateral agreement. The murder of Alexander Litvinenko in November 2006 ended any further discussions and the need for an MoU disappeared during the post-Litvinenko freeze in UK–Russia relations. The failure to agree the MoU in the years following the *Kursk* disaster, despite the existence of a clear imperative and much enthusiasm at the working level, probably cannot be attributed to a single reason but the following probably contributed:

- Fundamental disagreements on the format that such an agreement should take – the Russian system does not as a rule like MoUs although it had signed one on UK–Russia Naval Cooperation in 1998. It much prefers legally binding agreements that, by definition, are harder to agree and are met with nervousness by the UK side.
- The lack of real enthusiasm at the very highest levels of the RFN for engaging too closely with Western navies. By the time the dour and

suspicious Admiral Kuroyedov had been replaced by the much more positive Admiral Masorin, the window for an MoU was fast closing and was then stopped by the political fallout of the Litvinenko affair.
- Poor use of limited 'face-to-face' opportunities to move the MoU process forward. The relatively infrequent meetings, together with changeover of personnel, especially on the UK side, meant that too much time was spent on establishing relationships and cultural events to allow sufficient time to make substantive progress.
- The glacial rate of progress of staff work in the RFN Main Naval Staff where there was no clear direction from above. This was a common theme where friction between the more forward-leaning Russian entities and the dead hand of the more suspicious central staffs of the Navy and the Russian MoD, stymied real progress on many fronts.

The NSRS,[4] introduced in 2008, replaced work that the UK had undertaken bilaterally with Russia prior to the political fallout from the murder of Litvinenko, but it did not exclude the UK. NSRS is a tri-national project developed by France, Norway and the UK and provides a rescue capability primarily to the partner nations, but also to NATO and allied nations and to any submarine equipped with a suitable mating surface around its hatches. The interaction that had taken place between Russia, the UK and other partners, including NATO, on the theme of submarine search and rescue since the *Kursk* tragedy, led to a major NATO exercise in 2011 – Bold Monarch. It was the *Kursk* accident that had led to the development of a framework agreement between NATO and Russia on cooperation in the field of submarine search and rescue and was signed in February 2003.

By 2011, Russia had participated in NATO submarine search-and-rescue exercises in 2005 and 2008 but Bold Monarch was on a different scale. The exercise took place off the coast of southern Spain, near Cartagena, from 30 May to 10 June, and involved some two thousand participants from over twenty nations, including for the first time, a Russian *Kilo*-class submarine, *Alrosa*. Fully integrated in a NATO-led exercise, *Alrosa* was supported by three other Russian ships – a submarine-rescue vessel, a salvage vessel and a heavy-lifting vessel. The Russian Chief of Staff, Army General Nikolai Makarov, took part in the exercise during VIP day. He visited the *Alrosa*, while it was at a depth of 100 m, together with Admiral Giampaolo Di Paola, Chairman of the NATO Military Committee, and other high-level guests, including the RN's Commander-in-Chief Fleet, Admiral Sir Trevor Soar KCB OBE.[5] During the twelve-day exercise, submarines from Portugal, Russia, Spain and Turkey were bottomed in carefully chosen and surveyed areas. Rescue forces with a range of sophisticated debris-clearance and diver-assisted equipment and submarine-rescue vessels from Italy, Russia,

Sweden and the United States, and the jointly owned system of France, Norway and the United Kingdom worked to rescue the submariners.[6] Bold Monarch was an example of what can and was achieved with Russia despite political difficulties, summed up by Admiral Giampaolo Di Paola 'This demonstrates that at the military level, notwithstanding some political diversities and political challenges, [...] you can understand each other, you can work together, you can start help building that level of trust and confidence that eventually will also percolate up to the political level.'

Safe dived navigation of submarines

A further failed UK–Russia MoU attempt during the early 2000s was based on the theme of safe navigation between dived submarines. It was a theme that the Russians returned to time and again from as early as the Adderbury talks in 1989 and became a particular focus in 2004. The Russians argued in 1989/1990 that the dangers of submarines operating in close proximity to each other was as dangerous, if not more so than ships operating in close proximity, for which there was an INCSEA agreement – could there be the same for submarines? The UK, and others, opposed this idea seeing it as an attempt by Russia to better monitor allied sub-surface operations, as well as potentially undermining the location of the UK's strategic deterrent.

By 2004, however, after repeated discussions on the subject, the UK did put forward what it considered to be a workable MoU proposal which addressed these early concerns. At a meeting in Moscow in January 2004 the RN delegation, led by Rear Admiral Niall Kilgour, agreed to a possible MoU, but declined the Russian proposal that there should be a legally-binding treaty. The atmospherics between Rear Admiral Kilgour and Vice Admiral Oleg Burtsev, an anglophile following the failed attempt to rescue the crew of the *Kursk*, were excellent, but the meeting ended with neither side willing to offer real concessions. A further meeting was held in Moscow in December 2005, with the RN delegation led by Rear Admiral Matt Parr. Again the atmospherics were very good, but no substantive progress was made with the same sticking point of treaty versus MoU remaining. While neither set of talks achieved anything of substance, they were very useful from another perspective, in that they presented opportunities for high-level engagement and to discuss all issues of mutual interest.

Cooperation between training establishments

The 1998 MoU codified the nascent relationships between the MWC, HMS *Dryad* and the KNA, St Petersburg and also the two navies' junior-officer basic-training establishments – the SPNI and BRNC, Dartmouth. The MWC and KNA bond went on to become the 'jewel in the crown' of the relationship between the RN and RFN in the early 2000s. When not interrupted by funding issues on the RFN side, a steady rhythm of events was developed, usually three per year. This enabled real progress to be made in the scope and complexity of issues discussed and the paper-based exercises conducted. The strength of this relationship paid dividends in other areas, particularly as it became easier for the RN to assist the RFN in their preparations for RFN-hosted FRUKUS events such as that held in 2004, which led to a greater ambition in the scale of the at-sea phases of the exercises.

The key contributors to the success of the relationship during this period were:

- Strong support from senior officers in both the KNA and MWC.
- Continuity of personnel on both sides, but especially in the KNA, led to a high degree of mutual trust and respect and the ability to make real progress over time rather than 'reinventing the wheel' at every meeting.
- KNA staff officers were considered to be experienced and politically reliable, although all KNA delegations included an obvious GRU 'minder' whose brief probably included keeping an eye on fellow delegates as well as intelligence gathering. This relationship was therefore viewed by the RFN Main Naval Staff as being both safe and productive.
- Viktor Konusov, who as already mentioned had been recruited into the British Consulate in St Petersburg in 2003, had ended his naval career as a professor at the KNA. His input was invaluable and, as a key link who was well liked and trusted by both sides, was able to resolve problems that could otherwise have stalled progress.

Establishing a relationship between SPNI and BRNC was more problematic and in the early 2000s, a number of attempts were made to forge a closer relationship. However, the heavy lifting in this area of potential cooperation came almost exclusively from the UK side and the dead hand of the Russian Main Naval Staff managed, successfully, to stymie any real potential for engagement; the relationship was no further forward at the end of 2006 than it was at the start of the decade. This is not to say that specific serials did not take place, rather that they all occurred as piecemeal 'one-offs', rather than as part of a structured programme leading to increased mutual benefit and understanding. On every occasion, proposals to insert related serials into the annual naval cooperation programme were ignored and those that did get in were either because the UK was paying or because the

Russian side suggested events such as the visit of the training ship *Perekop* to BRNC in July 2006 that were 'safe', i.e., short in duration, scripted and unlikely to allow for close interaction between cadets of the two nations.

The most significant interaction during this period was one RN sub lieutenant who spent six months at SPNI learning Russian from January to July 2004. From the Russian perspective this was a purely financial transaction, i.e. the UK was buying a period of language training rather than engaging in a bilateral exchange that might lead to a Russian officer studying at BRNC. Although he spent six months at SPNI, the officer did not have a great deal of interaction with Russian junior officers, as the tuition was on a 'one-to-one' basis and his instruction and accommodation were in a separate part of SPNI for foreign students.

Gathering headwinds

By the second half of the decade, political headwinds between Russia and the West were gathering strength with a consequent effect on defence engagement. Navy-to-navy cooperation was taking place against the background of Russia's opposition to the Iraq war which started in 2003 and the ongoing war in Afghanistan, and its growing concern about what it perceived as 'colour revolutions' supported by the West in Russia's near abroad, seen as a direct threat to Russia itself. Putin's speech in 2007 at the Munich Security Conference clearly signalled frustration at the persistent ignoring by the West of Russia's concerns about NATO's expansion and a European security architecture that was not fit for purpose post-Cold War. This was further underpinned by then President Dmitry Medvedev stating in Berlin in June 2008, that it was 'hard to escape the conclusion that Europe's architecture still bears the stamp of an ideology inherited from the past'. These deep-rooted grievances and perceived slights against Russia, coupled with the launch of a well-funded military modernisation programme began to change the mood in bilateral military interactions and discussions. Other events during this period, such as the murder of Alexander Litvinenko in the UK in 2006 and the Russo–Georgia war of 2008, also affected defence cooperation programmes.

Nevertheless, RN and RFN interaction did happen even against this testing political backdrop. There were five ship visits to Russia, although none to the UK, including by the large amphibious platform, HMS *Albion*, to St Petersburg in May 2007. The ship then conducted an amphibious landing demonstration near Baltiysk, Kaliningrad. It was considered at the time that this demonstration played a part in the decision-making process by the

RFN to replace its ageing amphibious capability. In 2010, Russia signed a contract to procure the *Mistral*-class amphibious platform from France, an order subsequently cancelled after Russia's annexation of Crimea in 2014.

The year 2007 also saw a visit to the UK by the C-in-C of the RFN, Admiral of the Fleet V. V. Masorin, hosted by the First Sea Lord, Admiral Sir Jonathon Band. Admiral Band had come to know the Russians well and was very much respected by them. He had been a key interlocutor with the RFN in the late 1990s as Assistant Chief of Naval Staff (ACNS) and had led on the negotiations of the MoU on Naval Cooperation signed in 1998, as well as attending a number of annual staff talks and RUKUS events. Masorin's visit programme was ambitious and covered London, Portsmouth and Plymouth and even included a visit to one of the UK's strategic missile nuclear submarines, HMS *Victorious*, refitting in Devonport. One of the highlights of Masorin's visit was a morning spent at sea onboard a Type 23 frigate undergoing sea training during the Thursday War.[7] As with other Russian naval officers who had witnessed this exercise, Masorin was extremely impressed with the realism, particularly that of the firefighting and damage control exercises, and the quality of the younger members of the ship's company, which included females, a concept alien to the RFN. (See the text box below for more detailed observations of Admiral Masorin and his visit by Mr Robert Avery, who was acting as interpreter throughout the visit. Masorin's comments with regard to China are particularly interesting and highlight the uneasy historical relationship with China.)

For the return visit to Russia in June 2008, shortly before the Russo–Georgia war, Admiral Band was hosted in Moscow and Severomorsk, including a visit to a Victor III-class nuclear attack submarine, and St Petersburg where he gave a speech in the Kuznetsov Naval Academy.

Visit to UK of Admiral of the Fleet Masorin
Commander-in-chief Russian Federation Navy
Interpreter's observations

He came over as an extremely affable, good-natured and unpompous person with a good sense of humour and an almost sentimental streak. The relationship with his wife – who accompanied him on the visit – is central to his life and goes back to his youth.

He was most at home on HMS *Portland* during the Thursday War and viewed everything he saw with a sharp and practical seaman's eye; in particular, he was full of the little rubber hooters worn by everyone to attract attention when the wearer might be incapable of shouting for help and for the life jackets that fold out of a belt. FOST scored heavily by making him a present of each of these items. He told Vice Admiral Avdoshin that the hooter was such a simple, cheap and clever idea that he would order it to be brought into the Russian Navy forthwith. He greatly enjoyed the bridge simulator and the mini-gun at MWC (although he only got a single kill out of several minutes' firing!).

He seemed ill at ease when in other environments, for example public speaking, where he tended to ramble endlessly on in a slightly emotional way. I repeatedly heard his wife say to him 'Stop now, don't keep repeating yourself!' both under her breath and on a couple of occasions at full volume to him directly. When he was asked to propose the toast to the Queen by 2SL at the HMS *Victory* dinner, he misjudged the solemnity of the moment by turning it into a rambling speech about how he loved and admired the Queen, how her joys were his, how he felt her pain and how the Russian Navy sounded better when it was 'The Imperial Russian Navy', just as 'Royal Navy' sounds better than 'British Navy'. At the Admiralty House dinner hosted by 1SL, he occasionally turned around to speak to me directly and some interesting points emerged: I had heard that the First Deputy Commander-in-Chief since 2001, Admiral Mikhail Zakharenko, might be retiring on reaching 60, so I asked him to pass on my best wishes to him, having interpreted for him when he was Acting Commander Pacific Fleet in 1998. He said Zakharenko was retiring that Friday – 23 March on his birthday – and spoke warmly of him. I passed similar good wishes to his Chief of Staff, Admiral Mikhail Abramov (who came over as Admiral Kuroyedov's representative to the Trafalgar 200 events in 2005), I got a frosty response and his wife blanked me when I mentioned his name. I got the impression that there is little love lost between them. The orthodoxy has been that Abramov (born 6 July 1956) was being groomed as Masorin's successor but this reaction should give pause for thought to those who predicted a 'coronation' for Abramov when Masorin retires (on his sixty-first birthday, probably, on 24 August 2008). It will be interesting to see who is appointed First Deputy C-in-C to relieve Zakharenko. Masorin shows great loyalty to his erstwhile colleagues in the Black Sea Fleet (Capt First Rank Kalmykov, his personal secretary, whom he brought to the UK is such an example). A man to watch would be the current Commander Black Sea Fleet Admiral Tatarinov (born 25 October 1950). He would be an older counter-weight to Abramov – they would be of equivalent weight as the two First Deputy C-in-Cs – and even if Tatarinov succeeded Masorin, Abramov, being about six years younger than him, would still not be excluded from eventually taking the top post. In an interesting aside to me, Masorin said 'I was never in the queue to be C-in-C – nowhere near it – and when it was offered, it came as a big surprise. But perhaps I shouldn't have been so surprised: recent history has shown that the favourite to succeed usually hasn't!' He is probably referring to Admiral Khelmnov, tipped to succeed C-in-C Gromov in 1997 but ruined by being found guilty of gross financial improprieties, then First Deputy C-in-C Kasatonov in 1998 – squeezed out by Gromov (in favour of the obscure CommanderPacific Fleet Kuroyedov) for behaving as if he were already C-in-C – and even Abramov in September 2005 on Kuroyedov's retirement.

He often seemed at a loss for information about the RFN as a whole and relied heavily on the extremely capable and incisive Avdoshin for guidance. He frequently asked him for concrete data ('How many Ivan Rogov LPDs did we build?', 'How many nuclear-powered submarines did the USSR build?'). During the session on the sofa with 1SL after the dinner, Masorin looked at a loss on the submarine rescue issue and more or less let Avdoshin run with it. Masorin is an impulsive and emotional man and did not always give his comments adequate forethought; the invitation to send an RN SSN to Russia serves as a good illustration. During the dinner, he asked me what other interpreting serials I'd been involved in, as I seemed to know many Russian Navy officers and to remember all the dates when visits occurred. I told him I'd been lucky enough to see many 'firsts' – most notably the first RN submarine to visit Russia (HMS *Opossum* in August 1993). He asked me whether it was a nuclear boat and when I said no, he said it was high time to have another one. I explained that as we no longer operate SSKs, there could be some problems to overcome. To my surprise, he fired from the hip on this during his after-dinner speech, indicating his impulsiveness and the fact that this initiative had not been staffed at all.

He occasionally showed surprising ignorance – e.g. that the UK has Sovereign Base Areas in Cyprus. He is an extremely hard worker and his wife laments that he is in the office on Saturdays, Sundays and public holidays, although he said these were usually half-days.

He likes making jokes but then sometimes regrets having done so. At Lympstone, he told Colonel Stewart that the Royal Marines and the US Marines were probably better at what they do than the Russian Naval Infantry; however, the latter could fight 'without the need for toilet paper'. Afterwards, he told me he feared having offended the Marines (he hadn't) by implying their urge for toilet paper was caused not by a need for life's little comforts but because of the biological effects of cowardice. This so bothered him that he asked his NA to phone Colonel Stewart next day to correct the unintended slur. He told me, 'I got carried away – sometimes Russian humour doesn't carry across to other nationalities'. He then recounted the whole saga to general amusement at FOST's supper party.

In July of 2006 he was involved – with his wife – in a serious air crash near the Black Sea after running the exercise that caused him to cancel his visit to the UK. He was travelling in a military Tu-134 with nineteen other admirals when the aircraft suffered a bird strike on one of the engines during take-off. Although the pilot should have tried to stay airborne and gain height, he actually did a belly landing. In the process, the starboard wing hit a radar installation and was ripped off with '14 tons of fuel', the plane careered on at great speed (over 300 kph) for one-and-a-half kilometres. Luckily, there was clear ground ahead so it hit no further obstructions. However, on coming to rest, it exploded. The Masorins and everyone else inside managed to escape before this happened. Mrs Masorin nearly lost all her jewellery in the crash. He recounted this story to the assembled Fleet Air Arm team at Yeovilton, again beginning with thanks for a splendid visit but then drifting onto air safety and from that to nearly fifteen minutes on this tale, eventually leaving the aviators looking uneasy as they waited for it to end. The CO of 800 RNAS afterwards said it was classical post-crash trauma, released on finding a professional audience. He thought that Masorin had not really come to terms with his brush with death. The story also indicates that the RFN has learned little from the 1978 crash which wiped out virtually the whole Pacific Fleet command when twenty or so flag officers were travelling in a single aircraft.

Equipment and material

He told FOST that a fourth SSBN was being ordered to secure long-term funding, even though the first of class – *Yury Dolgorukiy* – had been in build since 1996. He acknowledged this might slow even further the completion of the lead boat but on balance believed that securing funding for a fourth of class was more important in the long term.

Every time he was asked about how the Russian naval shipbuilding programme stood, he avoided a direct answer about numbers/types of vessel in build and said there was no shipbuilding programme as such, only a State Armaments Programme for 2005–15 which depended on the continuing good health of the Russian economy for its full implementation. At no point did he state that there are currently about twenty-five units building. This was somewhat odd, given that it is a matter for national pride in the military/naval press in Russia.

He told some of the FAA pilots at Yeovilton – when quizzed about the carrier *Admiral Kuznetsov* – that she was currently in refit after problems with arrester wires. He said that a new (Su-33K?) had gone over the side of the carrier during flying trials at sea last summer; the aircraft's tail-hook had engaged on the third of four wires which had snapped, giving the pilot no time to recover height. He had ejected into the sea and been saved but the fighter was lost. Investigations had proved that the wires were all unable to restrain the one-hundred-ton breaking strain for which they had been designed. Some could only restrain ninety-five to ninety-eight tons. The result is that all the wires are being replaced and the arrester systems overhauled. This is turning into a lengthy process as the original production facility for the wires no longer existed and was having to be resurrected for manufacture of the replacement wires.

He stated that the current manpower of the Russian Navy was 'about 140,000', down from about 450,000 at the zenith of the Soviet Navy in the late 1980s.

China

In discussions with FOST, China loomed quite large. Masorin stated that if the Chinese were minded to invade Russia, then her twenty-nine divisions would find little meaningful resistance from the Russian side, now defended by barely one division. They could also achieve a territorial take-over by infiltrating large numbers of civilians (as is happening around Vladivostok in the Far East Maritime Province). When asked why Russia is selling weapons to China, Masorin replied these were just 'trivia' and had allowed Russian naval shipbuilding to survive through lean years.

Asked about Chinese intentions, he recounted the following tale. Last summer, when leaving Moscow for China after an official visit, the Chinese Chief of Naval Staff (CNS) was asked by an airport official to board the bus to the parked aircraft. He refused, indicating it was close enough for him to walk to on foot. When told this was the rule, he barged past the woman, knocking her to the ground and strode to the plane, ignoring her. Masorin observed 'You can draw your own inferences from this kind of behaviour, but I reckon neither you nor I could think of a single other CNS in the world who would behave like this.'

The Royal Navy

He ended the week highly satisfied and impressed, not least by the calibre of the people he met. He made a point of speaking to as many junior rates and marines as he could and was impressed by their confident manner, professionalism, good manners and good humour. In every case, he asked them how long they planned to serve and was without a single exception told 'the full twenty-two years'. The final time was in conversation with a Marines corporal in HMS *Albion* – this made Masorin wax lyrical: 'You are such an example of pride in your service – you are exactly what we need in the Russian Navy!'

He repeatedly said that before his visit he had expected the British to be formal, stiff and pompous – yet had been amazed to find smiling faces, openness and good humour everywhere. At the end he said this was his strongest impression of the Royal Navy – the quality, professionalism and courtesy of its personnel.

He was visibly struck by the quality of the real estate he saw, especially at Yeovilton and HMS *Collingwood*. He said to Avdoshin in mid-brief 'Just look how beautifully they keep everything maintained. Just compare it to what we've got at Kronstadt, say. And that bit (looking at me) is NOT to be translated!' (i.e. to the Commodore).

He particularly enjoyed the briefing on the first afternoon and the social events, but was especially at home in any practical 'hands-on' setting – most particularly with FOST in HMS *Portland*, with the aviators at Yeovilton and with the Royal Marines. He was moved by the trust in showing him an SSBN in refit (I believe he is the first Russian officer to set foot on a *Vanguard*-class SSBN – although many years ago a Soviet delegation visited a *Resolution*-class boat – HMS *Revenge* – in 1991). He also found 2SL's briefing of particular value and established a very good human rapport with him.

Robert Avery, Defence School of Languages,
Beaconsfield, 31 March 2007

Figure 4.3 Commodore Roger Lane-Nott (Deputy Flag Officer Submarines) at Severomorsk. HMS *Opossum* and *Kilo*-class diesel submarine in the background. August 1993. © Author – Robert Avery.

Figure 4.4 Royal Navy submariners from HMS *Opossum* enjoy Russian naval hospitality in the wardroom of the *Kilo*-class host submarine. Severomorsk. August 1993. © Author – Robert Avery.

Figure 4.5 HMS *Portland* and RFS *Admiral Chabanenko* sail into Norfolk, Virginia, to participate in exercise FRUKUS 2007. Public domain.

An attempt by the new Obama administration in 2009 to press the 'reset button' in the US relationship with Russia, provided another opportunity to improve Western defence engagement. Although this reset turned out to be short-lived, significant achievements were made in navy-to-navy cooperation. For example, with the exception of the cancellation in 2008 because of the Georgia crisis, FRUKUS took place with ships from each nation from 2005 until 2013.

From 2009, five consecutive FRUKUSes had sea phases as well as using shore-based training in damage control in 2011 in Norfolk, VA. The focus of these FRUKUS interactions was to build on the previous ten to fifteen years of experience of working together to build procedures for maritime task group planning, develop common ROE, and improve maritime domain awareness, anti-piracy and maritime interdiction operations. In 2013, the level of ambition grew still further with a move towards dealing with attacks on a maritime task group and employing coordinated offensive warfare. There was also an exercise which involved the evacuation of civilians from Morgat harbour in France using helicopters and sea boats.

Notes

1 Author: David Fields.
2 'Adventure Comes Home with Russian Navy', *Gov.uk*, 28 August 2013, www.gov.uk/government/news/adventure-comes-home-with-russian-navy (accessed 12 May 2023).
3 'Putin Honours Submarine Rescue Team', *Guardian*, 5 October 2005, www.theguardian.com/uk/2005/oct/05/russia.world
4 'The NATO Submarine Rescue System Factsheet', http://c69011.r11.cf3.rackcdn.com/b88a4d788a8746f8bbb89dc377fd0171-0x0.pdf (accessed 26 February 2024).
5 Soar was dual-hatted in this national post and as Commander of NATO's Allied Maritime Command.
6 'Russian Submarine Takes Active Part in NATO Exercise 'Bold Monarch 2011', NATO HQ, Brussels, 10 June 2011, www.nato.int/cps/en/natolive/news_75370.htm (accessed 12 October 2023).
7 A weekly exercise conducted by Fleet Operational Sea Training (known as Flag Officer Sea Training pre-May 2020), which tests the ship's ability to operate in a multi-threat environment and deal with any battle damage inflicted on it.

5

2010–14 Collapse of cooperation and return to confrontation

The Obama reset initiative of 2009 was further strengthened by the arrival of a new UK Prime Minister, David Cameron, in 2010. In similar fashion, he sought to reset the UK's relationship with Russia and to move on from the murder of Alexander Litvinenko in 2006 and the Russo–Georgian war in 2008. The London 2012 Olympics, the G8 summit at Loch Erne in June 2013 and the preparations for the Sochi Winter Olympics in February 2014 helped to provide some optimism for a so-called improved relationship, through trade and construction deals. Military cooperation also benefited from these resets. However, it could not hide the reality of the deep political divisions that existed between the two sides, nor that these resets were ultimately doomed to failure. These divisions manifested themselves in the Arab Spring of 2011, specifically the situation in Syria, Russia's close ally with its port at Tartus providing access to the Mediterranean, but also the overthrow of Gaddafi in Libya. Internally, the Bolotnaya protests in Moscow in 2011, which spread across the country, against what were perceived to be fraudulent elections, also led to protests against President Putin's own election in 2012. The spectre of a Western-backed 'colour revolution' in Russia was very real in the eyes of the Kremlin. By the end of 2013, that spectre was evident to the Russian leadership in its near neighbour Ukraine, where the Maidan protests against Yanukovych's refusal to sign a trade agreement with the EU led him to flee the country in February 2014. At this point, it seems enough was enough for Putin and he took the decision to annex Crimea at the end of February 2014, to, as he saw it, halt the West's meddling in Russia's near abroad and bring Ukraine back into Russia's sphere of influence.

In 2013, prior to the Maidan protests in Kyiv in November, Prime Minister Cameron had put 'his shoulder to the wheel' in trying to improve the relationship with Russia and build on the relationship he had been establishing with President Putin in the previous three years. The joint press conference in Downing Street ahead of the G8 summit at Loch Erne in June, acknowledged the differences in opinion about, for example, the situation in Syria, but at the same time spoke about ideas to get Britain and Russia working better together on science and space, on energy cooperation and on new business deals, especially to support Russia's Winter Olympics and the (2018) football World Cup in Russia.[1] Cameron also drew on the strong historical links of the Arctic Convoys which he said 'reminds us, when we overcome our differences we can be a powerful partnership'. This political atmosphere led to an increased optimism for improved defence engagement, including finalising a Military Technical Cooperation Agreement (MTCA) that was to be signed by the UK and Russia in 2014. Although the MTCA was in essence a token gesture which had been long in the negotiating process and offered neither side that much, it nevertheless provided a basis for further cooperation and demonstrated a political intent to improve the relationship.

Building on this apparently 'warming' political relationship, the short period from 2011 to early 2014 saw an effort to try to broaden RFN and RN cooperation through the development of bilateral programmes focused not only on Flag and ship visits but that also sought to develop links between personnel of lower ranks in both navies and to establish regular operational

Figure 5.1 Officers from the French ship *De Grasse*, Russian ship *Yaroslav Mudriy*, HMS *York*, USS *Normandy* and US Naval Forces Europe-Africa, walk in formation during a wreath-laying ceremony held at the Piskariovskoye Memorial Cemetery during Exercise FRUKUS 2012. Public domain.

communications between the two navies. The annual FRUKUS exercise took place in 2012, hosted by Russia, and included a visit by HMS *York* to the Baltic Fleet's base in Baltiysk, Kaliningrad, the first RN warship to visit Russia since 2009.

The tone for re-energising the RFN-RN relationship and cooperation programme was, however, set by two key meetings between the then First Sea Lord, Admiral Sir Mark Stanhope and Commander-in-Chief of the RFN, Admiral Viktor Viktorovich Chirkov. Stanhope had, through previous naval appointments and attending Arctic Convoy Op Dervish anniversaries, built a rapport with the RFN over a period of twenty years and a good working relationship. Chirkov, a quiet, personable man, wanted to engage and valued the relationship and friendship that existed between the two navies – 'we are told what to do by our politicians but we believe in genuine friendship'. Chirkov visited the UK in December 2012 and he was afforded significant 'red carpet' treatment. Roundtable discussions with Stanhope took place in the UK MoD, centring around ambitions for both the size and capability of the respective navies, with a focus on the in-build UK carrier HMS *Queen Elizabeth* and Russia's own, but distant aspirations for a nuclear-powered aircraft carrier. Chirkov was then taken to Faslane Naval base, where he visited the nuclear-powered submarine HMS *Astute*, and then on to Rosyth to see the HMS *Queen Elizabeth* and to be briefed on how the vessel was being built. The impact on Chirkov was said to have been quite profound. Some opined that he became quite reflective. It is worth recalling that at the time of this visit in 2012, the RFN had just taken the lion's share of the State Armament Programme 2010 to radically modernise the Russian fleet, a programme which has not yet fully delivered. Certainly aspirations for a Russian aircraft carrier remain some way off. Perhaps, in these two visits north, Chirkov foresaw the scale of the challenges he faced in delivering Russia's submarine and shipbuilding programme. Chirkov was then taken south to Plymouth to witness the weekly multi-threat, multi-environment 'war' conducted on a Thursday. It was reported that Chirkov was taken aback, like many Russian naval officers before him who have visited Fleet Operational Sea Training (FOST), by the scale and complexity of the training provided. The visit was completed in Portsmouth where Chirkov was awarded the rare honour of a dinner in Admiral Lord Nelson's cabin onboard HMS *Victory*, after which he indulged his love of whisky and enjoyed discovering the art of playing snooker.[2]

A return visit by Stanhope to Russia took place unusually quickly two months later, in February 2013. While not on the same scale as the visit by Chirkov to the UK, it nevertheless cemented the relationship between Stanhope and Chirkov. The visit was focused on the Northern Fleet (NF) in Severomorsk and meetings with both Chirkov and Admiral Korolyov, then commander of the NF. Stanhope visited a Sierra-class nuclear-powered submarine and the *Kirov*-class cruiser *Pyotr Veliky*, and then went to the prestigious Kuznetsov Naval Academy in St Petersburg, as well as the Admiralty Shipyard, the manufacturer of Russia's diesel-electric Project 636.3 *Varshavyanka*-class submarine (NATO:*Kilo*).

Both of these Flag visits gave direction and guidance to the staffs of the respective navies on the nature and ambition for the RFN-RN relationship. In what turned out to be the last RFN ship to visit the UK, May 2013 saw the *Udaloy*-class destroyer, *Vitse-Admiral Kulakov*, take part in the seventieth anniversary celebrations of the Battle of the Atlantic in Liverpool, underlining the importance of the historical links mentioned by Cameron a month later. In July, Flag Officer Sea Training, then Rear Admiral Ben Key, who went on to become the First Sea Lord in 2021, visited St Petersburg to attend the International Maritime Defence Show, and also met Admiral Chirkov. Although Chirkov retired in 2016, he still remains a key player in Russian maritime circles. In particular, he is the Chief Advisor to the President of United Shipbuilding Corporation and Chairman of the St. Petersburg Admirals' Club. As a former proponent of fostering better relations with the RN and other navies, he would be a good candidate for discreet conversations between retired personnel in re-establishing any future dialogue, which is examined in more depth in Chapter 8.

Naval Staff talks took place in London in September 2013. It was during these talks that ideas about developing working level contacts and interaction between more junior personnel were discussed, with a view to trying to break down prejudices on both sides about each other at an earlier stage in naval careers. These ideas included formalising student exchanges between training colleges and re-organising the trip for Officer Cadets from BRNC onboard the Russian cadets' yacht, *Adventure*, which had just been cancelled due to an engine defect incurred while alongside in Gosport. It also included discussion of personnel embarking in each other's ships during exercises such as FRUKUS planned for 2014, as well as in RFN ships transiting UK waters to the NF.

As a confidence-building measure and to improve the coordination of exercises between NF and RN units, the staff talks also raised the proposal to establish a Skype link between the NF HQ in Severomorsk and the RN operational HQ in Northwood. A telephone hotline was also proposed that would be tested daily between the headquarters, and which is still active and used today. This initiative mirrored similar arrangements between Norway and Russia. There was also enthusiasm from a Russian delegate, Captain First Rank Moloko, who worked in the Operational Directorate (Maritime) of the National Defence Management Centre (NDMC) in Moscow, to exchange telephone numbers with the UK NA[3] to improve coordination of exercises between RN and RFN units, primarily around the UK but also further afield, mindful that the dead hand of the External Relations of the Russian Ministry of Defence (GUMVS) would need to be kept informed. An opportunity to test this presented itself soon after the talks, with RFN and RN ships visiting Cork, Ireland at the same time. The UK NA phoned the NDMC, spoke to Captain Moloko and what usually took days, if not weeks to arrange, a short exercise was arranged and conducted by the ships when they sailed from Cork. However, that was the last time that happened and Moloko's phone number never worked again. Less supportive forces of increased cooperation between the navies had probably come into play.

Similarly there was suspicion, at least in Moscow, behind the UK's motives for establishing the Skype link, even if at the working level of the RFN there was genuine support. This was expressed during a meeting in November 2013 between the UK NA and then Deputy Commander of the NF, Admiral Yevmenov, subsequently C-in-C of the RFN.[4] Little did we know at the time that the Maidan protests, which had started in Kyiv in the same month against President Yanukovych's government, were to have a profound impact on the relationship between Russia and the West.

That meeting with Yevmenov was the last formal working, cooperative and friendly meeting between the RN and RFN. It was held in the naval headquarters of the NF in the bleak, run-down naval town of Severomorsk, which had changed little since the UK NA's first visit there as Assistant NA in 1997. The meeting coincided with the annual November wreath-laying ceremony at the Commonwealth War Graves' Vaenga cemetery where six airmen, five RAF and one Canadian Air Force, are buried. These November ceremonies conducted by the British Embassy still occur elsewhere in Russia, but mainly in Murmansk and Arkhangelsk. The ceremony was attended by local children, who read poems and sang songs in memory of the lost airmen.

Yevmenov had been appointed to the NF in 2012, having spent his career as a submariner in the Pacific Fleet. He was, therefore, one to watch as the NF was, and is, often the fleet that nurtures future C-in-Cs of the RFN. The HQ building where the meeting took place had not changed much in sixteen years and was similar to countless other buildings and rooms in which so many meetings had taken place between people from the two navies since the early 1990s. A tired two-storey block clearly in need of upkeep and maintenance, was matched by the ubiquitous decoration inside of brown wooden or formica panelled rooms, and dreary almost paper thin, brown curtains. Pictures of past naval glories and former stern looking, imposing Northern Fleet Commanders adorned the walls. Added to this jaded atmosphere was the odour which is so peculiarly Russian – musty, stale air infused with the smell of an odd kind of paint and bathroom facilities which might not be working as effectively as they could be. According to Yevmenov's staff he had not met a Western naval attache before nor, as far as anyone understood, someone from a NATO country. With hindsight this made the meeting unique.

So what was Yevmenov like, a man who then became the C-in-C of a maritime force unleashing waves of land-attack cruise missiles from ships and submarines in the Black Sea against Ukraine? As is often the case when first meeting any Russian, he maintained a granite-like composure with carefully chosen words, probably wary of at least one member of his staff – the GRU intelligence officer. However, the conversation warmed up and discussion turned to how a Skype link might work between his headquarters and the RN's operational headquarters in Northwood, which could be used to arrange exercises and for regular confidence building conversations. When asked how the deployment of his ships toward the Northern Sea Route in August/September, led by the *Kirov*-class cruiser *Pyotr Velikiy*, had gone, he commented that it was successful although not without its difficulties. Navigation in the region is challenging because of the ice even in so-called summer, and he felt comfortable, he said, for about six to eight weeks sending his surface ships to the region. Yevmenov then asked several questions about the UK's future aircraft carrier programme, but was most intrigued by the UK's decision in its defence review of 2010, to remove from service its Nimrod maritime patrol aircraft (MPA). Despite pointing out that as part of the NATO alliance the UK had access to MPA, this did not stop him smiling and commenting that it was anathema that as *the* premier maritime nation to which the RFN and many others aspired, the UK no longer had its own MPA. He added, smiling more broadly, that 'it did at least make his life a little easier'.

As is traditional, Yevmenov invited the UK three-person delegation into a separate room for vodka and *zakuski* – Russian appetisers. Friendship and families were toasted along with future cooperation between the two navies. Yevmenov's initial granite mask had already begun to slip earlier in the meeting, revealing a man with a good sense of humour and it slipped further still when he discovered the UK NA was a fly fisherman, as was he. This led to Yevmenov telling some fishing stories about the wonderful and bountiful salmon rivers on the Kola peninsula. Yevmenov, in a bear hug on bidding the UK NA farewell, suggested they should try one day to fish together.

About eight years later, in February 2022, Yevmenov was put on the European Union sanctions list for being 'responsible for actively supporting and implementing actions and policies that undermine and threaten the territorial integrity, sovereignty and independence of Ukraine as well as the stability or security in Ukraine'. Meeting Russians in these sorts of settings, such as the 2013 meeting with Yevmenov, followed by witnessing their politically directed actions, creates conflicting emotions. Although it is, of course, difficult to reach a conclusive judgement of a person from one two-hour meeting, Yevmenov, like many other senior RFN officers encountered over the twenty-five-year period of engagement, did not come across as a man who would necessarily feel entirely comfortable with waging war on a neighbouring Slavic country. But we are unlikely ever to know.

The activity, both political and military, in 2013 led to the development of an ambitious bilateral military cooperation programme for 2014 across all three UK services. For the RN this included proposed student exchanges between naval colleges, as well as ship visits and re-energising working level visits between the Royal Marines and Russian Naval Infantry. As this agreed bi-lateral programme was about to be signed off in March 2014, coinciding with the Defence and Foreign 2+2 ministerial meeting in London[5] to sign the Military Technical Cooperation Agreement, Russia annexed Crimea.

Table 5.1 Warship visits RN–RFN 1988–2014

RN ship (CO)	Place/event	Date	RFN ship (CO)	Place/event	Date
HMS *Bristol* (Capt P. M. Franklyn)	Leningrad/(Flag) First RN ship visit to Leningrad since 1966; first RN ship visit since May 1976 (HMS *Devonshire* to Odessa); first RN ship visit since Soviet invasion of Afghanistan (1979)	26–30 May 1989			
			Bezuprechny (C2R Vladimir Ivanovich Geletin)	Portsmouth/ (Flag) First Soviet warship to visit UK since *Obraztsovy* May 1976	– Jul 1990
HMS *London* (Capt M. Stanhope) and RFA *Tidespring* (Capt Jeremy Carew)	Murmansk/Arkhangelsk (Flag) fiftieth anniversary of first Arctic Convoy to USSR – Op Dervish First foreign warship of any nation to visit Soviet Union after the August Coup (a week before)	Aug 1991			
			Ivan Kruzenshtern	London (Flag)	Oct 1991

HMS *Fearless* (Capt S. R. Meyer)	Sevastopol/(Flag) First – and last – RN ship to visit Sevastopol in Soviet times	Nov 1991	
HMS *Battleaxe* (Cdr S. J. Scorer)	Baltiysk/(Flag) First RN ship ever to visit Baltiysk	Jul 1992	
HMS *Herald* (Cdr R. A. Mark)	St Petersburg/(Flag) First RN hydrographic ship to visit Russia since HMS *Vidal* (1967)	Oct 1992	
			Gremyashchy (C2R Viktor Leonidovich Belkin)	Liverpool/(Double Flag) fiftieth anniversary of the Battle of the Atlantic	May 1993
HMS *Opossum* (Lt Cdr J. R. G. Drummond)	Severomorsk/(Flag) First – and only – visit of an RN submarine to Russia since World War II	Aug 1993	
			Gangut (C1R Valery Imerikov and C1R Boris Grigor'ievich Kolyada – Deployment Cdr)	Dartmouth (Flag) First Russian warship visit to Dartmouth	Oct 1993
HMS *Glasgow* (Cdr R. C. Twitchen)	Baltiysk/(Flag)	May 1994	

(*Continued*)

Table 5.1 (Continued)

RN ship (CO)	Place/event	Date	RFN ship (CO)	Place/event	Date
			KILO 431 SSK (C2R Yevgeny Arkadievich Dvortsov) First – and only – Russian submarine to visit Portsmouth	Portsmouth/(Flag)	May 1994
750 RNAS (no ship) (Lt Cdr R. E. Drewett)	Kaliningrad Chkalovskoye	5–7 Sept 1994			
HMY *Britannia* (RAdm R. N. Woodard) and HMS *Glasgow* (Cdr R. C. Twitchen)	St Petersburg/(State visit and Flag) First ever State Visit to Russia. First Royal Visit to Russia since 1908	15–20 Oct 1994			
HMS *Lancaster*	St Petersburg/ (NATO)	1995	(*Bespokoiny* – host ship) (C2R Yevgeny Ivanovich Alyoshin) *Serebryakov*	Portsmouth/(Flag)	1995
HMS *Chatham* (Capt R. P. Boissier)	St Petersburg/1995 (Flag) fiftieth anniversary of the end of World War II in Europe	May 1995			
			Admiral Levchenko (Flag)(C1R Orest Yurievich Gur'yanov)	Portsmouth/(RUKUS)	May 1996
HMS *Cornwall* (Capt G. K. Billson)	St Petersburg/(Double Flag) three-hundredth anniversary of the Russian Navy	Jul 1996			

HMS *Iron Duke* (Cdr C. J. Bryning)	Severomorsk/28 May–3 Jun 1997 First RN surface ship to visit Severomorsk (?)	28 May–3 Jun 1997	(*Zadorny* – host ship) (C3R Yevgeny Ivanovich IRZA)
HMS *Richmond* (Cdr E. F. K. Seatherton)	Vladivostok/1997(Flag) First RN ship to visit Vladivostok since the Intervention (1920)	Jun 1997	
HMS *Somerset* (Cdr the Hon M. C. N. Cochrane) (HMS *Norfolk* – HOST/OOW EX) (Cdr B. N. B. Williams)	St Petersburg/ (Flag and HRH the Duke of York)	29 May–3 Jun 1998	*Besstrashny*	Devonport/22–26 Sept 1997	22–26 Sept 1997
			Bespokoiny (Flag) (C2R Vladimir Nikolayevich Sokolov)	Devonport	Jul 1998
HMS *London* (Cdr T. McBarnet)	Novorossiisk	3 Nov 1998			
HMS *Sheffield* (Cdr T. M. Lowe)	St Petersburg	Jun 2000			
HMS *Cornwall* (Capt T. P. McClement) and HMS *Newcastle* (Cdr S. J. Pearson)	Vladivostok	24–28 Aug 2000			
HMS *Campbeltown* (Capt D. A. Halliday)	Murmansk and Arkhangelsk sixtieth anniversary of first Arctic Convoy to USSR – Op Dervish	Aug 2001			

(*Continued*)

Table 5.1 (Continued)

RN ship (CO)	Place/event	Date	RFN ship (CO)	Place/event	Date
HMS *Campbeltown*	St Petersburg/ Kaliningrad Captain Tony Johnstone-Burt – Captain F6 visit to Twelfth Surface Division Baltic Fleet C1R Oleg Demyanchenko	Jul 2001			
			Vologda (*KILO* SSK) (Flag) (C2R Gennady Aleksandrovich Yesipov)	Faslane (RN Submarine Service Centenary)	1 Jun 2001
			Admiral Chabanenko (C1R Sergei Gennadievich Grishin)	Devonport Navy Days	22–27 Aug 2002
HMS *Ramsey*	Severomorsk	Jun 2002			
HMS *Southampton* (Cdr G. L. Doyle)	Novorossiisk	Oct 2002			
RM Delegation (no ship)	Baltiysk	Oct 2002			
			Admiral Chabanenko	Liverpool sixtieth anniversary of the Battle of the Atlantic)	May 2003

2010–14 Collapse of cooperation and return to confrontation 115

HMS *Atherstone* and HMS *Ramsey*	Baltiysk	Jun 2003	
HMS *St Albans* (Cdr M. KNIBBS)	Baltiysk and St Petersburg	Jul 2003	HRH Prince of Wales hands over yacht *Adventure* to Russian Navy and three-hundredth anniversary of Baltic Fleet and of St Petersburg
HMS *Atherstone*	Arkhangelsk	Jul 2003	
HMS *Cornwall* (Cdr S. B. Charlier)	St Petersburg	2003–4?	
HMS *Ramsey*	Severomorsk	Jul 2003	
HMS *York* (Cdr R. M. M. J. Harvey	Novorossiisk	Nov 2003	
HMS *Exeter* and RFA *Grey Rover*	Vladivostok	Jun 2004	
HMS *Newcastle* (Cdr J. J. F. Blunden)	Novorossiisk (NATO)	Jul 2004?	
HMS *Shoreham*	St Petersburg NATO MCMV Force	Oct 2004	
	Neustrashimy	2003	London coinciding with Putin State Visit
HMS *Sutherland* (Cdr P. J. Haslam)	Baltiysk then Murmansk	May 2005	(1SL and Duke of York) sixtieth anniversary of the end of World War II in Europe

(*Continued*)

Table 5.1 (Continued)

RN ship (CO)	Place/event	Date	RFN ship (CO)	Place/event	Date
			Admiral Levchenko (C1R Anatoly Petrovich Dolgov)	Portsmouth Trafalgar 200 Fleet Review	Jul 2005
			Admiral Chabanenko	Devonport	2006
HMS *Echo* (Cdr J. Churcher)	Vladivostok	Jan 2007			
HMS *Albion* (Capt T. M. Lowe)	Baltiysk (Roads) and St Petersburg	Jul 2007			
HMS *Middleton* (Lt Cdr S. Holloway)	St Petersburg (with NATO SNMCMG1)	Aug 2007			
HMS *Exeter* (Cdr P. Brown)	Severomorsk	May 2008			
HMS *Kent*	Vladivostok (FRUKUS) Cancelled due to annexation of South Ossetia and Abkhazia	Aug 2008			
HMS *St Albans* (Cdr A. Pierce)	St Petersburg (IMDS)	Jun 2009			
HMS *York* (Cdr R. J. Cox)	Baltiysk (FRUKUS)	2012			
			Vitse-admiral Kulakov	Last Russian warship to visit UK before the Russian annexation of Crimea on 18 Mar 2014	2013

Table 5.2 RN–RFN Flag/Delegation Visits 1988–2014

Serial	Date	Ship	Flag Officers visiting	Flag Officers receiving	Comments
Adderbury talks (Adderbury) (in Russia – Moscow and Sevastopol)	29–31 Jul 1988		Adm N. N. Amel'ko		First in Adderbury Series
	Sept 1988		Adm N. N. Amel'ko		Second in Adderbury Series
Flag visit to USSR	May 1989	HMS Bristol	RAdm J. F. Coward	RAdm K. A. Tulin	First visit to USSR since May 1976 (HMS Devonshire)
Adderbury talks (in UK – Adderbury and Plymouth)	Nov 1989	–	Adm N. N. Amel'ko VAdm M. D. P. Komarov RAdm Markov Adm W. MacDonald VAdm J. Lyons	Adm Sir J. J. R. Oswald (1SL) Adm Sir J. H. F. Eberle RAdm R. Hill VAdm Sir J. M. Webster (Flag Officer Plymouth)	Third in Adderbury series
Flag visit to UK	Jun 1990	–	Adm of the Fleet V. N. Chernavin (C-in-C Soviet Navy)	Adm Sir J. J. R. Oswald (1SL)	Marshal of the Soviet Union D. T. Yazov (Min Def) led delegation
Ship visit to Portsmouth	Jul 1990	Bezuprechny	RAdm V. P. Yeryomin (CDR Kola Flotilla)	RAdm J. J. R. Tod (Flag Officer Portsmouth)	Adm Sir J. J. R. Oswald (1SL) visited ship
Flag visit to UK	Nov 1990	HMS Lordon HMS Trenchant	Adm of the Fleet K. V. Makarov (Chief Main Naval Staff)	Adm Sir J. J. R. Oswald (1SL) VAdm Sir A Grose (Flag Officer Plymouth)	Five-day visit

(Continued)

Table 5.2 (Continued)

Serial	Date	Ship	Flag Officers visiting	Flag Officers receiving	Comments
Flag visit to USSR	Jun 1991	–	Adm Sir J. J. R. Oswald (1SL) visited Moscow MNS, Leningrad NB, Severomorsk and Sevastopol	Adm V. Chernavin Adm of the Fleet K. V. Makarov	First visit by a serving First Sea Lord to the Soviet Union
Ship visit to Murmansk	Aug 1991	HMS *London*	RAdm A. B. Richardson (FOF2)	VAdm I. V. Kasatonov	'Dervish 50' Commemoration and 1991 coup
Ship visit to Sevastopol	Oct 1991	HMS *Fearless*	RAdm A. B. Richardson (FOF2)		
Ship visit to London	Nov 1991	*Ivan Kruzenshtern*	VAdm Yu I. Zheglov (hydrographer of RFN)	RAdm J. A. L. Myres (hydrographer of the Navy)	HRH Duke of York visited First hydro-graphic exchange since HMS *Vidal* (1967)
Chief of General Staff Lobov visit to UK	4 Dec 1991	HMS *Revenege*	General of the Army V. N. Lobov Adm V. G. Yegorov (COMBALTFLOT)	VAdm Sir H. M. White (FOSNI)	First visit of Soviet officers to UK SSBN (Lobov sacked days later)
Ship visit to Baltiysk	2 Jul 1992	HMS *Battleaxe*	RAdm A. B. Richardson (COS to FOSF)	Adm V. G. Yegorov (COMBALTFLOT) VAdm V. I. Litvinov	
Ship visit to St Petersburg	Oct 1992	HMS *Herald*	RAdm J. A. L. Myres (hydrographer of the Navy)	VAdm Yu I. Zheglov (hydrographer of RFN) VAdm V. V. Grishanov	Return visit for *Ivan Kruzenshtern*

2010–14 Collapse of cooperation and return to confrontation 119

Flag visit to UK	May 1993	Embarked HMY Britannia for review	Adm F. N. Gromov (C-in-C RFN)	Adm Sir H. M. White (CINCFLEET) Adm Sir J. Kerr (CINCNAVHOME)	
Fiftieth anniversary of Battle of the Atlantic: Fleet Review off Anglesey	May 1993	Gremyashchy	VAdm Yu G. Ustimenko (DEP COMNORFLOT) RAdm A. S. Bogatyryov (Kola Flotilla)	VAdm M. C. Boyce (FOSF) RAdm R. N. Woodard (FORY) HRH Duke of Edinburgh	Ustimenko dined aboard HMY Britannia
RUKUS 93	May 1993	–	RAdm R. F. Cobbold (ACDS OR/SEA SYSTEMS)	VAdm Yu A. Kaisin (First Dep Chief Main Naval Staff)	Exercise 'Triple Trust'
SSK visit to Severomorsk	3–6 Aug 1993	HMS Opossum	Cdre R. C. Lane-Nott (DEP FOSM)	Adm O. A. Yerofeyev (COMNORFLOT) VAdm Yu G. Ustimenko (DEPCOMNORFLOT)	Only RN submarine visit to Russia
Flag visit to Portsmouth	Mar 1994	–	Adm I. V. Kasatonov (Dep C-in-C RFN)	VAdm M. C. Boyce (FOSF) RAdm A. B. Richardson (Ex FOST) Lt Gen Sir R. J. Ross (CGRM)	Red carpet predicted for next C-in-C RFN
Visit to Dartmouth	Oct 1993	Gangut	RAdm Arenochkin		Flag Officer presence not expected
RUKUS 94	May 1994	–	RAdm J. A. Trewby (ACDS OR/Sea Systems)	VAdm Yu A. Kaisin (First Dep Chief Main Naval Staff)	Held at US Naval War College Rhode Island – RAdm J. Strasser (President)

(Continued)

Table 5.2 (Continued)

Serial	Date	Ship	Flag Officers visiting	Flag Officers receiving	Comments
SSK visit to Portsmouth	May 1994	KILO 431 SSK	RAdm G. A. Titarenko (First Dep COS NORFLOT)	RAdm R. C. Lane-Nott (FOSM) RAdm N. E. Ranken (Flag Officer Portsmouth)	Adm H. M. White (CINCFLEET) and Adm Sir K. EATON (Controller) involved
Ship visit to Baltiysk	Jun 1994	HMS Glasgow	VAdm M. C. Boyce (FOSF)	Adm V. G. Yegorov (COMBALTFLOT) VAdm V. P. Komoyedov (Cdr Baltiysk Naval Base) RAdm V. V. Patrushev (MNS Moscow)	Visits to Yantar shipyard, to Baltic Higher Naval College (CDT G. P. Yasnitsky)
State visit to St Petersburg	Oct 1994	HMY Britannia HMS Glasgow	RAdm R. N. Woodard (FORY)	VAdm V. V. Grishanov (Cdr Leningrad Naval Base) Adm F. N. Gromov (C-in-C RFN)	HM the Queen and HRH Duke of Edinburgh embarked
Flag visit to Northwood	31 Mar 1995	–	Adm I. V. Kasatonov (DEP C-in-C RFN)	Adm Sir B. Bathurst (1SL) Adm Sir H. M. White (CINCFLEET) VAdm Sir M. C. Boyce (FOSF) RAdm R. C. Lane-Nott (FOSM)	Second red carpet predicted for next C-in-C RFN
Flag visit to Portsmouth	Mar 1995	Serebryakov	VAdm A. A. Komaritsyn (hydrographer of RFN)	RAdm N. R. Essenhigh (hydrographer of the Navy)	Met 1SL Adm Sir B. Bathurst in London

2010–14 Collapse of cooperation and return to confrontation   121

RUKUS 95	May 1995	–	RAdm J. A. Trewby (ACDS OR/SEA Systems)	Adm V. P. Ivanov (CDT Kuznetsov Academy) VAdm Yu A. KAISIN (First Dep Chief Main Naval Staff)	Hosted by Kuznetsov Academy St Petersburg. Visit to Northern Fleet – met Adm O. A. Yerofeyev (COMNORFLOT)
Ship visit to St Petersburg	May 1995	HMS *Chatham*	VAdm J. R. Brigstocke (FOSF)	VAdm V. V. Grishanov Admls Gromov, Kasatonov, Yegorov and Komaritsyn involved	VE Day fiftieth anniversary review ON NEVA
Flag visit to Moscow/St Petersburg	Sept 1995	–	RAdm N. R. Essenhigh (hydrographer of the Navy)	VAdm A. A. Komaritsyn (hydrographer of RFN)	Met by Gromov and Kasatonov in Moscow
Flag visit to UK	5 Mar 1996	–	Adm I. V. Kasatonov (Dep C-in-C RFN)	Adm Sir J. C. K. Slater (1SL) Adm Sir M. C. Boyce (2SL) Adm Sir P. C. Abbott (CINCFLEET)	Third red carpet for predicted next C-in-C RFN (met ten admirals in one day)
RUKUS 96	May 1996	HMS *Gloucester* RFS *Admiral Levchenko* USS *Samuel B. Roberts*	RAdm P. M. Franklyn (FOST)	VAdm V. V. Patrushev (First Dep Chief Main Naval Staff)	At Rusi Seminar devoted to three-hundredth anniversary of Russian Navy Admirals Oswald and Kasatonov involved

(*Continued*)

Table 5.2 (Continued)

Serial	Date	Ship	Flag Officers visiting	Flag Officers receiving	Comments
Three-hundredth anniversary of Russian Navy	Jul 1996	HMS *Cornwall*	Adm Sir J. C. K. Slater (1SL) Adm Sir P. C. Abbott (CINCFLEET)	Adm of the Fleet F. N. Gromov (CinC RFN) Adm V. G. Yegorov (COMBALTFLOT)	1SL met constellation of Soviet admirals incl Amel'ko, Selivanov, Khovrin, Khronopoulo, Mikhailin, Chernavin, Kapitanets, Makarov, Sorokin and Korobov
Visit to Northwood	Sept 1996	–	RAdm M. M. Yermilov	VAdm Sir J. J. R. Tod (DCINCFLEET) RAdm J. Perowne (FOSM)	
RUKUS 97	May 1997	–	RAdm P. M. Franklyn (FOSF)	VAdm V. V. Patrushev (First Dep Chief Main Naval Staff) RAdm V. F. Bessonov (Head Tactics Faculty Kuznetsov Academy)	Held at US Naval War College Rhode Island – RAdm J. Stark (President)
Ship visit to Vladivostok	Jun 1997	HMS *Richmond*	Adm Sir P. C. Abbott (CINCFLEET)	Adm V. I. Kuroyedov (COMPACFLOT) VAdm M. G. Zakharenko (Dep COMPACFLOT)	
RUKUS 98	May 1998	–	RAdm J. Band (ACNS)	Adm V. P. Yeryomin (CDT Kuznetsov Academy) VAdm V. V. Patrushev First Dep Chief Main Naval Staff)	Hosted by Kuznetsov Academy St Petersburg.

Ship visit to St Petersburg	23 May–3 Jun 1998	HMS *Somerset*	RAdm P. M. Franklyn (FOSF) LT CDR HRH Duke of York	Adm V. G. Yegorov (COMBALTFLOT) Adm A. A. Komaritsyn (hydrographer RFN)	
Ship visit to Devenport	Jul 1998	*Bespokoiny*	Adm V. G. Yegorov (COMBALTFLOT)	RAdm R. J. Lippiett (FOST) RAdm P. M. Franklyn (FOSF) Adm Sir J. R. Brigstocke (2SL)	Visit to HMS *Invincible* Portsmouth (Capt J. M. Burnell-Nugent) and to BRNC (Cdre R. A. Clare)
Signing Memorandum of Understanding on RN-RFN Naval Cooperation	Sept 1998	–	Adm Sir J. C. K. Slater (1SL)	Adm V. I. Kuroyedov (CinC RFN) Adm V. G. Yegorov (COMBALTFLOT)	
RUKUS 99	Sept 1999	–	RAdm J. M. Band (ACNS) Adm Sir J. H. F. Eberle	RAdm (retired) V. S. Pirumov	Substitute RUKUS improvised as result of RFN withdrawal (NATO Kosovo intervention) HRH Prince Michael of Kent attended two sessions

(*Continued*)

Table 5.2 (Continued)

Serial	Date	Ship	Flag Officers visiting	Flag Officers receiving	Comments
INCSEA talks London	Jun 2000		VAdm N. A. Konorev	RAdm J. M. Burnell-Nugent (ACNS) Adm Sir M. C. Boyce (1SL) VAdm Sir F. M. Malbon (DCF)	
Ship visit to Vladivostok	Aug 2000	HMS *Cornwall* HMS *Newcastle*	RAdm S. R. Meyer (COMUKMARFOR – had to cancel owing to Balkan crisis)		*KURSK* had just sank – awkward press conference questions inferring RN SSN involvement
RUKUS 2001 – INCSEA	Jan 2001	–	RAdm J. M. Burnell-Nugent (ACNS)	VAdm N. A. Konorev (First Dep Chief Main Naval Staff)	Held in London – bilateral talks and a serial at US Embassy RAdm S. Bryant (DCINCUS Naveur)
Flag visit to Fost Devenport	Mar 2001	–	RAdm O. N. Lazarev (FOST RFN)	RAdm A Backus (FOST) Adm Sir A. W. J. West (CINCFLEET) (at Northwood)	Thursday War (in HMS *Southampton*)
Ship visit to Murmansk and Arkhangelsk	Sept 2001	HMS *Campbeltown*	RAdm M. Stanhope	VAdm V. G. Dobroskochenko VAdm N. P. Pakhomov	'Dervish 60' Commemoration Ship ran aground Arkhangelsk

2010–14 Collapse of cooperation and return to confrontation   125

CDS visits Moscow	Apr 2002	–	Gen of the Army A. V. Kvashnin (CGS) Col-Gen V. S. Mikhailov (CDR RF Air Force) Maj-Gen A. V. Smelov	Adm Sir M. C. Boyce (CDS)	
CINCFLEET visits Severomorsk	Jul 2002	HMS *Ramsey*		Adm Sir A. W. J. West (CINCFLEET)	Navy Day
RUKUS 2002	Jun 2002	–	RAdm T. P. McClement (ACNS)	VAdm N. A. Konorev (First Dep Chief Main Naval Staff)	First true RUKUS since APR 98 First RUKUS with French involvement (renamed FRUKUS for following year)
Trafalgar Night Moscow	21 Oct 2002	–	–	Adm I. V. Kasatonov (DEP CinC RFN) RAdm V. V. Pepelyayev (Head Main Command Post) Maj-Gen A. Yunak (Head RF Armed Forces Environmental Services)	
Trafalgar Night Moscow	21 Oct 2003	–	Adm of Fleet Sir J. J. R. Oswald (1SL)		Main guest: Adm I. V. Kasatonov Adm Oswald also met the Fleet Chernavin and Gromov during his stay

(*Continued*)

Table 5.2 (Continued)

Serial	Date	Ship	Flag Officers visiting	Flag Officers receiving	Comments
Sixtieth anniversary VE DAY	May 2005	HMS *Sutherland*	Adm Sir A. W. J. West (1SL) CDR HRH Duke of York	VAdm M. L. Abramov (COMNORFLOT) VAdm V. G. Dobroskochenko (First DEP CDR NORFLOT) RAdm V. L. Kasatonov (CO *Pyotr Veliky*)	
Trafalgar 200	Jul 2005	*Admiral Levchenko*	Adm M. L. Abramov (COMNORFLOT)	Adm Sir A West (1SL) Adm Sir J. Band (CINCFLEET) VAdm A. Johns (2SL) RAdm P. Boissier	RAdm HRH Prince Michael of Kent visited *Admiral Levchenko*
Ship visit to St Petersburg	Jul 2005	HMS *St Albans*	HRH Prince of Wales	VAdm A. I. Komaritsyn (hydrographer RFN) VAdm Yu N. Sysuyev (CO Kuznetsov Academy) RAdm V. Yu Kudryavtsev (CDR Leningrad Naval Base)	
C-in-C RFN visits UK	Mar 2007	–	Adm of the Fleet V. V. Masorin (C-in-C RFN) VAdm V. V. Avdoshin (MNS)	Adm Sir J. Band (1SL) VAdm A Johns (2SL) Adm Sir J. Burnell-Nugent (CINCFLEET) and four RADMs	Red carpet treatment – London, Portsmouth, Plymouth, HMS *Victorious*, *Albion*, Royal Flight

2010–14 Collapse of cooperation and return to confrontation

1SL visits Russia	Jun 2008	Adm Sir J. Band	Adm V. V. Vysotsky (C-in-C RFN)	Visited Moscow, Severomorsk (inc SSN Victor III) and St Petersburg (speech at Kuznetsov Academy)
			VAdm N. M. Maksimov (COMNORFLT)	
			RAdm A. I. Lipinsky (CDR Leningrad Naval Base)	
			VAdm A. A. Rimashevsky (CO Kuznetsov Naval Academy)	
			RAdm Yu P. Yeryomin (CO St Petersburg Naval Institute)	
C-in-C RFN visits UK	Dec 2012	Adm V. V. Chirkov (CinC RFN)	Adm Sir M. Stanhope (CNS/1SL)	Visited MoD, Faslane and HMS *Astute*, HMS *QNLZ* in build, Rosyth. Witnessed Thursday War. Dinner in Nelson's Cabin, HMS *Victory*
(CNS/1SL) to Russia	Mar 2013	Adm Sir M. Stanhope	Adm V. V. Chirkov (CinC RFN)	Visited Kirov class *Pyotr Veliky*, *Akula* SSN and KNA
			Adm Korolev – Nor Flt cdr	
			Adm Maksimov – Kuznetsov Naval Academy	
FOST to Russia	Jul 2013	RAdm Ben Key	Adm V. V. Chirkov (CinC RFN)	International Maritime Defence Show, St Petersburg

Table 5.3 RUKUS/FRUKUS 1988–2014

Date	Venue	Key players	Theme	Notes	Ships
30–31 Jul 1988	Adderbury	Adm N. Amel'ko RAdm R. Hill (Retired) Eric Grove/Geoff Till			
20–21 Feb 1989	Moscow	Adm N. Amel'ko RAdm R. Hill (Retired) Eric Grove/Geoff Till			
17–20 Nov 1989	Adderbury	Adm Sir Julian Oswald Adm Wesley Macdonald Adm Nikolai Amel'ko			HMS *Avenger*
31 Oct–3 Nov 1990	Brown Univ Rhode Island	RAdm P. Hoddinott VAdm N. Markov Eric Grove/Geoff Till			
9–12 Nov 1991	Brown Univ Rhode Island	RAdm P. Hoddinott RAdm E. Baker RAdm A. Pauk			
22–26 Jun 1992	Moscow	RAdm R. Cobbold VAdm Yu Kaisin RAdms J. Strasser and E. Baker			
3–7 May 1993	Greenwich	RAdm R. Cobbold VAdm Yu Kaisin RAdm J. Strasser			
1–6 May 1994	Newport Rhode Island	RAdm J. Trewby VAdm Yu Kaisin RAdm J. Strasser			

2010–14 Collapse of cooperation and return to confrontation 129

17–22 Apr 1995	St Petersburg	RAdm J. Trewby VAdm Yu Kaisin RAdm J. Strasser		
29 Apr–4 May 1996	Greenwich Portsmouth Plymouth	RAdm P. Franklyn VAdm V. Patrushev RAdm J. Stark		HMS *Gloucester* USS *Samuel B. Roberts* RFS *Admiral Levchenko* RFA *Black Rover*
4–7 May 1997	Newport Rhode Island	RAdm P. Franklyn VAdm V. Patrushev	Rules of Engagement	
19–24 Apr 1998	St Petersburg	RAdm J. Stark RAdm J. Band VAdm V. Patrushev		
27–30 Sept 1999	Oxford	RAdm J. Stark RAdm J. Band HRH Prince Michael of Kent RAdm V. Pirumov (Retired)		Formally not a RUKUS (NATO Kosovo Intervention)
2000 and 2001				No RUKUS (Kosovo Crisis)
17–20 Jun 2002	Portsmouth	RAdm T. McClement VAdm N. Konorev RAdm S. Bryant (USN)		France involved for first time
2003 2004	France UK			First FRUKUS

(Continued)

Table 5.3 (Continued)

Date	Venue	Key players	Theme	Notes	Ships
2005	France				HMS Montrose RFS Admiral Levchenko USS Mahan FNS De Grasse
2006	English Channel				HMS Monmouth RFS AdmiralD Levchenko USS Barry FNS De Grasse
18–22 Jun 2007	Norfolk VA				HMS Kent RFN Marshal Shaposhnikov USS McCampbell FNS Vendemiaire
2008				No RUKUS – invasion of Georgia	
19–23 Jun 2009	Brest France				HMS York RFS Severomorsk USS Klakring FNS Tourville
22–25 Jul 2010	Plymouth				HMS Kent RFS Severomorsk USS Mount Whitney FNS Primaguet

2010–14 Collapse of cooperation and return to confrontation 131

20–24 Jun 2011	Norfolk VA		HMS *Dauntless* RFS *Admiral Chabanenko* USS *James E. Williams* FNS *Ventose* HMS *York* RFS *Yaroslav Mudry* USS *Normandy* FNS *De Grasse*
25 Jun 2012	Baltiysk	VAdm Chirkov	
27 Jun 2013	Brest		The last (F)RUKUS HMS *Sutherland* RFS *Sterecushchy* USS *Nicholas* FNS *Primaguet*
2014			No RUKUS. Annexation of Crimea

Into the deep freeze – 2014 to 2022

The collapse of military cooperation and consequently the RN–RFN relationship, was driven by many factors, not least the need to be seen to 'punish' Russia for its annexation of Crimea and support to Ukrainian separatists in the Donbas. Among the first reactions was the suspension by the UK, and other western allies, of all military cooperation and dialogue. While understandable with regard to practical cooperation, the suspension of dialogue was a grave mistake. The relationships and linkages that had been built up in the preceding twenty-five years were lost and even the in-country UK attaches were precluded from meeting their interlocutors in the Russian MoD or Military Districts. The 2014 rupture in dialogue was made worse in 2018, by the attempted poisoning of the former GRU officer Sergei Skripal in Salisbury. The UK and West's attempts to deter Russia from taking further action in Ukraine after the 2014 annexation of Crimea spectacularly failed on 24 February 2022, when Russia invaded Ukraine. What had been forgotten after 2014 was that effective deterrence is not just about taking active measures, such as implementing sanctions or bolstering NATO's military posture, but is also about conducting a dynamic dialogue with Moscow that evolves over time.[6] It would be naive to suggest that had military dialogue continued, Russia's invasion of Ukraine could have been avoided. However, the loss of that element of dialogue between the UK and Russia post 2014 denuded the UK of insight to Russian military thinking, and possibly planning, and exacerbated the risks of miscalculation and misunderstanding in a period of increased tension with Moscow. Even in the Cold War, *fora* existed in which sometimes very difficult military dialogue, especially at the working level, could take place, whereas now, except via occasional high-level contact,[7] there are none. The levels of distrust and the lack of confidence between both sides, exacerbated by alleged Russian war crimes, have reached such a low tide mark that it is hard to imagine circumstances where any meaningful dialogue between militaries could be re-established. But it will need to be.

Two non-official, in-country, working level meetings did take place in the immediate aftermath of the annexation of Crimea, one in March 2014 and the other in June 2015. These were between David Fields, then UK NA and the officer in the Western Military District in St Petersburg, responsible for the organisation of the UK/Russia bilateral defence programme of events for 2014, Captain First Rank Konstantin Gulnev. Both meetings were conducted not in uniform and in hotel lobbies over coffee. Gulnev was a quiet but engaging man with a great sense of humour and through his actions in 2013, an apparent promoter of an ambitious bilateral programme, and not just with the RN. The first meeting in 2014 was to inform Gulnev of the UK's decision to suspend all mil-mil cooperation and dialogue. Gulnev had come to the meeting believing that it was intended to put the final touches to the programme for 2014, which he had laid out on the table. The UK NA explained the situation and the UK Government's position and consequent decision on suspending military cooperation. At first, Gulnev did not believe it and went on to describe the berthing arrangements for the first ship visit and other issues before he was stopped and had it explained that no, it really was over. His reaction was bewilderment, naively, that the political fallout over 'a small piece of land that had always been Russian anyway', could cause such a rupture in the relationship. A year or so later in June 2015, that bewilderment had changed to depression and a lack of understanding on Gulnev's part of how the situation between Russia and the West had come to this and 'why did the West hate Russia so much' – a common refrain from our Russian interlocutors over this period, particularly, as NATO expanded to the East. He emphasised the importance of maintaining dialogue and conversation between the two sides before 'we ended up unintentionally and needlessly killing each other', adding words to the effect that 'we have more in common than divides us'. Neither of these two meetings are necessarily of earth-shattering importance in themselves, but they highlight that without dialogue or conversation mistrust builds, miscalculations and misunderstandings flourish, and deterrence measures, without dialogue, do not prevent conflict.

There were a few thin strands of military dialogue that remained after 2014 but which, since 2022, have snapped. Those strands were all maritime by nature and as will be discussed in Chapter 8, it is these strands that might well lead the way in any future defence dialogue with Russia. The treaty obligated meetings under INCSEA 1986 no longer take place, but a last face-to-face meeting did take place in Moscow in 2019, involving the UK Assistant Chief of Naval Staff. The Protocol of amendments signed in 2021, was conducted behind diplomatic closed doors and not through face-to-face meetings. This lack of interaction obligated by the INCSEA agreement represents a more serious degradation in the UK/Russia relationship than existed even in the Cold War.

The Arctic Convoys remained and still remains a key link, as was evident in 2020 when Rear Admiral Iain Lower, then the Assistant Chief of Naval Staff (Policy), and the Russian Defence Attache to the UK, Colonel Maksim Yelovik, met on the quarterdeck of *Belfast* in London for a fifteen-minute service of remembrance and thanksgiving. Throughout the entire 1988 to 2014 period of interaction between the two navies, the commemoration of the convoys remained a golden thread and often helped to smooth over political ruptures and maintain links. Although many of the veterans are no longer with us, their families and the organisations involved continue to commemorate them and the importance of this maritime historical link between Russia and the UK remains undiminished. The maritime Allied assistance to the Soviet Union through the Arctic Convoys played a key role in supporting the USSR and the commemoration of this effort remained the one, indeed only tenuous link between the UK and Russian military after 2014, but even this link has become stressed to breaking point. If and when defence engagement is restored with Russia, the history of the Arctic Convoys will, however, come to the fore and play an important role.

While the relationship between hydrographic departments waned after the MoU was signed in 1995, the UK Hydrographic Office (UKHO) was invited to St Petersburg in May 2017, three years after the annexation of Crimea. That Russia issued the invitation is in itself more proactive than usual, especially to an organisation with which GUNIO had hitherto had a relatively lukewarm relationship. The reason was that GUNIO wanted something, which was for the UKHO to buy their Electronic Navigation Charts (ENC), including the Crimean ones, for the UK to distribute. The GUNIO also wanted training from the UK in both cartography and hydrography. Clearly both demands were politically unacceptable. Similarly, UKHO's desire to obtain access to the Arctic Regional Hydrographic Commission, which was being blocked by Russia, was also not achieved. The visit, although light on deliverables, nevertheless maintained a form of dialogue around the issues of safe navigation and safety at sea. In the margins of cultural visits and hospitality events, relationships could be established and despite the presence of likely intelligence officers within the GUNIO delegation, these exchanges were cordial and polite.[8]

Notes

1. 'Press Conference: The Prime Minister and President Vladimir Putin', Cabinet Office, London, 16 June 2013, www.gov.uk/government/speeches/press-conference-the-prime-minister-and-president-vladimir-putin (accessed 12 June 2023).
2. These observations of Admiral Chirkov are drawn from discussions with Commodore Jim Perks CBE in July 2023, who, as the desk officer on UK's Naval Staff, accompanied Chirkov throughout the 2012 visit.
3. Author: David Fields.
4. Yevmenov was replaced as C-in-C by the Northern Fleet Commander Admiral Moiseyev in March 2024. 'Admiral Moiseyev naznachen vrio glavnokomanduyushchego Voyenno-morskim flotom RF', *TASS*, 19 March 2024, https://tass.ru/armiya-i-opk/20281675 (accessed 19 March 2024).
5. The 2+2 format includes the Foreign and Defence Ministers from each country.
6. A. M. Monaghan, *Dealing with the Russians*. Cambridge, UK, Polity Press, 2019, p. 84.
7. Inter alia these include UK CDS' hotline with Russia's Defence Ministry (www.independent.co.uk/news/uk/politics/russia-nuclear-direct-line-putin-b2029609.html) and limited interaction in the NATO-Russia Council and OSCE.
8. Discussions with Rear Admiral Tim Lowe CBE in July 2023, who in 2017 was the National Hydrographer and Deputy Chief Executive from 2015 before becoming the CEO of the UKHO in 2019.

6

What did the two navies learn about each other?

Some of the lessons that the RN learned about the RFN during two-and-a-half decades of cooperation have been touched on in previous chapters. Now we examine in greater detail, supported by anecdotal evidence, what these unequalled insights provided to the RN in understanding the RFN's ways of doing business and the culture of its people. Conversely, the RFN was also exposed to RN culture and practice. Both navies drew lessons from this prolonged interaction – some positive, others negative. Many of the examples provided of RFN behaviour span the entire twenty-five-year period of cooperation and it would be easy to suggest that in the 2020s the way RFN personnel behave and operate would have adapted or changed, given their exposure to operating with and observing the RN and other Western navies at close range prior to 2014. However, there were no significant changes in culture and behaviour noted during interaction right up to 2014 and many of the traits outlined below remained as they were when the RN first started its cooperation programme in the 1990s. Changing the culture of an organisation like the RFN into a more westernised model of empowerment and delegation of authority to junior ranks for example will not occur any time soon. Given the armed forces' personnel of any country tend to reflect the culture of the society it recruits from, we can expect a continuing paranoid, distrusting culture to pervade the RFN and a silo-based, centralised approach both to the way it operates and also in how it manages its people.

Turning first to the perceptions formed by the RN of the RFN. Russians are centralisers with even minor decisions routinely going to the top for approval. If an admiral is embarked, he dominates decision-making within the ship and eclipses the Commanding Officer (CO). When the *Sovremenny*-class destroyer *Gremyashchy* visited Liverpool in 1993, a junior officer asked the Deputy Commander Northern Fleet, Vice Admiral Ustimenko's, permission to take down the dressing lines of flags whilst the CO stood glumly and passively in the background. Flag officers frequently take over the control of the ship and give direct orders when coming alongside a jetty or to a buoy. Should an accident ensue, however, it would be the CO who would be held responsible. Ustimenko also gave a demonstration lesson to an ordinary seaman on how to blow a bugle call correctly on the destroyer's quarterdeck in full view of the guard of honour preparing to salute a visiting RN admiral.[1]

Another illustration of 'top-downism' occurred at the end of HMS *Campbeltown*'s visit to Odessa in 1997. Although this example relates to the Ukrainian Navy in its immediate post-Soviet incarnation, it still very much retained this element of Russian/Soviet Navy culture. On the final morning alongside, Captain Massey of HMS *Campbeltown* was due to take the ship out for Officer of the Watch (OOW) manoeuvring exercises with the corvette *Lutsk* but was concerned about the latter's seaworthiness as the vessel pumped out clouds of dense black smoke from the adjacent berth. The RN interpreter team were all leaving HMS *Campbeltown* to return to the UK by air before the ship put to sea. The CO was adamant that an interpreter had to be on hand on the bridge, and thus the Defence Attache (DA) brought a trilingual locally-employed interpreter from the embassy. On a leaving call, the Commander of the Odessa Military District, Colonel-General Shkidchenko came to the ship for breakfast during which Captain Massey asked if there was an interpreter in *Lutsk*. No, there wasn't. In that case, said the CO, he would be more comfortable if he could embark the embassy interpreter. But how would the interpreter get back ashore, asked Shkidchenko, given that HMS *Campbeltown* would not be returning to port on completion of the exercise? Captain Massey suggested a helicopter or boat transfer to get the interpreter back ashore. The general said this was out of the question, as it did not appear in the pre-agreed visit plan – such a change could only be authorised by the Chief of the Ukrainian General Staff. And why was an interpreter needed in any case? Captain Massey replied that it would be vital, should anything unforeseen happen. The Naval Captain of the Port replied without any visible irony: 'Nothing unforeseen is envisaged in this exercise.' Captain Massey pressed on. The solution? The general turned to his interpreter aide, an army major, and ordered him to put to sea with *Lutsk*. But as *Lutsk* was proceeding to Sevastopol on completion of the exercise, the major would have to make his own way back to Odessa, some 550 km. For the major, this must have come as unwelcome news: from a one-hour protocol call on HMS *Campbeltown* a short walk from his HQ, his task had turned into a two-day assignment of naval interpreting, which he quickly claimed was not his forte, with nothing but the uniform he stood up in: a good example of improvisation to get round near insurmountable bureaucratic obstacles, albeit with total disregard for subordinates.[2]

Blind adherence to established practices is characteristic of the RFN. An example is the procedure that flag officers must always use an accommodation ladder,[3] presumably to provide suitably dignified arrivals and departures when anchored or moored. When, on the eve of the Battle of the Atlantic Review off Anglesey in 1993, HMS *Cornwall*'s Cheverton-class sea boat was returning two flag officers and the CO of *Gremyashchy* to their ship after a reception given by Flag Officer Surface Flotilla (FOSF), the weather suddenly deteriorated. As the Cheverton approached the stern of the destroyer, the coxswain (helmsman) warned that using the accommodation ladder to board would be dangerous, given the two to three-metre rise and fall of the boat generated by the sea state when at the ladder. The Russian vice-admiral insisted on jumping across first. The CO and the rear-admiral were left with no choice but to follow, nearly resulting in the latter being crushed between ladder and boat, having slipped off the boarding platform with his legs dangling over its edge. The Cheverton was damaged as it repeatedly hit the ladder. At no point was a Jacob's ladder[4] considered, despite its Russian name loaned from Dutch, 'shtorm-trap', and this was a storm. But fixed procedure prevailed over commonsense and safety.[5]

The RFN's approach to training is quantitative rather than qualitative and often reduced to box ticking. There was always surprise expressed at the rigour and dynamism of Fleet Operational Sea Training (FOST) training, compared to the RFN approach seemingly based on fulfilling certain serials within set time-limits. This reflected a very Soviet-style quantitative approach, i.e. five-year plans and production targets set by Gosplan.[6] Asked for his impressions of the Thursday War he had just witnessed from HMS *Southampton* in 2001, Head of Combat Training Rear Admiral Lazarev's first observation was that he had not seen a stop-watch all day. Admiral Gorshkov is said to have kept long obsolete destroyers technically in service by having them towed to the exercise area for gunnery practice – their engines were unserviceable. Gorshkov had apparently served in vessels of this class as a younger officer and had a sentimental attachment to them, so he turned a blind eye to the practice.

A formalistic approach to training is also evident in highly choreographed exercise planning.[7] Predicted positions of units with corresponding times are meticulously fixed on hydrographic charts of the exercise area with painstaking artistry and copper-plate calligraphy. A 1996 handbook by two senior directing staff (both Captains First Rank) at the Kuznetsov Naval Academy prescriptively sets out the rules on how these charts must be drawn up, right down to the use of stencils and even how a pencil should, and should not, be sharpened with accompanying diagrams.[8] Much of the exercise debriefs were devoted to establishing why units did not end up in their prescribed positions on the chart rather than the quality of the training conducted or the ability to react to the unexpected (i.e. the unscripted).

This reflects a system of highly centralised command and control, which in wartime would depend heavily upon units carrying out their pre-assigned functions to the letter. It further highlights the very different approaches of each navy to command and control of their ships and submarines, the management of their people and the material state and technology gap between the navies' platforms. The RFN's autocratic top-down approach to commanding ships and submarines as well as managing their personnel, was (and is) in stark contrast to the RN's mission command approach.[9] That is not to say that the RFN is any less professional in its conduct of maritime operations, particularly underwater, where Russian submarines have always shown a high level of proficiency.[10] The difference in approach towards both individual training and collective training in surface ships was also particularly striking, and a number of visits to the RN's sea training organisation by RFN senior officers left the latter bewildered by the complexity of the training serials and the ability of seemingly junior people taking on responsibilities that would not be seen in the RFN. Was the lack of mission command in RFN culture and a lack of effective training in damage control and firefighting[11] evident in the sinking of the *Slava*-class cruiser *Moskva* in May 2022? Ordered to patrol a particular area in the Black Sea, despite the threat from shore-based Ukrainian *Neptune* anti-ship missiles, the CO might well have felt unable or unwilling to question his orders up the chain of command. It is not a natural Russian thing to do. The RN concept of a 'private ship' or mission command, in which a CO is able to take decisions of his or her own to fulfil assigned missions is alien and incomprehensible to RFN officers. Both terms are also not easily translatable into Russian.

The RFN favours depth over breadth in officer training. An officer specialises in a particular discipline early on and stays strictly in that groove or career path. For sea-going officers, it is commonplace for a junior officer to be appointed to a ship and for him to stay in the same ship – or class of ship – as he progresses to head of department, executive officer and commanding officer. A further progression may be to command a squadron of similar vessels. This leads to a great depth of knowledge about the specific ship, but to a narrowness of command or staff experience too. An alternative career route is that of 'flag specialist' – in effect, specialist staff officers tasked with HQ support. When Admiral Amel'ko, who had just retired after fifty-three years' service in the Soviet Navy was visiting HMS *Avenger* in Devonport in 1989, he asked the CO very specific technical questions. Standing on the forecastle, he asked 'What is the thickness of the shell-plating of the hull below us here?' then 'What is that cylinder halfway down the barrel of that (4.5') gun?' and then 'And how does it work (fume-extractor)?' The fact that the CO had to ask a senior rate for the answers to these questions appeared to appal the Admiral as 'not serious' – i.e. unprofessional.[12] When Admiral Yegorov was touring HMS *Invincible*, he was nonplussed to learn that her CO had been a submariner. This was a surface ship and in the RFN could only be commanded by a surface ship officer, not a submariner or aviator. He was even more amazed to learn that US Navy practice is that only naval aviators command aircraft carriers. The Russian Naval Air Arm is fundamentally a land-based organisation and its personnel, although wearing naval uniform, carry military rank.[13] Yegorov was also surprised to learn that the chef to whom he was speaking had an obvious damage-control role as well. In the RFN, specialist teams are assigned to damage control, perhaps a by-product of a conscription-based system. The same applies to disaster-relief training. Not every Russian warship is trained to carry out disaster relief operations as are RN ships. Russian admirals visiting disaster relief exercises at Portland and later Plymouth were surprised, and actually impressed, that all RN ships underwent such realistic training. They were similarly impressed by the realism of the Thursday War. The RFN was at one stage considering sending a Russian ship to FOST in 2007 after Admiral Masorin's visit, but the deterioration of UK–Russia relations following Alexander Litvinenko's murder in 2006, precluded this event.

When it comes to appointing officers to posts in the RFN, a long-term view is very evident. A commanding officer's appointment can last routinely for four to five years, sometimes extending to seven. Merchant naval appointments in Russia's logistics auxiliary fleet tend to last even longer. One Pacific Fleet tanker master has just completed twenty-four years in command. Similarly, admirals stay in post much longer than in the RN. Five years is common and Admiral Yegorov commanded the Baltic Fleet from 1991 to 2000. The former Minister of Defence Sergei Shoigu was in post for over twelve years and a minister since April 1991. The supreme example is Gorshkov, who was C-in-C of the Soviet Navy for nearly thirty years from 1956 to 1985. While this brings consistency and long-term vision as positives it may also lead to complacency and stagnation, as it did in the Soviet political system under Leonid Brezhnev.

Common across all branches of the Russian armed forces is the lack of an established senior rates cadre and culture.[14] In the RFN, junior officers carry out tasks routinely fulfilled by senior rates in the RN. The personnel profile of the RFN still resembles an hour-glass, with a preponderance of officers at the top, including over two hundred admirals and naval generals and of short-service conscripts at the bottom with a relatively small cadre of professional senior rates in the middle. With the gradual shift from conscription to contract service, this is changing. Of note, however, the ship's companies of nuclear-powered submarines and the Russian Naval Infantry have no conscripts and a stronger senior rate component. This shift, however, is a slow process.

The RFN's platforms are resilient and its people good at technical improvisation. Most of their surface fleet dates back to the 1980s and earlier, yet they manage to keep even forty-/fifty-year-old amphibious ships like the *Alligators*, *Ropuchas* and the *Krivak*-class frigates running. This is helped by the fact that many of their legacy Soviet-era platforms rely on analogue and not digital technology and by personnel who know their ships thoroughly by virtue of their length of service on board. This resilience is being demonstrated in the conflict with Ukraine. Both new and old ships and submarines have maintained a high level of operational tempo during operations in the Black Sea in a way that would challenge the high-tech, high maintenance demands of more modern platforms, including some of those operated by the RN.

Bureaucratic inflexibility in Russia is a well known phenomenon, especially hampering communications between different ministries and agencies. This was very evident during the *Priz* submersible rescue in 2005 described in more detail in Chapter 4. The RFN had done all that was necessary to get the UK Scorpio rescue Remotely Operated Vehicle (ROV) to Kamchatka by overflight of Russian territory. However, on its arrival, the local customs officer insisted on going through every separate item on the C17 cargo manifest, including the ROV itself, demanding to know its exact monetary value and warning that any item left behind on completion of the operation would incur a fine. And all this as the seven Russian submariners were running perilously short of breathable air. A seething Commander Riches, in charge of the rescue team, was persuaded by the NA, Captain Holloway, to comply with the bureaucratic idiocy, who later recounted the procedural nightmare he had been through when trying to clear entry for the musical instruments of a Royal Marines band coming into Moscow for a performance. This is an example of cultural awareness being applied by Captain Holloway to good effect.[15]

A further example of the Russian 'silo' mentality, where adherence to one's own chain of command prevailed regardless of the bigger picture, was the refusal of the guard on the gate to let the Scorpio ROV and the RN team into the dockyard at Petropavlovsk. It turned out that this was a civilian facility and no one had warned the guard to open the gates, resulting in more lost time. This ingrained reaction to comply with 'vertical' authority at all costs and to fail totally to communicate with other authorities 'horizontally' is very characteristic of Russian bureaucracy across the board. The left hand frequently has no idea of what the right hand is doing. Russian commentators identify this phenomenon but inertia prevents change. In this context, 'mission command' and initiative are alien, even dangerous concepts.

Another example of procedural inflexibility was apparent during the *Priz* rescue operation. When the RN team finally got into the dockyard and onto the support vessel *KIL-27*, they found the deck on which they needed to mount the deployment crane for the Scorpio ROV was rusted through and needed reinforcing. The master of the tug was totally passive, so they were forced to forage for scrap metal in the darkness on the pierside. When they found suitable pieces of steel, they asked the civilian master for welding support. One oxy-acetylene torch was produced plus a welder. When Captain Holloway requested three more sets plus welders he was told that state regulations allowed only one welder at any one time to be used in that space. Again, more time was lost by prioritising observance of pettifogging regulations over the main effort – saving men's lives.[16]

The RFN is a conservative organisation. Despite the revolutionary origins of the Soviet Navy, its senior officers were appalled that the RN could even consider decommissioning the Royal Yacht *Britannia* and the naval college at Greenwich. Women do not serve at sea in the RFN and there is even a widespread superstition that women on board bring bad luck. They retain the rates system of the wooden sailing naval era. Cruisers and nuclear submarines are 'First Rates' down to 'Fourth Rates' for minor war vessels. There is some logic to this. The three principal ship-command ranks, namely Captains First, Second and Third Rank (Captain, Commander and Lieutenant Commander are the RN equivalents) by and large command ships of the corresponding 'Rank'. The Russian term 'rang', a loan from the Dutch language, is common to ship and rank.

Like many Russians, RFN personnel are secretive and often for no good reason. Information is kept close to the chest. During the celebration of the three-hundredth anniversary of the Russian Navy in 1996, over fifty heads of navy from all over the globe came to St Petersburg for an event on a grand scale. At no point were they given a comprehensive briefing as to what to expect in advance; the expectation was that they would turn up at stated times and places to be shepherded through the programme.

For example, there was much interest in a rumoured fly-past by aircraft of Russian Naval Aviation but exactly when and with what aircraft were questions left open to speculation. Yet the liaison officers had chapter and verse on this event, but one needed to know who they were and how to ask them for it (in Russian, of course). By taking the initiative, the interpreter was able to see a detailed diagram of the composition of the flypast with exact timings.[17] There was no particular resistance to providing the information when asked for it, but the culture was not to give it voluntarily.

The RFN is also accident-prone. The loss of *Kursk* and its entire ship's company in 2001 is the prime example of modern times but is just one of a catalogue of accidents which include: major fires on the strategic nuclear missile submarine *Yekaterinburg* refitting in the PD-50 floating dock in 2011 and the missile cruiser *Kerch* in 2014, writing the ship off as a total loss; in October 2018, the sinking of the PD-50 with the refitting air-capable cruiser *Admiral Kuznetsov* in it. This resulted in one of PD-50's travelling cranes crashing through the carrier's deck and deprived the Navy of a key asset, the only one capable of docking the very largest surface ships and submarines; in December 2019 *Admiral Kuznetsov* was further ravaged by fire. Even senior officers have been observed smoking near fuel-bowsers on airfields. There is no concept of 'health and safety' – or even a fixed term for it. There is, however, a Ministry for Emergencies (or Ministry of Disasters, depending on how it is translated). Poor maintenance leads to reliability problems, which is why task groups are invariably accompanied by a powerful salvage tug in case of breakdown away from home waters. This indeed did happen to *Admiral Kuznetsov* in the Bay of Biscay in 2012 and it had to be taken in tow back to the Northern Fleet's base in Severomorsk.

Despite their apparent granite-faced frostiness at first encounter, Russians place great emphasis on making the human connection. This is often achieved through bonding in Olympic-scale vodka bouts, although this is perhaps less the case under the austere Putin as Supreme Commander-in-Chief. As one officer explained, 'I can't fully trust someone I haven't been drunk with.' Similarly, the institution of the *banya* (sauna) often played a positive role in building good relations and results, as witnessed by the presentation of previously classified charts to the UKHO in 1992, which took place after a shared *banya* experience, with alcohol, the day before. The human connection generated through the warmth of vodka and *banyas* is often vital in successfully navigating Byzantine bureaucracy, as Captain Holloway found in the *Priz* rescue. Captain First Rank Podkopayev appeared in the dockyard and emerged as a valuable problem-solver. Crucially, he knew members of the UK team. They had worked together in a NATO exercise in Taranto two months previously.

Vodka and *banyas* are the currency for 'getting things done' and building trust in Russia – in the naval context this was no different. Everything from arranging ships' visits to the conduct of those visits and other events relied to a large extent on the bonds formed during a session of vodka drinking. Indeed, there is a set protocol for these sessions of which one should be mindful. The first toast is usually reserved for the host to propose, the second for the senior person present to reply, and the third, considered to be the most reverential, is for anyone to make but is always *Za tekh, kto v more* – for those at sea – i.e. in their ships at sea, battling with the elements with their duty preventing them from being present. Another more sombre toast and one which would need sensitive timing, is *Za tekh, kogo s nami net* – For those who are not with us – i.e. the departed. After the third toast it is a free for all on toasting and with three toasts consumed and with the hospitality and sense of goodwill flowing, these can quickly become long sessions and a test of stamina, which some feel they are up to and often quickly find they are not.

The importance to Russians of the human connection is further illustrated by the encounter between Vice Admiral Boyce (then Flag Officer Surface Flotilla) and Vice Admiral Komoyedov (Commander Baltiysk Naval Base) during HMS *Glasgow*'s visit to Baltiysk in 1994. At the end of a long day, Admiral Boyce invited Komoyedov for a nightcap in his cabin. Instead of the usual subjects, Komoyedov steered the conversation onto religion. Perhaps the absence of the Russian interpreter encouraged him to do so. Although a life-long Communist, his interest in religion had been sparked by conversations with the Baltic Fleet chaplain. He was intrigued but not convinced by the chaplain's assertion that upon death, every human soul 'recalibrates' to the age of thirty-three – the age of Jesus Christ on the Cross – regardless of their earthly age. He found this too mechanistic. A nearly hour-long conversation ensued, with Komoyedov much appreciating Admiral Boyce's thoughts. Many years later, about 2015–16, a Russian veteran visiting the UK passed a pocket watch to Admiral Boyce – with best wishes from Admiral Komoyedov. So it turned out that the Communist Head of the Defence Duma Committee – which Komoyedov had become on retiring from the navy – was passing a heartfelt gift to a British Admiral of the Fleet and member of the House of Lords. That encounter in Baltiysk had not been forgotten.[18]

However grim-faced Russian Navy personnel, like many Russians, may seem at first meeting, they have a refined sense of humour which reveals itself over a longer working relationship. In 1989 Admiral Amel'ko, during a briefing at Devonport and just retired after fifty-six years' service in the Soviet Navy, was told HMS *Avenger* had used her 4.5' gun to shoot down an Exocet missile in the Falklands War. 'Pure luck', he said, 'during the siege of Leningrad, the one and only elephant in the city zoo took a direct hit from a German shell'. Later, touring the frigate, the CO recounted the same story, adding that the 4.5' had a limited anti-missile capability, depending on the proximity of the target. Amel'ko, speaking in Russian through the interpreter, threw up his arms with a smile and said 'Well, the more elephants there are...' without completing the sentence. The interpreter realised this comment was meant for him as one 'in the know' on the elephant joke and not the CO. The interpreter rendered his words as 'I agree with your tactical evaluation of the weapon'. It was a nice piece of irony on Amel'ko's part.[19]

The phenomenon of *vranyo* is frequently encountered in dealing with any Russian and the RFN is not immune. There is no English translation that conveys its essence, which lies somewhere between telling preposterous lies and making up tall stories in the manner of 'blarney'. There is another verb for 'lying' in Russian, where the intention is more evidently malevolent. *Vranyo*, however, may not necessarily have evil intent. It may be playful, or used for concealment or even to create a bond with the person on the receiving end, who becomes complicit by tacitly going along with the confection. An example of the latter relates to the *Gremyashchy* accommodation-ladder episode previously related. In the following year, Robert Avery accompanied Commodore Lane-Nott to the Northern Fleet HQ in Severomorsk, where he met Vice-Admiral Ustimenko. Somewhat to Avery's embarrassment, he was greeted by Ustimenko like a long-lost friend, with the Commodore cast in the role of spectator. Ustimenko wanted to reminisce about getting back onto *Gremyashchy* in a force nine gale and related a version of events, in which he was first to leap across from the Cheverton, followed by the interpreter. But the interpreter never got back onto *Gremyashchy*, nor even attempted to. He then explained that just the two of them made the death-defying leap across the foaming abyss 'and the others just chickened out'. Having to translate this to the somewhat baffled Commodore Lane-Nott, the interpreter became complicit in the *vranyo* but it was evidently meant to show us as comrades in adversity.[20]

Sometimes concealment is the motive for *vranyo*. During the 1997 RUKUS talks at the US Naval War College at Newport Rhode Island, a day-long visit to New York was organised by the hosts for the head of the Russian delegation, Vice-Admiral Viktor Patrushev. The next day, the following informal exchange between the interpreter and the Admiral took place:

Int: Did you enjoy your trip to New York yesterday?
Pat: I didn't go to New York.
Int: Oh, I was told you were there.

Pat: No, I went to the aircraft-carrier USS *Intrepid*.
Int: But the *Intrepid* is berthed in New York.
Pat: I didn't notice.

The whole exchange was conducted without any trace of irony or humour by Patrushev. He was obviously anxious to dispel any rumours he'd been on a 'jolly' to a museum ship in New York, especially amongst his subordinates who were not part of that outing.[21] One should be aware that the convention of *vranyo* is that obvious big lies of this kind are not challenged.

A further example of *vranyo*, but one met with 'counter *vranyo*' occurred during the three-hundredth anniversary celebration of the Russian Navy in St Petersburg in 1996. Heads of Navies were being ushered through a checkpoint to board one of the despatch vessels which would pass through the lines of warships moored in the Neva. The First Sea Lord, Admiral Sir Jock Slater, was told in no uncertain terms by the C-in-C RFN's personal assistant, Captain Andreyenkov, that he could not bring his interpreter on board, despite the fact the Russians had supplied no interpreters at all for the foreign VIPs. Admiral Slater challenged this but was told the presence of the interpreter would upset the stability of the vessel. This was patently ludicrous *vranyo*, given this was a substantial vessel able to accommodate fifty or sixty people. The admiral, demonstrating a very Russian quality of persistence, would not let it go, reducing Andreyenkov to despair: 'These are the orders of the Commander-in-Chief Gromov.' The admiral pressed on: 'Are there no exceptions?' 'Only security personnel' was the reply. 'Ah, but my interpreter is also my personal protection officer and I must have him next to me at all times.' Andreyenkov threw up his arms in desperation: 'Then go through.' The interpreter accompanying the US Secretary of the Navy Dalton was not let through despite his boss's pleadings.[22]

Russians are extremely proud of their Navy's role in making Russia a global power and knowledgeable about both its history and also the RN's. It was the Navy, under Peter the Great, which gave Russia access to the high seas and made Russia a global power with which to be reckoned. There is also pride in the technical achievements of the Navy. Since Peter the Great, the navy has been a national symbol of modernity, perhaps *the* national symbol of engineering achievement before the Space Race eclipsed it in the national consciousness. Witness the icebreaker *Lenin*, the world's first nuclear-powered surface vessel, the *Typhoon*-class SSBNs, the *Alpha*-class SSNs, the *Kirov*-class nuclear-powered cruisers. Portraits show Peter's father and predecessor, Tsar Aleksei Mikhailovich, in ceremonial robes of mediaeval style, whereas Peter chose to be married in the elegant western-style uniform of a Rear-Admiral.

Figure 6.1 Old adversaries meet at the Catherine Palace reception marking the three-hundredth anniversary of the Russian Navy: From left to right: Admiral Vladimir Mikhailin (Commander Baltic Fleet 1967–75, Deputy Commander Warsaw Pact Navies 1978–83), Admiral Sir Jock Slater (First Sea Lord), Admiral Nikolai Khovrin (Commander Black Sea Fleet 1974–83), Admiral Nikolai Amel'ko (Commander Pacific Fleet 1962–69, Deputy C-in-C Soviet Navy 1969–78, Deputy Chief of Soviet General Staff, 1979–87), Admiral of the Fleet Aleksei Sorokin (last chief zampolit of the Soviet Navy 1981–91), Robert Avery (Interpreter). July 1996. © Author – Robert Avery.

Much attention is devoted to demonstrations of naval 'power' every July on Navy Day, focusing heavily on visual and photographic impact, with beautifully painted warships forming into line ahead like dreadnoughts of another age as they pass Kronstadt or firing salvoes of rockets from anti-submarine rockets launchers (RBU) from inside the harbour at Sevastopol. One is reminded of the great Royal Naval reviews at Spithead in Victorian and Edwardian times which definitely inspired great public awareness of, and support for, the Navy. However, the Edwardian fixation with a smart turn-out predominated over realistic battle training, as illustrated by the notorious 1907 Paintwork Incident between Admirals Beresford and Scott. As noted by Andrew Gordon in *The Rules of the Game* regarding the pre-World War I Royal Navy, these words might equally applicable to the post-Soviet Russian Navy: 'Snow-white decks, the spotless enamel, the gleaming brass tompions plugging the gun muzzles, were accepted as the hallmarks of naval quality; the punctilious perfection of time-honoured ceremonial as the evidence of efficiency.' And also apposite for the RFN is: 'a spirit of swagger; and its signs are a love of ostentation and of theatrical showing-off, a mania for doing everything at great pace in order to break the record and get one's name mentioned as a smart officer, a passion for doing all work with a margin for safety cut to the quick'.[23]

Many of the behaviours described here are part of the seventy-five-year legacy of a centralised top-down Soviet way of doing things, in managing its politics, its economy and its armed forces. Others are much more deeply embedded in Russian culture. Some of them we can easily identify with, while others are totally alien. Perhaps crucially, this naval interaction over such a lengthy period, gave Russian officers a human face for their RN counterparts after decades of distant encounters on the high seas when the adversaries observed each other through periscopes, binoculars and gunsights. Admirals like Amel'ko, Gromov, Yegorov, Kasatonov, Patrushev, Konorev and Lazarev, to name but a few, came across as thoughtful, enlightened and erudite. Yegorov, in particular, was an officer of great integrity and charisma who commanded the Baltic Fleet for a decade and turned down the offer of relieving Gromov as Commander-in-Chief in 1997 to stay with his people,[24] who evidently held him in high regard.

While the RN might have learned lessons from this twenty-five-year period of interaction, it might equally have also drawn some wrong conclusions. Although there was rarely open gloating by RN personnel at a former enemy who had 'lost' the Cold War, a certain complacency became evident in assessing Russian naval capabilities. In the 1990s Russian naval harbours

Figure 6.2 Rear Admiral John Lippiett (Flag Officer Sea Training) and Admiral Vladimir Yegorov (Commander Baltic Fleet) on board destroyer *Bespokoiny* during her visit to Plymouth. July 1998. © Author – Robert Avery.

Figure 6.3 Rear Admiral John Lippiett (Flag Officer Sea Training) and Admiral Vladimir Yegorov (Commander Baltic Fleet) on board HMS *Norfolk* during the visit of destroyer *Bespokoiny* to Plymouth. July 1998. © Author – Robert Avery.

were full of rusting and even sunken surface ships. Of Krivak, *Udaloi* or *Sovremenny* operations rooms,[25] the quiet aside 'just like the Ops Room of a 1960s RN County-class destroyer' was often articulated, on the assumption that Russian warships were designed for the same roles as their Western counterparts and that digital systems were superior and more robust than the more analogue systems. The fact that only four submarine visits took place in this period meant that assessments of weakness were often made purely on observations of the surface fleet, and not the powerful submarine arm, where the RFN has always performed better.

While the RN might have developed its perceptions of the RFN during this period, so too did the RFN of the RN. A common theme throughout the period was the high regard in which the RN was held both for its history and the way it operated. The UK was often referred to as the 'premier maritime nation' against which the RFN, and others, benchmarked their own navies. One of the many occasions that serve to highlight this point was onboard the *Slava*-cruiser *Marshal Ustinov*, moored on the River Neva for the fiftieth anniversary of victory in World War II in 1996. Both authors were present at a formal lunch at which many other navies were also represented. The then C-in-C RFN, Admiral Gromov, raised the first toast, describing the prowess and professionalism of one particular navy at the table, with his audience held in suspense as to which one he was describing. He concluded, 'to the aristocrats of the sea – the Royal Navy'. There was much eye-rolling and raised eyebrows from the assembled gathering.

What did the two navies learn about each other? 149

Figure 6.4 Admiral Sir Hugo White – Commander-in-Chief Fleet – welcomes Commander-in-Chief Russian Federation Navy Admiral Feliks Gromov to the Northwood Command Centre. This was a historic occasion – Admiral Gromov was the first Russian admiral to go 'down the Hole' into the command bunker. May 1993. © Crown Copyright.

On the positive side of the lessons learned by Russian naval personnel was that the pay and conditions, particularly for RN junior and senior rates, were incomparably superior when set against those in the RFN. They found it difficult to comprehend that there had been no conscription since 1961. The multi-skilling and educational level of junior and senior rates also surprised them, especially the universal competence required in damage control on top of their specialisation. Those Russians who witnessed a DISTEX or Thursday War at first hand were unfailingly impressed by the realism and dynamism of the training process. They were also surprised that RN officers were not the emotionless stereotypes they had been led to believe they were. It also became clear early on that despite their publicly antagonistic ideological stance at the time, the British operation to retake the Falkland Islands in 1982 was followed closely as it unfolded, especially by directing staff at the Kuznetsov Naval Academy. There was grudging admiration for the success of an operation that seemingly defied the laws of 'Military Science' (*Voyennaya nauka*).[26]

This understanding and insight into the RN and its people took time. Soviet conditioning and mirror-imaging had initially made them think they were being deceived by carefully contrived theatre: how, for example, can there be a bar with alcoholic drinks in the Wardroom or senior rates' areas (messes)? However, the length of the interaction with the RN, often with the same Russian officers, made them believe they were not being tricked by 'show ships'.

As well as positive observations made by the RFN about the RN there were also negative ones. They were inclined to regard the length of RN appointments as too short, potentially leading to amateurism and superficiality. They were universally horrified that women were serving at sea. When pressed to give a reason, they routinely fell back on the superstition that it was bad luck. When confronted with reality, they were not always beyond changing their minds. Admiral Ustimenko was highly impressed by the coolness and professionalism of a female Leading Hand on board the Cheverton in the episode described earlier and reiterated his admiration subsequently to his own people.

As stated earlier, they found the concept of Rules of Engagement incomprehensible and admitted publicly at RUKUS 97 that they had nothing of the kind. They were willing to train individual ships' companies in the concept if they were going to take part in joint peace-keeping operations but the lingering impression was that they regarded ROEs as legalistic niceties hampering the business of killing the enemy.

The senior hierarchy of the RFN were baffled by the numerical weakening of the RN throughout the entire period. In 1998 Admiral Yegorov was in disbelief to learn that the Batch 2 Type 22 frigates were being disposed of after barely thirteen to fifteen years' service. The four Batch 3 Type 22s followed them in 2010–11. The significance of the premature demise of these ten anti-submarine frigates together with their signals intelligence capability (SIGINT) cannot have been lost on the Russians.

For successful interaction with the RFN at some indeterminate point in the future, it is vital to ensure appropriate cultural and language training is provided for UK Forces personnel. In the meantime, while the RN–RFN relationship is adversarial, this training is no less important in attempting to interpret Russian thinking. In this regard, the establishment of the Defence Centre for Languages and Culture at Defence Academy Shrivenham in 2014 has proven a very positive development, especially in view of the 2011 decision to scrap MoD Russian language training altogether: a decision thankfully reversed, Russian is now the biggest department at DCLC. The Centre combines the language training capabilities of Defence School of Languages (DSL) with many other aspects of attache training, including cultural, in a single space under the aegis of the Defence Engagement School (DES).

DCLC is a valuable platform for systematic training of linguists and analysts who in turn would be able to brief visiting flag officers, ships' companies and others about Russian culture and behaviour. These include help with interpreting body language, not misreading the apparent frostiness of Russian senior officers at first encounter as hostility when on the Russian side it is appropriate formality and being aware of the tactility and emotionality of Russians. This training and practice was followed throughout the period under review and proved most effective. In the 1990s the RN was particularly fortunate to have been able to draw on a powerful cadre of up to forty Russian interpreters, trained during the Cold War who could be rapidly re-purposed for the new environment. This cadre atrophied to nearly zero in the early 2000s as language training at DSL Beaconsfield (forerunner of DCLC) focused on training hundreds of Pashto and Dari speakers for Afghanistan operations. It is now vital to rebuild this capability but that will not be achieved overnight. As Admiral Cunningham said, it takes three years to build a warship but three hundred years to build a tradition. It will take decades to restore the RN's lost Russian linguistic capabilities and corporate knowledge but at least the process has now begun.

Notes

1 Witnessed by author Robert Avery as interpreter, May 1993.
2 Witnessed by Robert Avery as interpreter, September 1997.
3 A portable staircase hinged to a platform attached to the side of a ship and which can be positioned to provide easier access to the ship.
4 A Jacob's ladder consists of wooden rungs and ropes. It is a roll-up ladder that hangs freely down the side of a ship.
5 Witnessed – and experienced – by Robert Avery as interpreter, May 1993.
6 Gosplan – the state planning commission of the former Soviet Union responsible for coordination and development of the economy, social services, etc.
7 Witnessed by Robert Avery as interpreter: conversation Admiral Sir Alan West-Lazarev, Northwood, March 2001.
8 V. F. Kupreyenkov and I. V. Solovyov, 'Morskiye operativniye karty', St Petersburg, 1996, pp. 60–61.
9 Mission Command is the delegation of authority to personnel to execute orders from a higher authority in what they consider to be the most efficient and effective manner to complete the assigned mission or task.
10 T. Sharpe, 'Putin Has One Deadly Weapon Left, and I Saw First Hand the Threat It Poses', *Telegraph*, 19 May 2023, www.telegraph.co.uk/news/2023/05/19/putin-has-one-deadly-weapon-left-seen-threat-it-poses/ (accessed 22 May 2023).
11 Damage control refers to firefighting and dealing with floods and other damage caused either by enemy action in war or accidents in peacetime.
12 Witnessed by Robert Avery as interpreter, November 1989.
13 Witnessed by Robert Avery as interpreter, conversation Capt J. Burnell-Nugent-Yegorov, HMS *Invincible*, July 1998.

14 Senior Rates are non-commissioned officers who are experienced and well trained.
15 F. Pope, *72 Hours*. London, Orion/Hachette UK Press, 2012, pp. 138–139.
16 F. Pope, *ibid.*, pp. 158–160.
17 Witnessed and experienced by Robert Avery as interpreter.
18 Conversation Boyce-Komoyedov HMS *Glasgow* in Baltiysk June 1994 witnessed by Robert Avery as interpreter and in subsequent conversations with VAdm Boyce.
19 Witnessed by Robert Avery as interpreter, November 1989.
20 Witnessed – and experienced – by Robert Avery as interpreter, conversation Cdre R. Lane-Nott-Vice Admiral Yu G. Ustimenko. Northern Fleet Headquarters, Severomorsk, August 1993.
21 Informal conversation Robert Avery – Vice Admiral V. V. Patrushev, US Naval War College, Rhode Island, May 1997.
22 Witnessed – and experienced – by Robert Avery as interpreter in exchange Admiral Sir Jock Slater-Captain First Rank V. Ye Andreyenkov, St Petersburg, July 1996.
23 A. Gordon, *The Rules of the Game*. London, John Murray, 1996, pp. 174–175.
24 Revealed to Rear Admiral John Lippiett in informal conversation with Admiral Yegorov (interpreter Robert Avery) Devonport, July 1998.
25 The operations room is where the conduct of military operations is conducted from. Sensor information from radar and sonar, for example, is analysed here and weapons directed accordingly.
26 Conversation Robert Avery – Captain 1 Rank S. V. Aprelyev, Kuznetsov Naval Academy, St Petersburg, May 1995.

7

The Russian Navy – future prospects

Policy (ends)

The aspiration of the UK's 2021 Integrated Review (IR), its Refresh and updated Defence Command Paper in 2023, is of a Global Britain that seeks, in a post-Brexit world, to deepen the UK's diplomatic and prosperity links with allies and partners worldwide. Defence plays a key role in support of this aspiration and its stated aim, beyond its main Euro-Atlantic focus, is that it must prepare for more persistent global engagement with non-NATO allies, such as Japan and South Korea, and other regional alliances such as the Five Power Defence Arrangement.[1] In September 2021, AUKUS, a trilateral security pact for the Indo-Pacific region, was signed between Australia, the UK and the US which will also see the US and the UK assisting Australia in acquiring nuclear-powered submarines. Also in 2021, the aircraft carrier, HMS *Queen Elizabeth*, undertook one of the most ambitious global deployments in twenty years, visiting the Mediterranean, the Middle East and the Indo-Pacific. Another aircraft carrier deployment to the region is scheduled for 2025. The purpose of such deployments is to demonstrate interoperability with allies and partners, in particular the US, and to project military power in support of NATO and international maritime security. In May 2023, the First Sea Lord, Admiral Sir Ben Key, highlighted the persistence of this task for the RN in the future, noting that 'as a navy we also have to be able to support our commitments to NATO and the Euro-Atlantic, to be able to deploy globally to engage with and reassure our partners and allies wherever they are, and to ensure that the people who share our values, likeminded around the world, can see us as reliable, dependable and engaged'.[2]

However, it is not just the UK that has global maritime power projection aspirations. So too Russia, and thus the RN and other navies as they go about their 'daily business' across the globe will continue to confront and interact with units of the RFN both above and below water. Regarded more as a continental land power, this element of power projection in Russian strategy is often overlooked but the latest maritime doctrine published in

July 2022, updated from 2015, is explicit.[3] The doctrine takes other national strategic and planning documents into account in setting the direction for Russia's maritime policy, with the key assumptions being that:

- The use of the sea is intensifying around the world.
- The importance of the sea will increase as land resources (natural resources) are depleted and the Arctic ice melts.
- As a great maritime power, Russia's interests extend worldwide.
- The main threat to those interests comes from the US and NATO.

The claim that Russia should have the capability to protect its national interests worldwide ranks the Arctic and Pacific oceans before the Atlantic, unlike the previous iteration, while its contiguous waters are assigned the highest priority. As a reflection of this priority, many of the new nuclear submarines, and conventional submarines have been sent to the Pacific Fleet, with a commensurate level of investment in new basing facilities and infrastructure, thereby boosting the RFN's capability in the Indo-Pacific region.

The doctrine, therefore, provides the RFN with its traditional defensive role of Russia and its CNI, but also the task of challenging and competing on the high seas and to hold adversaries at risk with new capabilities above and below water. This task is expressed in more detail in Russia's Naval Policy 2017.[4] The core aim of the policy remains consistent with that of Admiral Gorshkov: to protect Russia with a set of capabilities that can be deployed at range to deter and to defeat an adversary. There also remains an aspiration for an aircraft carrier capability and amphibious expeditionary forces. As with Gorshkov's fleet, submarines remain the key component, with strategic ballistic-missile submarines the indisputable priority.[5] What is interesting, however, is that the objectives in the policy would not look out of place in a UK maritime doctrine. That should not be surprising. The level of interaction between the RN and other western navies between 1988 and 2014, helped to shape RFN thinking about its role and future structures, as it emerged from the Cold War. Indeed, a key architect of the 2017 naval policy and an advisor to the Chief of the General Staff and the President on maritime matters, was, and may still be, Admiral Igor Kasatonov. He was the Deputy C-in-C of the RFN and a key interlocutor with the RN in the 1990s, and frequently visited the UK. In sum, those objectives are:

- Delivery of the strategic nuclear deterrent.
- Protection of the nuclear deterrent (in the bastions[6] of the Barents Sea and Sea of Okhotsk).
- Conventional deterrence, enhanced by long-range precision guided missiles launched from the air, surface and sub-surface, as well as shore-based anti-ship missiles.

- Protection of Russia's maritime economic zone in coordination with other state agencies.
- Projecting power in areas of national interest in support of allies, including defence diplomacy visits.

For now, the 2017 version of the policy remains extant, although it was announced in November 2024 that a new draft Strategy for the Development of the Russian Navy will be produced in 2025.[7] Compared to previous iterations, the 2017 policy sets out clear objectives for the RFN against a much more clearly defined set of threats and dangers facing the Russian Federation. There is a specific emphasis on the threat posed by 'strategic high-precision sea-based non-nuclear weapons systems, as well as sea-based ballistic missile defence systems in the waters adjacent to the territory of the Russian Federation'. Thus, the main objective for Russia is the maintenance of 'naval capabilities that guarantees deterrence of aggression against the Russian Federation from the [sea], and the ability to inflict unacceptable damage on any potential adversary'. These core themes are likely to remain in the 2025 strategy to which will be added lessons learned from the 'special military operation', with particular emphasis on the development of surface and underwater drones. Russian analysts also predict that the Arctic, Baltic and Far East will be key regions to strengthen, especially the Baltic, given all countries around it have joined NATO.

The ability to inflict unacceptable damage on an adversary is something we have witnessed in Ukraine through Russia's numerous attacks on its CNI through the employment of, amongst other capabilities, the *Kalibr* LACM fired from surface and sub-surface units in the Black Sea. The deployment of the *Kalibr* missile system on a range of different platforms, from frigates and corvettes to diesel-electric and nuclear submarines provides the RFN with considerable flexibility, not only to defend its own territory and CNI but also to hold adversaries at risk worldwide. In November 2023, Defence Minister Shoigu underlined this land-attack capability as remaining an important goal for the Russian military.[8] The deployment of the hypersonic cruise missile *Tsirkon* will only enhance this capability to project force. Russia's highly capable submarine force and underwater capabilities that can threaten undersea cables and other CNI, will also remain a persistent challenge to the UK and Western alliance.

Since February 2022, there has been significant commentary about the failings and weaknesses of Russia's conduct of its military campaign in Ukraine. This brush frequently tars all elements of the Russian military machine, with some commentators remarking that there is nothing to fear from Russia's armed forces; that they have been shown to be 'four feet tall rather than ten feet tall', as had been believed before the invasion. This is a dangerous assumption. There have indeed been significant losses and failings, but large elements of the impressively sized Russian armed forces remain intact. The Military Industrial Complex (MIC), still continues to produce weaponry and other military hardware, albeit perhaps of lower quality. The RFN, other than in the Black Sea, has not been fully committed to the campaign and, where it has been, has actually demonstrated resilience, maintained platform availability and had operational success in Russia's 'special military operation' in Ukraine. The RFN has, for example, validated its maritime land attack concept by attacking Ukraine's CNI with *Kalibr* missiles and has also established sea denial in the Sea of Azov. Although there have been Ukrainian maritime successes and Russian naval losses, most notably the *Slava*-class cruiser *Moskva*, and a large quantity of *Kalibr* missiles have been expended, the RFN still remains able to project force within the Black Sea, maintaining a cycle of ships and submarines to support Russia's campaign, as required, in Ukraine. While it has been less able to establish sea denial or control in the western Black Sea, the threat of mines still poses significant risks to commercial shipping exporting Ukraine's grain from Odessa and Russia has yet to escalate to targeting vessels with torpedoes fired from its submarines. While the latter could come with significant diplomatic risks from Russia's allies reliant on Ukrainian grain exports and also threaten the use of the Black Sea for its own exports from any Western alliance response, politically driven statements that Russian naval losses and adjustments to basing its assets in the face of Ukrainian success amount to the 'functional defeat of the Black Sea Fleet' should be treated with caution.[9]

The war is also driving innovation and procurement for both sides and no more so than in the use of sea-based drones with which Ukraine has targeted units of the Black Sea Fleet. In February 2024, the then Minister of Industry and Trade, Denis Manturov, stated that Russia intends to build up both competencies and production volumes across a wide range of drone products from heavy UAVs to First Person View (FPV) drones, and also, in particular, sea-based drones.[10] To that end, Kingisepp Machine-Building Plant (KMZ), St Petersburg, is set to begin serial production in 2024 of the *Oduvanchik* drone which can carry an explosive payload of up to 600 kg, with a range of up to 200 km, enabling potential strikes of Odessa from Crimea. It is also suggested that a more stealthy version of the *Oduvanchik* is being developed, *the Vizir-M* which could be equipped with a missile launcher, machine guns and an electronic warfare system to combat enemy naval drones, as well as air targets.[11] Russia is also developing an underwater attack drone which could be used in the Dnipro river and in particular for mine clearance operations on bridge supports. With a payload of up to

The Russian Navy – future prospects

5 kg, it has an operating range of up to 1 km and was planned to be tested in February 2024.[12]

Despite the war, the RFN has continued delivering against all its stated naval policy objectives from delivery of the strategic nuclear deterrent through to defence diplomacy. In early 2023, the *Admiral Gorshkov* frigate conducted exercises with units from South Africa, Pakistan, China and Iran, with Admiral Yevmenov, then C-in-C of the RFN, visiting the latter in May 2023.[13] The ship also conducted a rare port visit to Jeddah, Saudi Arabia in March 2023. At the end of 2023, the *Udaloy*-class frigates *Admiral Tributs* and *Admiral Panteleyev* participated in exercises with a frigate and a corvette from Myanmar's navy, before conducting a port visit to Bangladesh for the first time in fifty years.[14] In March, 2024, the *Udaloy*-class *Marshal Shaposhnikov* arrived in Qatar to take part in the maritime defence exhibition, DIMDEX-2024,[15] before taking part in joint naval exercises with Iran and China in the Gulf of Oman, with observers from Pakistan, Kazakhstan, Azerbaijan, Oman, India and South Africa.[16] These visits and exercises exemplify the utility of the RFN as an effective tool in supporting Russia's diplomatic, political and economic lines of effort amongst its 'friends' in the Global South for its campaign in Ukraine, while reinforcing the priority it places on the Indo-Pacific region, as stated in its 2022 maritime doctrine

Moscow, therefore, has an ambitious, future oriented strategy in which the sea and the navy play an important role. The growth of the importance of the sea to Russia, including the expansion of its CNI on or near the Russian coast means that the navy has an important defensive role to protect it. This reflects a traditional defensive task, as does the protection of Russia's nuclear deterrent. Equally, though, the navy now has a larger, more forward-leaning, even offensive role in Russian military strategy.[17]

Delivery (ways)

While the logic and objectives of the Maritime Doctrine (2022) and the Naval Policy (2017) are clear, the full implementation remains challenging. The increased funding in the State Armament Programme GPV-2020 begun in 2010, revitalised the shipbuilding industry, with the RFN reportedly allocated 25 per cent of the whole of the budget to modernise and build new ships and submarines. This marked an increased emphasis on rejuvenating a navy which, as we had witnessed first hand in the 1990s, had largely fallen into disrepair at the end of the Cold War, with many platforms obsolete or unserviceable. By the start of GPV-2020, Russia had also developed its thinking on the utility of maritime power, in part derived from the West's interaction with it, and had likely noted the reduction in platforms amongst Western navies, particularly the UK.

This section will provide an overview of the ways in which the RFN intends to meet its ends (as of late 2024) in terms of the platforms it is aiming to procure, their delivery timelines and constraints but will not address the overall organisation of Russian shipbuilding.[18] It was envisaged that between 2011 and 2020 over fifty new surface vessels and twenty-four submarines would be built.[19] Fifteen modernised late Soviet-era major surface warships, such as the *Udaloy*-class and *Sovremenny*-class destroyers and around twenty modernised submarines, would complement these new vessels. However, the shipyards have struggled to deliver platforms on time, and delivery schedules have been further impacted by US and allied sanctions since 2014, following Russia's actions against Ukraine, and these difficulties are likely to continue, despite claims by senior officials that Russia has reached 100 per cent import substitution in warship building.[20]

Submarines

GPV 2020 aimed to recapitalise the underwater force with a combination of new nuclear-powered Project 955 *Borei*-class strategic ballistic missile submarines (SSBNs) and Project 885 *Yasen*-class cruise-missile submarines (SSGNs) on the one hand, and modernised Project 949 *Antei*-class (NATO: *Oscar*) and Project 971 *Shchuka B*-class (NATO: *Akula*) attack submarines on the other. Project 636.3 *Varshavyanka-class* (NATO: *Kilo*) and Project 677 Lada-class diesel-electric powered submarines were to form the backbone of the conventional submarine force. Table 7.1 shows that twenty-five new submarines have been delivered to 2024, including one special purpose submarine, *Belgorod*, able to deploy the nuclear unmanned underwater drone (UUV), *Poseidon*. Together with two out of twenty refurbished Soviet-era platforms, this represents only about 60 per cent of the GPV-2020 target, but over 90 per cent of the deliveries are modern, capable platforms.

The delivery rate of new submarines has largely been driven by the production of conventionally-powered ones, almost 50 per cent through one class alone – Project 636.3 *Varshavyanka*, built by the experienced Admiralty Shipyard, which takes two to three years to produce each one. Production rates of submarines have, in general, been better than that of surface warships. This is because Russia is less reliant on imported goods to build its submarines and is thus less impacted by Western sanctions. Historically too, Admiral Gorshkov's policy that submarines were the prime reason for the navy's importance, and surface combatants and aircraft were constructed to protect the submarine force, still remains relevant today. To that end,

Table 7.1 Submarine deliveries 2011–24

Type	GPV 2020 goal	Delivered 2022	Delivered 2023	Delivered 2024	Under construction	Delivered between 2011 and 2024
SSBN						
Borei-class (Project 955/955A)	8	1	1	1	3	7
Nuclear-powered multirole/special purpose						
Yasen-class (Project 885/885M)	7		1		4	5
Belgorod (Project 09852)	Unknown	1			0	1
Khabarovsk (Project 09851)	Unknown				1	0
Ul'yanovsk (Project 09853)[1]	Unknown				1	0
Diesel-electric submarines						
Lada-class (Project 677)	9–15			1	3	1
Varshavyanka-class (Project 636.3)	3 6 (12)	1	1		1	11
Upgraded legacy units						
Shchuka-B-class (Project 971M)					5	1
Antey-class (Project 949AM)					2	0
Paltus-class (Project 877B)						
Alrosa		1				1

Author David Fields' calculations from Russian media reports.

[1] 'SMI uznali o stroitel'stve tret'yego nositelya "Poseydonov"', *Flotprom.ru*, 15 January 2021, https://flotprom.ru/2021/%D0%A1%D0%B5%D0%B2%D0%BC%D0%B0%D1%88I/ (accessed 16 January 2021).

the submarine force attracts significant funding, delivering Russia's maritime strategic nuclear deterrent through the *Bulava* ICBM, as well as capabilities that can target CNI covertly underwater, and overtly through *Kalibr* LACM, while also holding at risk, globally, NATO's maritime forces. From 2028, it is hoped to reduce nuclear submarine production by a year to about six years, with the introduction of new building methods.[21]

Submarine build programmes

Nuclear-powered

Project 955 and 955AM – *Borei and Borei-AM* – the delivery of *Imperator Aleksander III* in November 2023, brings the total in service to seven with three more in build at the Sevmash yard, due for delivery by 2030. Two additional units are planned to be laid down in 2024.[22]

Project 885 and 855M – *Yasen* and *Yasen-M* – the delivery of *Arkhangelsk* in December 2024 brings the total in service to five. A further four are in build, with the next, *Perm*, due for delivery in 2025, which could be the first submarine carrier of the *Tsirkon* hypersonic cruise missile. Reporting suggests that a further three additional platforms might be built, bringing the overall total to twelve.[23]

Project 09852 *Belgorod* – entering service in July 2022, four years behind schedule, this new platform represents a significant milestone and a step forward to the deployment of the *Poseidon* UUV. Leaked reports in 2021 suggested that it will take until at least 2026 to complete the development of the combined submarine and *Poseidon* system.[24] This does not mean the submarine, which is still assessed to be on trials in the Northern Fleet before its transfer to the Pacific Fleet, will be without a mission. It is also capable of fulfilling a number of intelligence tasks for the Main Directorate of Deep-Sea Research (GUGI), such as targeting undersea cables, using nuclear-powered mini-submarines. A second special purpose submarine *Khabarovsk* has been under construction since 2014 and could enter service in 2024, although there has been limited open-source reporting to confirm this.

Diesel-electric powered

Project 636.3 *Varshavyanka* – production of these quiet, capable submarines (NATO: *Kilo*) has maintained a steady rate of two to three years per unit. Six are in service with the Black Sea Fleet and have been extensively used in the Ukraine conflict to launch LACM against Ukraine's CNI. The fifth of six for the Pacific Fleet was delivered in November 2023 and a further six are to

Table 7.2 Submarines under construction at Sevmash, Severodvinsk

Type	Laid down	Launched (* est.)	Official estimated commission date
Borei-class – SSBN (Project 955A)			
Knyaz' Pozharsky	Dec 2016	Feb 2024	Jun 2025
Dimitry Donskoy	2021	–	2026
Knyaz Potyomkin	2021	–	2027
TBC – contract expected in 2022	2024*		
TBC – contract expected in 2022	2024*		
Yasen-class (Project 885M)			
Perm'	Jul 2016	–	2025
Ul'yanovsk	Jul 2017	–	2026
Voronezh	Jul 2020	–	2027
Vladivostok	Jul 2020	–	2028
Speculation three more to be laid down[1]			
Special Purpose-class (Project 09851)			
Khabarovsk (based on small Project 955 Borei)	Jul 2014	2022	2024

Author David Fields' calculations from Russian media reports.

[1] 'Istochnik: chislo mnogotselevykh APL tipa "Yasen"' dovedut do 12 yedinits', *Flotprom.ru*, 20 November 2023, https://flotprom.ru/2023/%D0%A1%D0%B5%D0%B2%D0%BC%D0%B0%D1%8816/ (accessed 26 February 2024).

be built for either the Baltic Fleet or Northern Fleet, although reporting suggests the latter.[25] They are to be named after cities in what Russia considers to be its new regions in the Donbas.

Project 677 Lada – production has been plagued by chronic delays. It was intended that the *Lada* would represent a step change in capability to the Project 636.3 class, including the use of the ultra-quiet air-independent propulsion (AIP) system. The lead submarine *Sankt Peterburg* was laid down in 1997 and commissioned in 2010, but fell far short of the Navy's requirements and is scheduled to be scrapped due to costs for repairs. Following a number of re-designs, including no AIP, the *Kronshtadt* has now entered service[26] and *Velikye Luki* is expected to follow in 2024,[27] with two more in build. All are expected to be based in the Northern Fleet.

Soviet-era legacy submarines

Deliveries have fallen well short of the intended target of twenty and Table 7.4 shows little progress to improve the situation, with only about nine reportedly in the yards for upgrades. Soon after Russia's invasion of

Table 7.3 Submarines under construction at Admiralty Shipyard, St Petersburg

Type	Laid down (* est.)	Launched (* est.)	Official estimated commission date
Lada-class (Project 677)			
Velikiye Luki	Nov 2006	2022	2024
Vologda	Jun 2022		
Yaroslavl	Jun 2022		
Varshavyanka-class (Project 636.3)			
Yakutsk	2021	2024	2024
Mariupol (First for the Northern Fleet?)	2024*		
Contract for 3 signed at Armiya 2022			

Author David Fields' calculations from Russian media reports.

Table 7.4 Upgraded legacy sub-surface units

Type	In service	Shipyard	Refit began	Official estimated commission date
Delfin-class (Project 667BDRM)				
Bryansk	1988	Zvezdochka	2018	2026
Shchuka-B-class (Project 971)				
Leopard	1992	Zvezdochka	2011	2024
Samara	1995	Zvezdochka	2014	2023?
Tigr	1993	Nepra	2019	2023?
Volk	1991	Zvezdochka	2014	2028
Magadan	1990	Zvezda	2019	2022?
Bratsk	1989	Zvezdochka	2014	Likely to be scrapped
Antei-class (Project 949AM)				
Irkutsk	1988	Zvezda	2001	2025
Chelyabinsk	1990	Zvezda	2014	?
Tomsk	1996	Sevmash	2022	?

Author David Fields' calculations from Russian media reports.

Ukraine,[28] senior officials made statements to indicate certain platforms would be delivered in 2023, including the Project 949AM *Antey*-class (*Oscar*) *Irkutsk*, which has been awaiting its upgrade since 2001, but reports in January 2024 indicate this is likely to slip further to 2025.[29] Two *Shchuka-B*-class SSNs (NATO: *Akula*) have also been delayed, *Leopard* to the end of 2024 and *Volk* to 2028 – an additional five years.[30]

By the early part of the next decade, based on official Russian projected in service dates (ISDs), we can expect to see a continuing strengthening of the sub-surface fleet, including up to three additional *Borei-A* class SSBNs and four additional *Yasen*-class SSGN.

Surface platforms

While a number of surface ships have been laid down, build progress has been slow, especially in warships larger than corvettes. The result has led to a continued reliance on the deployment of forty-year-old, legacy Soviet-era platforms, such as the deployments of Pacific Fleet *Udaloys* in the Indo-Pacific region, with the numbers of new surface platforms well down on what was planned.

Russian media reporting, however, suggests that the surface fleet might have expanded by 2030, built mainly around the *Admiral Gorshkov*-class frigate armed with *Tsirkon* and *Kalibr* missiles, with the following additional units:

- *Admiral Kuznetsov* aircraft carrier from 2024/2025.
- Six more *Admiral Gorshkov*-class frigates, making ten in total.
- Six Soviet-era legacy units *Kirov*-class (Project 1144) *Admiral Nakhimov*, *Udaloy 1*–class (Project 1155) *Admiral Vinogradov* and *Admiral Levchenko*, *Udaloy 2*–class (Project 1155.1) *Admiral Chabanenko* and *Yastreb*-class (Project 11540) *Yaroslav Mudriy*.
- Two Project 23900 Universal Landing Ships (UDK) *Ivan Rogov* and *Mitrofan Moskalenko*.
- Two Project 1171Ms *Vladimir Andreyev* and *Vasily Trushin* (modified *Ivan Gren*-class).
- Four further Project 23130 *Akademik Pashin*-class oilers, making six in total.
- Seven to ten corvettes of various classes.

However, these optimistic delivery forecasts broken down in Tables 7.6 to 7.21 should be treated with some caution. A combination of adverse factors on shipbuilding delivery rates, such as shortages of skilled workers and low levels of unemployment in the wider economy, systemic corruption, and the rising prices of commodities, such as steel, plus sanctions imposed on Russia, make these targets ambitious and challenging to achieve. It is also very probable that resources could be diverted away from the RFN to aid the reconstitution of other capabilities, particularly in the land environment, lost or expended during the Ukraine conflict. The high rate of expenditure of *Kalibr* during the conflict, a key capability with which the RFN projects power, will impact generating sufficient stocks to replenish in-service platforms, as well as equipping the new units due to come into service.[31]

Table 7.5 Surface ship deliveries from 2011–24

Type	GPV 2020 goal	Delivery 2022	Delivery 2023	Laid down 2022	Laid down 2023	Under construction	Delivered from 2011–24
Universal Landing Ships							
Ivan Rogov-class (Project 23900)						2	
Ivan Gren-class (Project 11711M)						2	
Frigates	**12**						**6**
Admiral Gorshkov-class (Project 22350)	6		1			5	3
Admiral Grigorovich-class (Project 11356R)	6					1	3
Corvettes	**22**						**9**
Gremyashchiy-class (Project 20385)	16 (2)			2		4	1
Steregushchiy-class (Project 20380)	12 (20)		2			3	8
Merkuriy-class (Project 20386)						1	
Small missile ships	**8–10**						**15**
Buyan-M-class (Project 21631)	8–10	1	1		1	1	11
Karakurt-class (Project 22800)	0		1			11	5
Patrol ships	**6**						**4**
Vasily Bykov-class (Project 22160)	6	1				2	4
Minesweepers							
Alexsandrit-class (Project 12700)		2	1	1		2	8
Upgraded legacy units							
Admiral Kuznetsov						1	0
Kirov-class (Project 1144)						1	0
Udaloy 1-class (Project 1155)						2	1
Udaloy 2-class (Project 1155.1)						1	0
Sovremenny-class (Project 956)						3	0
Yastreb-class (Project 11540)						1	1

Author David Fields' calculations from Russian media reports.

All this makes it very difficult to forecast with any confidence the number of ships that will likely be delivered to the RFN over the next five to ten years. Furthermore, there exists another constraint on Russia's future global maritime ambitions – at sea logistic support. Replenishment at sea of its warships continues to be a weak area of operations for the RFN, and it uses out-of-date, ageing platforms. This makes the RFN heavily reliant on friendly host-nation support. This capability and the other platforms that offer a truly global maritime capability are worthy of further examination.

Aircraft carriers

An important capability for a 'blue water' navy[32] is the aircraft carrier, a key platform from which to project power. There has always been a Russian aspiration to build new large aircraft carriers to replace the ageing *Admiral Kuznetsov*, which former C-in-C RFN Admiral Yevmenov underlined again in early 2024.[33] But these are expensive platforms and with the current shipbuilding programme and shipyard capacity, their build is unachievable in the medium term.

The present

The only platform that has been capable of delivering (limited) air power ashore is the *Admiral Kuznetsov*. However, under repair and modernisation since 2018, its return to service has been plagued by mishaps most notably the loss of the PD-50 floating dock and a subsequent large-scale fire and damage caused by a falling crane. Sanctions and poor engineering standards have also hindered its return to service. Repeated official statements suggest that *Admiral Kuzentsov* will return to service in 2024/2025. However, there will be significant skill fade in its aircrew being able to operate from the deck, further complicated by the loss of a carrier-based training facility at Saki in Crimea, following the Ukrainian attack in August 2022. It is unlikely that the ship will reach Full Operational Capability (FOC) until at least 2025/2026.

The future

Three possible designs have appeared for a future aircraft carrier, each one becoming successively smaller.[34] They include Project 23000 *Shtorm*, Project 11430E *Lamantin* and the *Varan*. Of the three variants, *Varan* at thirty thousand tons emerges as the most likely platform that could be developed further, although not for at least ten years or more. Its design has been described as quite radical and not just an easy, lazy fallback on old Soviet designed aircraft carriers like the larger *Shtorm* and *Lamatin*. It is also of a size that would not require the wholesale renovation of Russian shipyards.[35] However, significant barriers remain to realising such a project, not least the cost, but also the increased difficulty of obtaining basic construction supplies like steel, the cost of which has been rising and could, according to the then Deputy PM Borisov, increase costs of shipbuilding by 25 per cent.[36] Other factors include the impact of western sanctions on specialised equipment for such a modern ship and, given the demographic pressures in Russia, enough manpower to operate them.

Ultimately, ambitious plans will come down to both money and requirement. In 2019, Deputy Prime Minister Yuri Borisov at the International Maritime Defense Show (IMDS), St Petersburg, explained that the current armament programme did not contain financing for 'such warships' (i.e., aircraft carriers) but 'this does not mean a ban on their development'.[37] Ahead of the IMDS in 2021, a member of the board of the Military-Industrial Commission, Vladimir Pospelov went further.[38] He suggested a feasibility study was ongoing, that Russia would require three aircraft carriers and that the first would take ten years to build, once a decision had been taken. He also seemed to suggest that a second platform would not be built at the same time but would take another ten years after the first. The cost would be at least five hundred billion rubles per platform ($5.5 billion at March 2024 exchange rates), although likely to rise, with experts suggesting that there should be a separate funding line in the state armament programme so as not impact on other shipbuilding projects. Pospelov also stated that the Zvezda yard in the Far East was the most viable option to build the platforms or Sevmash but the latter is already fully loaded with submarine orders.

Both Borisov and Pospelov's comments highlight the ongoing debates in the RFN and amongst Russian defence analysts about the requirement for aircraft carriers, given the rapid development of naval strike weapons such as *Kalibr* on smaller, cheaper platforms. Prior to Russia's invasion of Ukraine in February 2022, there was certainly no shortage of articles[39] debating whether there was a requirement for aircraft carriers, citing the costs, the impact on the submarine building programme and distorting the achievement of a balanced fleet, as reasons for not building them.[40]

Amphibious capability

The Ukraine conflict has demonstrated the limitations of an ageing Soviet-era amphibious fleet. The backbone of the current fleet are Project 775 (NATO:

Ropucha) and *Tapir*-class (NATO: *Alligator*) landing ships.[41] Their average age is forty years old, none are helicopter-capable, all were built for assaults through bow doors and a ramp on to gentle sloping, undefended beaches. However, two new large landing ships *Ivan Gren* and *Piotr Morgunov* are now in service, with the former supporting the Northern Fleet, deploying troops and equipment along the NSR, and the latter operating in the Black Sea. Modified, larger versions of these ships, *Vladimir Andreyev* and *Vasily Trushin*, laid down in April 2019, are expected to be in service by 2026, and a further two might be laid down in 2025/2026. All these large landing ships are designed, like the *Ropucha*, to beach in order to offload their equipment which makes them vulnerable in any contested battlespace.

Two Project 23900 Universal Landing Ships (UDK) *Ivan Rogov* and *Mitrofan Moskalenko* were laid down in July 2020. The vessels have been designed to replace the controversial procurement of the *Mistral*-class helicopter carriers from France, a deal which was cancelled in 2015 following Russia's annexation of Crimea. There are several barriers to their completion which are much the same as those facing any future aircraft carrier project and the in-service dates are already slipping to 2028 and 2029 respectively. Evidence suggests that since the laydowns, adjustments to the original design specification have also been considered, with the size of the vessels increasing from twenty five thousand tons to thirty thousand tons[42] and there was an indication that a modern propulsion system for the ships was still being discussed in 2020.[43] Supply of engines and other high-tech equipment has been a key weakness for Russian shipbuilding because of the sanctions imposed by the West. It was suggested that the 'moving design targets' were as a result of the relatively inexperienced Zelenodolsk Design Bureau (ZPKB) taking the lead,[44] rather than the more experienced Nevskoye Design Bureau. Despite the positive stories of what the ships might be equipped with, such as drones and a command system enabling C2 of task group operations, Russian analysts still question the efficacy of building such ships and whether or not a 'true' self-sustaining amphibious capability can ever be realised. In 2021, the defence commentator, Alexander Timokhin,[45] noted the project is 'senseless' raising the issues of money, a lack

Table 7.6 Amphibious vessels under construction at Yantar, Kaliningrad

Type	Laid down	Launched (* est.)	Official estimated commission date
***Ivan Gren*-class (Project 11711/M)**			
Vladimir Andreyev	Apr 2019	2024*	2026
Vasily Trushin	Apr 2019	–	2026
Two more may be laid down	2025*		

Author David Fields' calculations from Russian media reports.

Table 7.7 Universal Landing ships under construction at Zaliv, Crimea

Type	Laid down	Launched (* est.)	Official estimated commission date
UDK-class (Project 23900)			
Ivan Rogov	Jul 2020	–	2028
Mitrofan Moskalenko	Jul 2020	–	2029

Author David Fields' calculations from Russian media reports.

of aircraft and landing craft capability, a lack of a powerful enough propulsion system, and the lack of a robust logistic support chain both for the landing forces and the ships themselves at sea. His conclusion, however, was that 'failure is now unacceptable for political reasons but remains very likely'.

Frigates

For all the discussion about procuring large platforms for the RFN, both former Defence Minister Shoigu and Admiral Igor Kasatonov, made statements on 17 April 2017, ahead of the publication of the 2017 naval policy, which clearly indicated a more pragmatic approach to the shape and size of the future navy. Shoigu said that frigate class ships and not destroyers, cruisers or aircraft carriers would form the basis of the Russian Navy.[46] He went on to say 'in the near future, these multi-purpose frigates [i.e. the Project 22350 *Admiral Gorshkov*-class frigate] which are equipped with long-range precision-guided weapons, must become the Navy's main surface combatants'. Kasatonov, the key architect of the 2017 policy, went on to explain that naval sea battles and engagements are no longer envisaged but rather 'the conduct of strikes against coastal targets using cruise missiles is becoming the primary mission [of the navy]'.[47]

The RFN envisages three batches of Project 22350 frigates based on the number of vertical launch (VLS) cells fitted, which are capable of deploying a mix of *Kalibr* LACM, and *Tsirkon* and *Oniks* anti-ship missiles (although these have also been used to attack land targets in Syria and Ukraine). As of December 2023, only the first three platforms are in service with others at various stages of build or yet to be laid down:

- Batch 1 – sixteen VLS cells – Hulls one to four (*Admirals Gorshkov, Kasatonov, Golovko, Isakov*).
- Batch 2 – thirty-two VLS cells – Hulls five to ten5 to 10 (*Admirals Amel'ko, Chichagov, Yumashev, Spiridonov, Gromov, Vysotsky*).
- Batch 3 Project 22350M *Super-Gorshkov* – 48 VLS cells – Hulls nine to twelve (all TBC).

It has been suggested that the first Project 22350M *Super-Gorshkov* might be laid down in 2024 at Severnaya Verf, where the much delayed new construction hall is being built.[48] The hall was due for completion first in 2019, then in 2021 and then in 2024, following the appointment of a new (third) contractor. However, problems persist.[49] The new contractor, RusGuard, was sacked in September 2023. The hall is only 28 per cent finished, costs are spiralling and there is no clear plan on how and when it will be completed. The project had relied on imported equipment, including air conditioning, power supply, ventilation and electrical supply systems, that are no longer available due to sanctions. Completion is critical for the modernisation of the surface combatant fleet. Due to the limited slipway capacity at Severnaya Verf' and the issues with the construction hall, there is an indication that a contract for building some *Admiral Gorshkov*-class frigates will be awarded to the Amur shipyard in the Far East, where two slipways could be refurbished ready to begin building the frigates in 2024.[50] Amur currently builds corvette size vessels, so this would need additional expertise in the work force and more efficient processes than hitherto shown in their corvette production, which is regularly delayed.

Optimistically, reports indicate that up to twelve *Super-Gorshkov* will be built by the middle of the next decade. However, the picture is far from clear. It was claimed in 2019 that funding for eleven of these twelve was allocated to the RFN in GPV-2027, but other reports have suggested only four. This debate over numbers preceded Russia's invasion of Ukraine, so it remains to be seen what funding may be available to progress this programme and at what scale, if there is to be a diversion of funds to other areas of the RFN or defence more widely.

The other large surface platform that has been discussed in recent years is the Project 23560 *Lider*-class nuclear powered destroyer. Designed by the Severnoye Design Bureau and the Krylov State Scientific Center, the ships are expected to displace up to nineteen thousand tons and carry a combination of at least two hundred missiles of different variants. Models of the ship have been displayed at several recent arms exhibitions. Despite rumours that the project had been cancelled, the head of OSK said in 2022 that the project was still moving forward but emphasised that the Russian Ministry of Defence will only choose one large warship project for construction, and that the Project 22350M *Super-Gorshkov* frigate appears to be the likely option.[51] It seems highly likely that plans for the *Lider*-class destroyer will be shelved.

Table 7.8 Frigates under construction at Severnaya Verf', St Petersburg

Type	Laid down	Launched (* est.)	Official estimated commission date
Admiral Gorshkov-class (Project 22350)			
Admiral Isakov	Nov 2013	Sep 2024	2024
Batch 2 (32 VLS)			
Admiral Amel'ko	Apr 2019	–	2026
Admiral Chichagov	Apr 2019	–	2026
Admiral Yumashev	Jul 2020	–	2027
Admiral Spiridonov	Jul 2020	–	2027
Admiral Gromov	2022*		2029
Admiral Vysotsky	2022*		2029
Super-Gorshkov-class (Project 22350M)	2023*		
Admiral Grigorovich-class – in Yantar shipyard			
Admiral Kornilov		Nov 2017	2026 (likely to be sold)

Author David Fields' calculations from Russian media reports.

Soviet-era legacy units

An over-reliance on the repair and modernisation of legacy Soviet units to plug the gaps while new builds were ongoing has not been very successful. It remains painfully slow due to a lack of material and human resource, as well as yard availability, which focus on the production of easier and more profitable-to-build civilian ships. It has been argued by many Russian commentators that the vast effort and funds required to refurbish, for example, the *Kirov*-class cruiser *Admiral Nakhimov*, would be better spent on delivering more modern, capable platforms fit for the twenty-first century. They might have a point. In August 2023, a source indicated that the cost of the refurbishment had so far reached a staggering 200 billion rubles ($2.2 billion at March 2024 exchange rates) and that costs were still rising.[52] However, as a political symbol of Russia's naval power, the appearance of *Admiral Nakhimov* back on the world's oceans might prove irresistible and therefore the platform, which first came into service in 1988, is scheduled to be completed in 2026 – twenty-seven years after being laid up to start the refit in 1999.[53] Upgrades to other Soviet-era legacy units, which are still relied upon to deploy globally, continue to proceed very slowly, but it would be no surprise if, as a result of financial constraints from the Ukraine conflict, some of these plans are also reviewed.

Table 7.9 Upgraded legacy surface units

Type	In service	Shipyard	Refit began	Official estimated commission date
Admiral Kuznetsov	1991	Murmansk	2017	2024
Kirov-class (Project 1144)				
Admiral Nakhimov	1988	Sevmash	1999	2026
Udaloy 1-class (Project 1155)				
Admiral Vinogradov	1988	Dalzavod	2021	2024/25
Admiral Levchenko	1988	Nerpa	2014	2022?
Udaloy 2-class (Project 1155.1)				
Admiral Chabanenko	1999	Murmansk	2013	2025
Yastreb-class (Project 11540)				
Neustrashimy – in service April 2023	1993	Yantar	2014	2023
Yaroslav Mudriy	2009	Yantar	2021	2022?
Sovremenny-class (Project 956)				
Burny	1988	Dalzavod	2005	TBC
Nastoychivy	1992	Baltiisyk	2019	TBC
Ushakov – in service August 2021	1993	Zvezdochka	2018	2021

Author David Fields' calculations from Russian media reports.

Corvettes

Rather than frigates and destroyers, it has been the corvettes that have provided the backbone of Russia's surface capability in recent years. The current corvette fleet is made up of several classes: Project 22160 *Vasily Bykov*, Project 21631 *Buyan-M*, Project 22800 *Karakurt*, Project 20380 *Steregushchiy*, Project 20385 *Gremyashchiy*, some of which (e.g. *Vasily Bykov* and *Buyan-M*) have been used extensively as launch platforms for *Kalibr* missile attacks against Ukraine. The focus on producing these class of vessels is likely to continue, given they are able to operate both in defence of Russia and in offence holding NATO countries and forces at risk through the use of *Kalibr*.

However, the fate of the Project 20386 class corvette seems to have been sealed. Based on the *Steregushchy* and *Gremyashchiy* classes, this new class was to be larger and incorporate a more stealthy design. There were plans to build a series of at least ten such corvettes. The first, *Derzky*, laid down in 2016 will be the only platform to be built, if indeed it is completed. Sources indicated in July 2023, that due to high costs and 'new technologies of the

Table 7.10 Corvettes under construction at Severnaya Verf', St Petersburg

Type	Laid down	Launched (* est.)	Official estimated commission date
Steregushchiy-class (Project 20380)			
Strogiy	Feb 2015	-	2023??
TBD			
TBD			
TBD			
TBD			
TBD			
TBD			
Gremyashchiy-class (Project 20385)			
Provorny	Jul 2013	Jun 2024	2025 after a major fire in Dec 2021.
Merkuriy-class (Project 20386)			
Merkuriy	Oct 2016	-	2023/4

Author David Fields' calculations from Russian media reports.

Table 7.11 Corvettes under construction at Zelenodol'sk, nr Kazan

Type	Laid down	Launched (* est.)	Official estimated commission date
Karakurt-class (Project 22800)			
Taifun	Sep 2019	May 2024	2022?
Vasily Bykov-class (Project 22160)			
Viktor Veliky	Nov 2016	May 2024	2022?
Nikolai Sepyagin	Jan 2018	2022*	2022?
Buyan M-class (Project 21631)			
Stavropol	Jul 2018	2024	2024?

Author David Fields' calculations from Russian media reports.

corvettes' the programme was cancelled.[54] If true, this would represent a pragmatic decision when in the past a key weakness of the Russian naval shipbuilding industry has been the generation of too many different classes of vessels, stretching both limited resources and the capacity to build them.

Minesweepers

The Project 12700 *Alexsandrit*-class minesweepers have represented a more successful build programme for the RFN with eight entering service since

2016 and a further four in build at the Srednye-Nevsky yard. This delivery rate has been due to new digital production technologies and modernisation of the yard's facilities. The ships have a monolithic fibreglass hull and carry tele-guided and autonomous unmanned underwater vehicles (UUV) and unmanned surface vehicles (USV) to disable or destroy mines at range. On the face of it the *Alexsandrit* minesweeper might not be an eye-catching unit, but they highlight the layered defensive approach adopted by the RFN, inherited from the Soviet Naval tactical handbook, which is designed to deter attack from a 'blue water' navy, through forward deployed guided missiles ships and submarines, land-based aircraft with anti-ship missiles, offensive/defensive mining, fast attack craft and coastal shore batteries, supported by space, radar and EW capabilities. To underline this defensive posture three of the eight *Alexsandrit* minesweepers have been based at the strategic submarine base in Kamchatka to replace the ageing Soviet Project 266–M *Natya* class minesweepers.[55] The total number in the class is planned to reach around thirty to forty by 2050.

Table 7.12 Corvettes laid down and launched at Morye, Crimea (fitted out at Pella)

Type	Laid down	Launched (* est.)	Official estimated commission date
Karakurt-class (Project 22800)			
Kozelsk (ex-Shtorm)	May 2016	Oct 2019	2021?
Okhotsk	Mar 2017	Oct 2019	2021?
Vikhr	Dec 2017	Nov 2019	2021?

Author David Fields' calculations from Russian media reports.

Table 7.13 Corvettes under construction at Pella, St Petersburg

Type	Laid down	Launched (* est.)	Official estimated commission date
Karakurt-class (Project 22800)			
Burya	Dec 2016	Oct 2018	2021?

Table 7.14 Corvettes under construction at Zaliv, Crimea

Type	Laid down	Launched (* est.)	Official estimated commission date
Karakurt-class (Project 22800)			
Askold	Nov 2016	Sept 2021	Damaged by Ukranian missile strike 4 Nov 23 – likely beyond repair

Author David Fields' calculations from Russian media reports.

Table 7.15 Corvettes under construction at Amur, Far East

Type	Laid down	Launched (* est.)	Official estimated commission date
Steregushchiy-class (Project 20380)			
Grozny	2021		2024
Braviy	2021		
Karakurt-class (Project 22800)			
Rzhev	Jul 2019	Sept 2023	2026
Udomlya	Jul 2019	Sept 2023	2026
Ussuriysk	Dec 2019	—	2027
Pavlovsk	Jul 2020	—	2027
Gremyashchiy-class (Project 20385)			
Buyniy	Aug 2021		2028
Razumniy	Jun 2022		
Bystriy	Jul 2022		
Retivy	Jun 2023		

Author David Fields' calculations from Russian media reports.

Table 7.16 Minesweepers under construction at Srednye Nevsky, St Petersburg

Type	Laid down	Launched (* est.)	Official estimated commission date
Alexsandrit-class (Project 12700)			
Afanasy Ivannikov	Sept 2021	Aug 2024	
Polyarny	Jun 2022		
Dmitry Lysov	Jun 2023		
Semyon Agafonov	Jan 2024		
Viktor Korner	Jul 2024		
Contract for further ten signed at Armiya – 2021			

Author David Fields' calculations from Russian media reports.

Propulsion plants

A key constraint in the delivery of surface platforms has been the manufacture and supply of engines, in particular, for the *Admiral Gorshkov*-class frigates which were manufactured in Ukraine prior to 2014. The imposition of sanctions necessitated an import substitution programme for manufacturing a propulsion plant to maintain delivery of these ships. The *Admiral Golovko*, launched in May 2020 without a propulsion system, finally entered service on 25 December 2023.[56] It is equipped with a new domestically produced M55R propulsion plant, which includes the M90FR gas turbine (produced by Saturn), the RO55 gearbox (produced by Zvezda) and the 10D49 diesel engine (produced by Kolomensky Zavod). This represents a real achievement in domestic production, which could begin to increase the delivery rate of these important vessels, but problems persist. Zvezda has reportedly delayed supply of the gearbox for the the sixth frigate *Admiral Chichagov* which could impact its delivery, scheduled for 2026.[57] Furthermore, the 10D49 diesel engine is used by many warships under construction and it has been suggested that the factory will struggle to keep producing the engines in the required numbers once those that have already been built have been fitted.[58] Indeed, in June 2022, Russia's struggles with import substitution for engine production were illustrated by reports suggesting that the order for a second batch of six Project 22160 *Vasily Bykov*-class ships had been cancelled.[59] It was said this was 'due to the discrepancy between the tactical and technical characteristics of the combat conditions of use' of the diesel engines supplied by Kolomensky Zavod. Or in other words, domestically produced engines are not good enough. Another diesel engine manufacturer, Zvezda, is also struggling to meet demand for the *Karakurt*-class corvette. Only four vessels are currently in service. Twelve vessels are in various stages of construction, with many waiting for their engines to be delivered.

Logistic support ships

A logistics fleet of ships to support global maritime operations remains an unfulfilled ambition and the RFN remains poor at conducting underway replenishment of its warships. This is unlikely to change in at least the next five to ten years. The RFN has for forty-five to sixty years been relying on ageing ocean going oilers and other support ships such as the *Olekma* and *Uda* class oilers. Although these vessels do deploy in support of naval operations in areas such as the North Atlantic, Gulf of Aden and the Mediterranean, it tends to be in support of small groups of one to two frigates/corvettes and always with a tug in support in case of breakdowns of any of the units.[60] These are not logistic support vessels that can sustain a true global strategic reach capability of, for example, a carrier strike group or amphibious task group but rather a somewhat ramshackle collection of venerable units in a poor engineering condition that, so long as there is a 'friendly' port in the region, can support certain time/space limited maritime operations.

The class and size of logistic vessels under construction or coming into service still do not appear to reflect the requirement for long-term, self-sustaining global maritime operations. The Project 23130 *Akademik Pashin* tanker is the largest that could support task group operations with fuel but it only has a limited dry and food stores capability. According to Russian open sources the fleet is expected to consist of six vessels by 2027 but only the lead ship is in service. Three more have been laid down since 2021 but build progress is glacially slow. This has been partly due to Western sanctions, since the main power plant (Wärtsilä diesel engines) and a significant part of the auxiliary mechanisms of this vessel were imported, but going forward import substitution is supposed to accelerate production. Other new logistics ships coming in to service appear to have a freighting role in harbours and roadsteads plus a multiplicity of other non-replenishment taskings, operate at low speed, have no helicopter hangar and no gantries for underway refuelling or transfer of stores.

Table 7.17 Logistic support ships under construction

Type	Laid down	Launched (* est.)	Official estimated in service date (ISD)	Fleet
Project 23130 (Oiler)				
Akademik Pashin	2014	2016	Jan 2020 (in service)	Northern
Vasily Nikitin	2021	Oct 2023	2023?	Black Sea
Inzhener-Admiral Kotov	2022	Dec 2024	By 2027	TBD
Aleksey Shein	2023		By 2027	TBD
TBD	Ordered		By 2027	TBD
TBD	Ordered		By 2027	TBD
Project 23131 (Oiler)				
TBD	2014			
TBD	2014			
Project 23630 (Oiler)				
Argun	2024			
Project 23120 *Elbrus*-class (Support)				
Captain Shevchenko	2014	Cancelled	Cancelled	Cancelled
Project 03182 (Support)				
Vasily Nikitin	2017	TBD	TBD	Black Sea
Mikhail Barskov	2015	2019	2021*	Pacific
Boris Averkin	2018	2021*	TBD	Pacific
Project 20360M (Ammunition)				
Gennady Dmitriev	2017	Jun 2021	Delayed from 2019	Black Sea
Vladimir Pyalov	2018	TBD	Delayed from 2020	Baltic

Author David Fields' calculations from Russian media reports.

As with the Soviet Navy, this lack of a robust sea-based logistic support capability and a reliance on using a network of 'friendly' ports to enable global operations is a potential Achilles' heel in the development of a modern RFN. Whereas the Soviet Navy could call on a massive world-deployed Soviet-flagged merchant fleet whose ships could be ordered to replenish warships whenever necessary, but using the simplest methods, that is not the case now. This Soviet-era culture has perhaps led to lack of development of a strategic maritime reach capability by Russia compared to Western navies. The RFN, therefore, will continue to conduct at sea replenishment in only benign weather conditions and to rely on agreements with other nations to utilise their ports for logistic support to deployed units. On 6 March 2023,[61] however, an announcement that a new line of logistic support vessels were to be built, indicated there is at least a recognition that something needs to be done to fill the capability gap. The main requirement for the new vessels is that they must be built using only Russian supplied components. No timelines were given, nor designs shown at the time but could be related to the laying down in April 2024 of *Argun* the lead unit of Project 23630 oilers.[62] However, the ships are small at 86 m and relatively slow (top speed 12 kts), and the same building constraints as outlined above are likely to apply to such a project. Thus the RFN will continue to struggle to conduct long-term self-sustaining global deployments and not being part of an alliance has fewer allies to backfill capability gaps, unlike the RN. The UK aircraft carrier deployment to the Indo-Pacific region in 2025 is reported to require logistic support from Norway, following the RN's only solid support stores platform RFA *Fort Victoria*, being placed into 'extended readiness' and with replacement solid support ships not due until at least 2031.[63]

Icebreakers and ice-class patrol ships

The strategic importance to Russia of the High North and control over the use of the NSR is well documented. The continuing militarisation and resource exploitation of the High North requires a large fleet of nuclear and conventionally powered icebreakers to enable the year-round supply of materiel to new military bases, and the export of resources from the region to support Russia's economy. Nuclear powered icebreakers owned by Rosatomflot (a subsidiary of Rosatom) are a key enabler in exploiting the transit potential of the NSR, and the icebreakers and armed ice-class patrol ships of the RFN are also designed to support convoy operations along the NSR, supply military bases and conduct search and rescue operations as necessary.

However, a Presidential Decree in February 2023 suggests that Russia has lowered its ambitions for nuclear powered icebreakers, with plans to build three *Lider*-class vessels in the Far East reduced to just the lead vessel, *Rossiya*.[64] These vessels, twice as powerful as the Project 22220 *Arktika*-class, were designed to break ice up to 4 m thick, thus giving Russia year-round access along the NSR. The announcement coincided with EU imposed sanctions against Russia's state nuclear icebreaker operator, Rosatom. The *Lider* is also very complicated to build and comes at a high price. Russia allocated 127 billion rubles ($1.4 billion at March 2024 exchange rates) for the construction of the lead ship, *Rossiya*, alone. However, new contracts were signed for the *Arktika* class icebreaker in 2023, bringing the total to seven in the class. Hull six, *Leningrad*, was laid down in January 2024, attended by President Putin and coinciding with the eightieth anniversary of the liberation of Leningrad from the German blockade in 1944.[65] The seventh, *Primorye*, is due to be laid down in October 2025. *Arktika*, *Sibir* and *Ural* are in service – *Yakutiya* and *Chukhotka* are due to be delivered in 2024 and 2026, respectively.

It is not only sanctions that might have affected the *Lider*-class programme and completion of the lead vessel, *Rossiya*. According to Kommersant's sources,[66] the minutes of a meeting with the Deputy Head of the Ministry of Industry and Trade Viktor Yevtukhov, dated 13 March 2023, showed there were delays in the production of large hull components, and the cost and timing of work on the production of other individual parts of the icebreaker's nuclear power plant were leading to 40 to 60 per cent growth costs on an initial projections. One other reason for the slow down and cost growth may be that Russia is alleged to have bombed the EnergoMashSpetsStal plant in Kramatorsk, Donetsk, in May 2022, which was supplying the large hull components for the *Rossiya*.[67] EnergoMashSpetsStal is part of the Atomenergomash company of the Russian state-owned company Rosatom.

In October 2021, the Deputy Chief of Staff of Logistics Support of the Russian armed forces, Andrey Yefimov, outlined the programme to deliver five ice capable ships for the RFN, in order 'to deliver goods to polar regions'.[68] The five vessels are made up of one Project 21180 *Ilya Muromets* (in service) and two Project 21180M *Yevpatiy Kolovrat* icebreakers and two Project 23550 *Ivan Papanin* ice-class patrol ships (under construction).

Project 21180 Ilya Muromets *and Project 21180M* Yevpatiy Kolovrat

The diesel-electric powered icebreaker *Ilya Muromets* was accepted into service in 2017. It was the first purpose-built icebreaker for the Russian Navy (RFN) for forty-five years. With a displacement of six thousand tons and the

Table 7.18 Icebreakers under construction at Baltzavod, St Petersburg

Type	Laid down	Launched (* est.)	Official estimated commission date
Arktika-class nuclear-powered icebreakers (Project 22200)			
Yakutiya	May 2020	Nov 2022	2024
Chukotka	Dec 2020	Dec 2024	2026
Leningrad	Jan 2024		2028
Stalingrad Contract signed Feb 2023	Oct 2025*		2030
Project 227700 (Nuclear service vessels)			
			2029
TBC Contract signed Dec 2022 (3 by 2035)			
TBC			
TBC			

Author David Fields' calculations from Russian media reports.

Table 7.19 Icebreakers under construction at Zvezda, Far East

Type	Laid down	Launched (* est.)	Official estimated commission date
Lider-class (Project 10510)			
Rossiya –	Jul 20		2030
TBD – cancelled			
TBD – cancelled			

Author David Fields' calculations from Russian media reports.

ability to penetrate ice 1.5 m thick, its role is to escort Russian warships and provide materiel support to Russian military bases in the region. However, due to high costs the defence ministry cancelled the order for a further three vessels and instead developed the Project 21180M *Yevpatiy Kolovrat* which is a smaller, cheaper version (six billion rubles – $65.5 million at March 2024 exchange rates).[69] The ship was launched at the Almaz shipyard in November 2020 and is now in service in the Pacific Fleet.[70] At four thousand tons versus six thousand tons, it has more limited functionality and can only break through ice of 1 m. A second Project 21180M, *Svyatogor*, was laid down on 1 September 2023 and is scheduled to join the Northern Fleet by 2027.[71]

Project 23550 Ivan Papanin

While not designated as icebreakers, Russia is also investing in diesel-electric powered vessels termed ice-class patrol ships for operations in the Arctic and other ice-prone regions of Russia's coastline. For the RFN the *Ivan Papanin* is due to enter service in 2024[72] and the second ship *Nikolai Zubov* was launched in December 2024, with an in service date of 2027. These dates represent a five-year delay due to sanctions. At nine thousand tons the vessels have an endurance of about seventy days with a cruising range of up to ten thousand miles. The thickness of ice it can operate in is 1.5 m. The armament includes an automatic AK-176MA gun mount and it has stern space to house containerised weapons, including *Kalibr* missiles.[73] In addition, a helicopter and UAVs, as well as two *Raptor* high-speed patrol boats can be carried on board.

However, not only is the delivery rate of these two classes of ice capable ships slow but when delivered will be sub-optimal for the RFN's needs. Given the Arctic ice can be as much as 3 m thick they would be limited in their support to warships or military facilities along the NSR in the event of a military conflict in the region.

For navies wishing to exercise Freedom of Navigation (FoN) rights in the High North and the NSR specifically, the challenges will not only be bureaucratic (and political) but also practical. On the bureaucratic hand,[74] the Russian Ministry of Defence in July 2022, reportedly submitted amendments to the Federal Law 'On Inland Sea Waters, the Territorial Sea and the Russian Federation's Owned Zone'. Its purpose is to determine the legal regime for the passage of foreign warships and other government ships operated for non-commercial purposes in the internal sea waters of the Russian Federation. According to the new procedure, these ships and vessels will be

Table 7.20 Ice-class patrol ships under construction at Admiralty Yard, St Petersburg

Type	Laid down	Launched (* est.)	Official estimated commission date
Ice-class patrol (Project 23550)			
Ivan Papanin	Apr 2017	Oct 2019	2024
Nikolay Zubov	Nov 2019	Dec 2024	2027

Author David Fields' calculations from Russian media reports.

Table 7.21 Icebreakers under construction at Almaz Shipyard, St Petersburg

Type	Laid down	Launched (* est.)	Official estimated commission date
Muromets-class Icebreaker (Project 21180M)			
Svyatogor	Aug 2023		2027

Author David Fields' calculations from Russian media reports.

able to enter the internal sea waters of the NSR, which belong to Russia, only after receiving special permission ninety days in advance of the date of passage. The entry of foreign warships and vessels in the waters of the NSR will have to pass strictly along the established route and with compulsory pilotage.

On the practical hand, navigation in the High North and NSR is difficult all year round. Admiral Yevmenov's comments to the UK Naval Attache in November 2013 concerning the dangers of navigation in the region, chiefly from small and large icebergs, and fears for the safety of his ships, coupled with Russia's drive to build ice capable ships underlines the navigational challenges in the region. Director of the NSR Directorate, Vyacheslav Ruksham's comments in July 2021 added further emphasis to the dangers from ice in the region. He noted that over the previous five to seven years, despite weather forecasters' predictions, the volume of ice in the Arctic had not decreased, which means that unhindered year-round navigation remained a challenge.[75] Indeed, the CEO of Atomflot, Mustafa Kashka, went further, stating in September 2021 that despite global warming, there was a large amount of residual ice that particular year which had not thawed and fresh ice had already started to form. This presents significant navigational challenges. According to the forecast of the Institute of the Arctic and Antarctic, the volume of ice in 2030–50 will be approximately the same as it is now.[76] It could be argued that Russian officials would say this but the risks versus benefits of a FoN undertaking would need to be carefully assessed. The optics of a NATO or UK warship seeking Russian assistance, particularly from icebreakers, on the NSR may not be the desired outcome of such an undertaking. The US has recognised that in terms of available icebreakers it is outnumbered in the High North by Russia. In March 2024, General Gregory M. Guillot, the commander of US Northern Command and North American Aerospace Defence Command, warned of limited manoeuvrability in the region due to an icebreaker 'gap', adding that 'the US currently has really only one heavy icebreaker ship for Arctic operations while Russia has approximately 40 available'.[77]

Finance and people (means)

The wider Russian economy has shown remarkable resilience since the invasion of Ukraine in February 2022, driven by exports of both hydro-carbon and non-hydrocarbon commodities. This has led to a post-Soviet record level of defence spending and a shift from a temporary to a permanent programme of militarising society. Predictions that the economy would see a 10 per cent or even 25 per cent drop in GDP after the invasion did not materialise and instead the economy saw only a modest reduction of 2.1% in GDP in 2022.[78] This resilience was driven by booming exports, especially from high oil and gas prices.[79] In October 2023, Russia announced a significant uplift in military spending for 2024 which is set to rise to 10.8 trillion rubles, (about $118 billion at March 2024 exchange rates), which at the purchasing power parity (PPP) rate is close to $300 billion.[80] This represents 6 per cent of GDP or about 30 per cent of all federal spending and supports the 'Everything for the Front policy'.[81] As Alexandra Prokopenko, a former adviser at Russia's central bank, stated 'the war has become existential for the Russian economy because a big part of demand is now spread through the expanded military-industrial sector'.[82] The most dangerous scenario for the Russian economy is the state's heavy involvement in it and the drive towards militarisation of society that threatens the longer-term sustainability of the apparent economic recovery. In the near term, Russia looks set to be able to fund both 'guns and butter' but in the two- to four-year period, priorities are likely to have to be made between the two commodities.

Against this economic backdrop, complex balance of investment decisions will need to be made when Russia comes to re-constituting its armed forces after the Ukraine conflict. These may or may not have an impact on Russia's submarine and shipbuilding programme. However, as well as increasing defence spending, Russia is also adopting measures to develop its 'technological sovereignty'[83] and import substitution programme and it continues to utilise a complex system of sanction avoidance to import vital components through third parties and other illicit means. Shipbuilding, both civilian and military, is one of the priority areas for projects that support the 'technological sovereignty' project.[84] Projects within the priority areas of the economy will receive preferential lending terms. It is estimated that this initiative will provide up to ten trillion rubles (about $110 billion at March 2024 exchange rates) of additional funding to support Russia's 'technological sovereignty'. A shake-up of the management of the state-owned OSK also indicates that stricter financial oversight is being introduced, maybe in light of this new initiative. In August 2023, Putin signed a decree that transferred the state-owned stake in OSK to VTB, with the bank managing 100 per cent of OSK shares for five years. Andrey Puchkov, who previously held the position of First Deputy Chairman of the Management Board of VTB Bank, was appointed as the new General Director of OSK, replacing Alexei Rakhmanov who had been in post since 2014.[85] The CEO of VTB Bank, Andrei Kostin was made Chairman of the Board of Directors of OSK and instigated a six-month audit in September 2023, part of which was completed in May 2024[86] with indications that major work will be undertaken to modernise St Petersburg shipyards. Denis Manturov, then Minister of Industry and Trade, commented that this transfer of OSK to the management of VTB 'will contribute to the long-term stabilisation of the financial condition' of the company. OSK has often been accused of financial profligacy, poor management, slow rates of delivery and outdated methods of operating. But over a year on, the audit is still not complete and, in exasperation, Kostin stated in September 2024 that obtaining a clear picture of what has been going on at OSK, both in the civilian and military sectors, and its financial health is extremely challenging.[87] In May 2024, in a further attempt to get a grip on shipbuilding in Russia, former Secretary of the Security Council Nikolai Patrushev was replaced by former Defence Minister Sergei Shoigu, and handed the role of the Kremlin's aide on shipbuilding. Some analysts 'mocked' this as a demotion. This misses the point. What it actually indicates, taken together with all the other measures being adopted, is the strategic importance of military and civilian shipbuilding to the Russian state and the timely delivery of its ambitious global maritime strategy. A visit by Patrsuhev to a potentially failing or corrupt shipyard is likely to focus minds. Although it is still too early to tell what the impact of this change in management of OSK, Patrushev's appointment and the outcome of the audit might mean for naval shipbuilding, future expensive vanity projects, such as the refit of *Admiral Nakhimov*, might become a thing of the past.

However, for all the money that is 'being thrown' at defence, the human factor remains a key concern in maintaining high rates of output of military equipment. According to a report in January 2023,[88] the Russian Labour Ministry admitted that the MIC lacked at least twenty thousand skilled workers such as locksmiths, turners, machine operators and IT specialists, although some put this figure much higher. The conscription of hundreds of thousands of people into the army and the mass exodus abroad, along with the direct victims of the conflict, has aggravated the manpower resources in the MIC. The same figure was quoted in August 2023 by Deputy General Director of Rostec, Nikolai Volobuev, who added that Rostec intends to expand its number of engineering colleges of which it currently has nine.[89] Other reports suggest that the education system more broadly and university curriculums are being adapted to increase the labour force for the MIC. Other ways of attracting workers into the MIC also include a new law, which provides preferential mortgage rates of 5 per cent.[90]

Despite the challenges, the most likely scenario is for the Russian economy to keep growing and for the militarisation of society to be maintained for at least the next two years. The overall picture is of a Russia that continues to dig in for the long term in its war against Ukraine and its allies. It is a country that is seeking to adapt and re-orientate its economy both towards supporting the current conflict and also operating in the aftermath, leading to what may be a very different Russia to the one we see today.

So what?

It would be easy to draw the conclusion from all this that the RFN will be unable to meet its maritime ambitions as outlined in its strategic planning documents, based on unpredictable future economic shocks, delays in manufacturing, labour and skills shortages and other constraints, such as at sea logistic support. While official documents do point towards a desire to become a global sea power, their emphasis remains weighted towards the protection of geo-economic interests closer to Russia and the defence of Russia itself.[91] To deliver these missions the RFN is well equipped, through on the one hand the modernisation of its strategic nuclear deterrent and production of other highly capable sub-surface assets, which amongst other tasks are able to hold nations' CNI at risk, to corvette-sized vessels able to conduct 'sea on shore' attacks with *Kalibr*. It is in many ways a force that is already able to execute a broader range of missions than it could in the past without building large ocean-going vessels. That is not to say that Russia is not pursuing a construction programme of larger vessels, which it clearly is, but the tempo of delivery is not critical to achieving its current maritime ambitions and it is able even now to project a degree of force through a range of surface and sub-surface assets.

Within the context of the Russo–Ukrainian war, the path that Russia takes to reconstitute its armed forces, and given the change in management of OSK, it is probably reasonable to assume that the RFN in the medium term will aim to:

- Re-generate stocks of *Kalibr* LACM.
- Finish work already started on both new and modernised vessels.
- Accept a more modest rate of production for the *Admiral Gorshkov* frigates.
- Maintain the steady drumbeat of submarine production.
- Produce larger quantities of smaller vessels.
- Postpone the construction of any genuinely new classes of large vessels, such as aircraft carriers and expensive upgrades of Soviet-era vessels.

While the RFN, for sure, faces a number of ongoing problems and debates about its character, what vessels it needs and how it will build them, the horizon will remain global and focused on the imposition of costs on an adversary. To achieve this, it maintains an ambitious warship and nuclear and conventional submarine build programme that can still meet its overall objectives outlined in its 2017 naval policy. It will thus pose a persistent challenge to the UK and its allies and worthy adversaries or even colleagues to many future generations of naval personnel.

Notes

1 Five Power Defence Arrangements (FPDA) – a series of multilateral agreements between Australia, Malaysia, New Zealand, Singapore and the United Kingdom.
2 'First Sea Lord's Keynote Address to his Annual Sea Power Conference in London', *Royalnavy.mod.uk*, 17 May 2023, www.royalnavy.mod.uk/news-and-latest-activity/news/2023/may/17/20230517–first-sea-lords-key-note-speech (accessed 22 May 2023).
3 'Morskaya doktrina Rossiiskoi Federatsii', *Publication.pravo.gov.ru*, 31 July 2022, http://publication.pravo.gov.ru/Document/View/0001202207310001?index=1&rangeSize=1 (accessed 5 September 2022).
4 'Ukaz Prezidenta Rossiyskoy Federatsii ot 20.07.2017 № 327 'Ob utverzhdenii Osnov gosudarstvennoy politiki Rossiyskoy Federatsii v oblasti voyenno-morskoy deyatelnosti na period do 2030 goda', *Publication.pravo.gov.ru*, 20 July 2017, http://publication.pravo.gov.ru/Document/View/0001201707200015?index=0&r (accessed 4 March 2018).
5 K. Bogdanov and I. Kramnik, 'The Russian Navy in the 21st Century: The Legacy and the New Path', *CNA*, 1 October 2018, https://www.cna.org/reports/2018/10/IOP-2018-U-018268-Final.pdf, p. 21 (accessed 1 April 2019).
6 Russia's bastions became an important element of the USSR's maritime strategy to protect its ballistic missile submarines during the Cold War in the Northern and Pacific Fleets. They remain important today.
7 M. Solopov, J. Leonova, and R. Kretsul, '"Tak sderzhat": novuyu Strategiyu razvitiya VMF podgotovyat v 2025 godu', *Izvestiia*, 14 November 2024, https://iz.ru/1790536/maksim-solopov-ulia-leonova-roman-krecul/tak-sder-zat-novuu-strategiu-razvitia-vmf-podgotovat-v-2025-godu (accessed 16 November 2024).
8 'Shoigu Sees Maintaining Nuclear Forces in Permanent Readiness as an Important Goal', *TASS*, 21 November 2023, https://tass.com/defense/1709497 (accessed 22 November 2023).
9 A. Gregory, 'Russia Facing "Functional Defeat" in the Black Sea – But Kyiv Allies Warn They Are Running out of Ammunition', *Independent*, 5 October

2023, www.independent.co.uk/news/world/europe/russian-black-sea-fleet-ukraine-defeat-b2424347.html (accessed 5 October 2023).
10. 'Supplies of Drones to Russian Military to Grow in 2024 – Deputy Prime Minister', *TASS*, 5 February 2024, https://tass.com/defense/1741863 (accessed 6 February 2024).
11. E. Trishin, 'Rossiya nachinayet proizvodit' morskiye drony. Chto za modeli postavili v seriyu?', *Dzen.ru*, 1 February 2024, https://dzen.ru/a/ZbpiU8Itomb4gcDv (accessed 3 February 2024).
12. 'Istochnik: novyy rossiyskiy podvodnyy dron pristupit k ispytaniyam v fevrale', *Flotprom.ru*, 13 December 2023, https://flotprom.ru/2023/%D0%92%D0%BC%D1%8439/ (accessed 15 December 2023).
13. 'Glavkom VMF Rossii posetil Iran', *Flotprom.ru*, 23 May 2023, https://flot.com/2023/%D0%9C%D0%B5%D0%B6%D0%B4%D1%83%D0%BD%D0%B0%D1%80%D0%BE%D0%B4%D0%BD%D0%BE%D0%B5%D0%A1%D0%BE%D1%82%D1%80%D1%83%D0%B4%D0%BD%D0%B8%D1%87%D0%B5%D1%81%D1%82%D0%B2%D0%BE19/ (accessed 25 May 2023).
14. A. Pasricha, 'Russia Steps Up Presence in Indian Ocean', *VOANews.com*, 30 November 2023, https://www.voanews.com/a/russia-steps-up-presence-in-indian-ocean-/7378276.html (accessed 11 March 2024).
15. 'Russian Warship Arrives in Qatar for Defence Exhibition, Interfax Reports', *Reuters*, 4 March 2024, https://www.reuters.com/world/russian-warship-arrives-qatar-defence-exhibition-interfax-reports-2024-03-04/ (accessed 11 March 2024).
16. 'Minoborony RF soobshchilo o starte voyenno-morskogo ucheniya Rossii, Irana i Kitaya v Omanskom zalive', *Interfax*, 12 March 2024, https://www.militarynews.ru/story.asp?rid=0&nid=613251&lang=RU (accessed 12 March 2024).
17. Discussion and correspondence with Dr Andrew Monaghan, May 2023.
18. For further reading on the organisation of Russian shipbuilding, see A. Monaghan and R. Connolly, *The Sea in Russian Strategy*. Manchester, Manchester University Press, 2023, pp. 146–160.
19. R. Connolly and M. Boulègue, 'Russia's New State Armament Programme Implications for the Russian Armed Forces and Military Capabilities to 2027', Chatham House, May 2018, p. 6.
20. 'Russia Achieves 100–Percent Import Substitution in Warship Construction', *TASS*, 31 January 2024, https://tass.com/defense/1739617 (accessed 2 February 2024).
21. 'Sroki postroyki rossiyskikh atomnykh submarin poobeshchali sokratit' na god', *Flotprom.ru*, 27 February 2023, https://flotprom.ru/2023/%D0%9E%D1%81%D0%BA7/ (accessed 1 March 2023).
22. 'Keels for Two *Borei-AM* Nuclear Subs to Be Laid at Sevmash Shipyard This Year – source', *TASS*, 27 March 2024, https://tass.com/defense/1766441 (accessed 7 June 2024).

23 'Istochnik: chislo mnogotselevykh APL tipa "Yasen" dovedut do 12 yedinit', *Flotprom.ru*, 20 November 2023, https://flotprom.ru/2023/%D0%A1%D0%B5%D0%B2%D0%BC%D0%B0%D1%8816/ (accessed 22 November 2023).
24 A. Ramm and A. Lavrov, '«Poseydon» v lodke: submarinu gotovyat k ispytaniyam yadernykh robotov', *Izvestiia*, 11 February 2021, https://iz.ru/1123160/anton-lavrov-aleksei-ramm/poseidon-v-lodke-submarinu-gotoviat-k-ispytaniiam-iadernykh-robotov (accessed 15 February 2021).
25 'Novym podlodkam proyekta "Varshavyanka" prisvoyat imena gorodov novykh regionov Rossii', *Russkoye Oruzhie*, 25 April 2023, https://rg.ru/2023/04/25/reg-szfo/tass-novym-podlodkam-proekta-varshavianka-prisvoiat-imena-gorodov-novyh-regionov-rossii.html (accessed 25 April 2023).
26 'Kronshtadt submarine joins Russian Navy', *TASS*, 31 January 2024, https://tass.com/defense/1739523 (accessed 31 January 2024).
27 'Velikie Luki Submarine to Join Navy This Year', *TASS*, 31 January 2024, https://tass.com/defense/1739573 (accessed 31 January 2024).
28 'Ministr oborony Rossii provel selektornoye soveshchaniye s rukovodyashchim sostavom Vooruzhennykh Sil', *Ministry of Defence*, Moscow, 29 March 2022, https://function.mil.ru/news_page/country/more.htm?id=12415196@egNews (accessed 30 March 2022).
29 'Russia Reportedly Postpones Return of *Irkutsk* Nuclear Submarine Till 2025', *TASS*, 10 January 2024, https://tass.com/defense/1730413 (accessed 17 January 2024).
30 'Istochnik nazval sroki vozvrashcheniya v stroy mnogotselevoy APL "Volk"', *Flotprom.ru*, 5 March 2024, https://flotprom.ru/2024/%D0%97%D0%B2%D0%B5%D0%B7%D0%B4%D0%BE%D1%87%D0%BA%D0%B06/ (accessed 6 March 2024).
31 Reporting in 2023 suggests that Russia has doubled its monthly output of *Kalibr* to twenty-five but even with this rate of production it will take some years to meet the RFN's current and future demands.
32 Blue Water Navy – a maritime force that can be deployed globally, operate across the full spectrum of maritime activities from defence diplomacy to high-intensity warfare and be a self-sustaining force not relying on host nation support.
33 'Russia Likely to Build New Aircraft Carrier', *TASS*, 10 January 2024, https://tass.com/defense/1730443 (accessed 11 January 2024).
34 '«Varan» protiv «Lamantina»: kakim budet rossiyskiy avianosets novogo pokoleniya', *Voyennoye Obozreyniye*, 1 February 2021, https://topwar.ru/179537-varan-protiv-lamantina-kakim-budet-rossijskij-avianosec-novogo-pokolenija.html (accessed 5 May 2021).
35 P. Goble, 'Moscow's Plans for New Kind of Aircraft Carrier Unlikely to Be Realized', *Jamestown.org*, 11 March 2021, https://jamestown.org/program/moscows-plans-for-new-kind-of-aircraft-carrier-unlikely-to-be-realized/ (accessed 5 May 2021).

36. 'Proizvodstvo sudov v RF podorozhalo na 25% na fone rosta tsen na metally – Borisov', *Interfax*, 16 June 2021, www.militarynews.ru/story.asp?rid=1&nid=551682&lang=RU (accessed 16 June 2021).
37. 'NPKB Unveils Alternative Carrier Design for Russian Navy', *AINOnline.com*, 25 July 2019, www.ainonline.com/aviation-news/defense/2019–07–25/npkb-unveils-alternative-carrier-design-russian-navy (accessed 15 June 2021).
38. 'Vladimir Pospelov: novyy avianosets mozhet stoit' ot 500 milliardov rubley', *RIA Novosti*, 18 May 2021, https://ria.ru/20210518/pospelov-1732345158.html (accessed 15 June 2021).
39. K. Sivkov, 'Zryachiy flot – sil'nyy flot', *VPK-news.ru*, 14 June 2021, https://vpk-news.ru/articles/62547 (accessed 15 June 2021).
40. M. Klimov, '«Podvodnoye lobbi» topit sbalansirovannyy rossiyskiy flot', *VPK-news.ru*, 8 June 2021, https://vpk-news.ru/articles/62478 (accessed 15 June 2021).
41. Three *Ropucha* and one *Alligator* have been destroyed during the Ukraine conflict to date (26 February 2024).
42. 'Nazvany kharakteristiki rossiyskikh korabley proyekta 23900', *Russkoye Oruzhiye*, 4 March 2021, https://rg.ru/2021/03/04/nazvany-harakteristiki-rossijskih-korablej-proekta-23900.html (accessed 12 March 2021).
43. 'A New Modern Propulsion Will Equip Russian Project 23900 Amphibious Assault Ships', *Navy Recognition.com*, 2 November 2020, www.navyrecognition.com/index.php/news/defence-news/2020/november/9220–a-new-modern-propulsion-will-equip-russian-project-23900–amphibious-assault-ships.html (accessed 12 March 2021).
44. 'Istochniki: k proyektirovaniyu rossiyskikh UDK neobkhodimo privlech' Nevskoye PKB', *Flotprom.ru*, 7 September 2020, https://flotprom.ru/2020/%D0%92%D0%BC%D1%8452/ (accessed 12 March 2021).
45. A. Timokhin, 'Bessmyslennyy russkiy «Mistral'»', *VPK-new.ru*, 18 January 2021, https://vpk-news.ru/articles/60437 (accessed 3 March 2021).
46. A.Rezchikov, 'Rossiya bol'she ne mozhet pozvolit' sebe okeanskiy flot', *Vzglyad*, 21 April 2017, https://vz.ru/politics/2017/4/21/324418.html (accessed 23 February 2024).
47. *Ibid.*, p. 1.
48. 'Interv'yu general'nogo direktora Ob'yedinonnoy sudostroitel'noy korporatsii gazete «Kommersant»', *BMPDLivejournal*, 30 December 2021, https://bmpd.livejournal.com/4459763.html (accessed 6 January 2022).
49. 'Prodolzheniye bedlama s rekonstruktsiyey Severnoy verfi', *BMPDLivejournal*, 19 September 2023, https://bmpd.livejournal.com/4753627.html (accessed 20 September 2023).
50. 'Istochnik: novyy zakaz na fregaty proyekta 22350 mozhet poluchit' Amurskiy sudostroitel'nyy zavod', *Flotprom.ru*, 2 February 2023, https://flotprom.ru/2023/%D0%92%D0%BC%D1%846/ (accessed 5 February 2023).
51. 'Modernizirovannyy proyekt 22350M mozhet stat' bazovym dlya serii fregatov dal'ney morskoy zony – glava OSK', *Interfax*, 15 August 2022, www

.militarynews.ru/story.asp?rid=1&nid=579320&lang=RU (accessed 5 September 2022).

52 'Istochnik nazval stoimost' remonta i modernizatsii kreysera Admirala Nakhimova', *Flotprom.ru*, 24 August 2023, https://flotprom.ru/2023/%D0%A1%D0%B5%D0%B2%D0%BC%D0%B0%D1%889/ (accessed 25 August 2023).

53 'TASS: kreyser "Admiral Nakhimov" vyydet na ispytaniya ne ran'she 2025 goda', *Flotprom.ru*, 19 June 2024, https://flotprom.ru/2024/%D0%9C%D0%B2%D0%BC%D1%817/ (accessed 20 June 2024).

54 'TASS: Proyekt 20386 zakryt', *Flotprom.ru*, 7 July 2023, https://flotprom.ru/2023/%D0%90%D0%BB%D0%BC%D0%B0%D0%B71/ (accessed 8 July 2023).

55 A.Ramm, R. Kretzul, B. Stepovoy 'B minnom pole voin: bazy APL na Kamchatke zashchitit novyy tral'shchik', *Izvestiia*, 6 July 2020, https://iz.ru/1031774/roman-kretcul-bogdan-stepovoi-aleksei-ramm/v-minnom-pole-voin-bazy-apl-na-kamchatke-zashchitit-novyi-tralshchik (accessed 12 March 2024).

56 'Sostav VMF Rossii popolnili srazu tri korablya', *Flotprom.ru*, 25 December 2023, https://flot.com/2023/%D0%92%D0%BC%D1%8441/ (accessed 6 January 2024).

57 'Problemy s proizvodstvom reduktorov dlya fregatov proyekta 22350', *BMPDLivejournal*, 15 February 2024, https://bmpd.livejournal.com/4802509.html#cutid1 (accessed 29 February 2024).

58 A. Timokhin, 'Mobilizatsionnyy korabl′ dlya VMF v usloviyakh sanktsiy', *TopWar*, 21 June 2022, https://topwar.ru/197950-mobilizacionnyj-korabl-dlja-vmf-v-uslovijah-sankcij.html (accessed 25 June 2022).

59 'Istochnik soobshchil ob otkaze VMF ot dopolnitel'nykh patrul'nykh korabley proyekta 22160', *Flotprom.ru*, 15 June 2022, https://flot.com/2022/%D0%92%D0%BC%D1%8412/ (accessed 16 June 2022). However, in September 2024, the director of Ak Bars Shipbuilding Corporation suggested that the Project 22160 corvettes might be reprieved/re-designed 'through the upgrade of air defence systems and the installation of missile armament'. https://tass.com/defense/1835691 (accessed 30 September 2024).

60 A. Ramm and B. Stepovoy, 'Pri podderzhke tankerov: VMF poluchit universal'nyye zapravshchiki', *Izvestiia*, 13 May 2020, https://iz.ru/1010314/aleksei-ramm-bogdan-stepovoi/pri-podderzhke-tankerov-vmf-poluchit-universalnye-zapravshchiki (accessed 15 May 2020).

61 'SMI uznali o razrabotke novoy lineyki vspomogatel'nykh sudov dlya VMF', *Flotprom.ru*, 6 March 2023, https://flot.com/2023/%D0%92%D0%BC%D1%849/ (accessed 8 March 2023).

62 'In the Nizhny Novgorod Region, the Small Sea Tanker "Argun" of Project 23630 Was Laid Down for the Russian Navy', *Topwar*, 18 April 2024, https://en.topwar.ru/240803-v-nizhegorodskoj-oblasti-zalozhili-malyj-morskoj-tanker-argun-proekta-23630-dlja-vmf-rossii.html (accessed 7 June 2024).

63 D. Sheridan, 'Carrier Strike Group Reliant on Foreign Support Ships at Sea amid Staffing Crisis', *Telegraph*, 13 October 2024, https://www.telegraph.co.uk/news/2024/10/13/carrier-strike-group-reliant-foreign-support-ships-staffing/?ICID=continue_without_subscribing_reg_first (accessed 13 October 2024).

64 .'Ukaz Prezidenta Rossiyskoy Federatsii ot 27.02.2023 g. № 126', *Kremlin.ru*, 27 February 2023, http://www.kremlin.ru/acts/bank/48967 (accessed 15 October 2024).

65 'Na Baltiyskom zavode zalozhili atomnyy ledokol *Leningrad*', *Sudostroenie.info*, 26 January 2024, https://sudostroenie.info/novosti/41447.html (accessed 26 January 2024).

66 'Problemy s postroykoy golovnogo atomnogo ledokola «Rossiya» proyekta 10510', *BMPDLivejournal*, 29 March 2023, https://bmpd.livejournal.com/4678703.html (accessed 30 March 2023).

67 'Putin Was Told That It Is Impossible to Build the Flagship Nuclear-Powered Icebreaker "Russia" Because Shoygu Bombed the Plant in Ukraine', *X* (formerly Twitter), 28 March 2023, https://twitter.com/nexta_tv/status/1640820163472662528?t=tYors21eHyCk90MCtuH8FQ&s=09 (accessed 3 April 2023).

68 I. Voron, 'Dlya VMF Rossii v Arktike postroyat pyat' ledokolov', *Profile.ru*, 13 October 2021, https://profile.ru/news/protection/army/dlya-vmf-rossii-v-arktike-postroyat-pyat-ledokolov-941794/ (accessed 31 October 2021).

69 'Ledokoly doshli do "Almaza" Chastnyy zavod postroit dlya Minoborony udeshevlennyy variant "Il'i Muromtsa"' *Kommersant*, 13 April 2017, www.kommersant.ru/doc/3269247 (accessed 31 October 2021).

70 'Ledokol "Yevpatiy Kolovrat" vzyal kurs na Petropavlovsk-Kamchatskiy', *Flotprom.ru*, 25 January 2023, https://flot.com/2023/%D0%A2%D0%B8%D1%85%D0%BE%D0%BE%D0%BA%D0%B5%D0%B0%D0%BD%D1%81%D0%BA%D0%B8%D0%B9%D0%A4%D0%BB%D0%BE%D1%825/ (accessed 26 January 2023).

71 'Dlya VMF Rossii zalozhen ledokol *Svyatogor*', *BMPDLivejournal*, 3 September 2023, https://bmpd.livejournal.com/4745860.html (accessed 5 September 2023).

72 'V 2024 godu VMF Rossii peredadut pervyy patrul'nyy ledokol proyekta 23550', *Flotprom.ru*, 24 January 2024, https://flotprom.ru/2024/%D0%90%D0%B4%D0%BC%D0%B8%D1%80%D0%B0%D0%BB%D1%82%D0%B5%D0%B9%D1%81%D0%BA%D0%B8%D0%B5%D0%92%D0%B5%D1%80%D1%84%D0%B8/ (accessed 26 January 2024).

73 'Arkticheskoye transportnoye sudno mogut vooruzhit' "alibrom"', *Rambler.ru*, 15 October 2021, https://news.rambler.ru/army/47390609-arkticheskoe-transportnoe-sudno-mogut-vooruzhit-kalibrom/ (accessed 16 October 2021).

74 I. Petrov, 'Zakonoproyekt: Rossiya opredelit poryadok prokhoda inostrannykh voyennykh korabley po Severnomu morputi', *Rossiyskaya Gazeta*, 25 July 2022, https://rg.ru/2022/07/25/zakonoproekt-rf-opredelit-poriadok-prohoda

75 D. Safonov, 'Atomnyy ledokol'nyy flot Rossii uvelichat v neskol'ko raz', *Nezavisimaya Gazeta*, 29 July 2021, https://nvo.ng.ru/realty/2021-07-29/3_1151_fleet.html (accessed 31 July 2021).
76 'Ledenyashchiy tur: vdol' Sevmorputi desantiruyut morpekhov i motostrelkov', *Izvestiia*, 9 September 2021, https://iz.ru/1219056/anton-lavrov-roman-kretcul-anna-cherepanova/ledeniashchii-tur-vdol-sevmorputi-desantiruiut-morpekhov-i-motostrelkov (accessed 25 September 2021).
77 E. Sherman, 'The US Military Doesn't Have the Icebreakers to Compete in the Arctic and Is "Severely Outnumbered" by Russia, Commander Warns', *Business Insider*, 14 March 2024, https://www.yahoo.com/news/us-military-doesnt-icebreakers-compete-193233164.html#:~:text=Gregory%20M.,Russia%20has%20approximately%2040%20available (accessed 18 March 2024).
78 'Rosstat predstavlyaet vtoruyu otsenku VVP za 2022 god', *Rosstat.gov.ru*, 7 April 2023, https://rosstat.gov.ru/folder/313/document/203214#:~:text=%D0%92%D0%92%D0%9F%20%D0%B7%D0%B0%202022%20%D0%B3%D0%BE%D0%B4%20%D0%B2,%D0%B3%D0%BE%D0%B4%D0%B0%20%E2%80%93%20115%2C8%25 (accessed 5 February 2024).
79 Oil benchmark rose from $56 p/b in November 2021 to $125 in May 2022. Gas – $15 per MMBtu in August 2021 to a peak of $70 per MMBtu a year later.
80 PPP – a measure of the price of specific goods in different countries and used to compare the absolute purchasing power of the countries' currencies.
81 '"Everything for the Front": Russian MPs Back 68% Rise in Military Spending', *Euronews*, 26 October 2023, www.euronews.com/2023/10/26/everything-for-the-front-russian-mps-back-68–rise-in-military-spending (accessed 30 January 2024).
82 *Ibid*.
83 'Pravitel'stvo utverdilo Kontseptsiyu tekhnologicheskogo razvitiya do 2030 goda', *Government.ru*, 25 May 2023, http://government.ru/docs/48570/, (accessed 7 June 2024). The new Defence Minister, Andrei Belousov, was a key architect of the 'technological sovereignty' programme.
84 'Sudostroyeniye vklyuchili v perechen' prioritetnykh napravleniy proyektov tekhnologicheskogo suvereniteta', *Flotprom.ru*, 17 April 2023, https://flotprom.ru/2023/%D0%9E%D0%B1%D0%BE%D1%80%D0%BE%D0%BD%D0%BA%D0%B08/ (accessed 17 April 2023).
85 'OSK vozglavil zamestitel' glavy pravleniya banka VTB', *Flotprom.ru*, 23 August 2023, https://flotprom.ru/2023/%D0%9E%D0%A1%D0%BA18/ (accessed 25 August 2023).
86 'VTB zavershil audit "Ob"yedinennoy sudostroitel'noy korporatsii', *Interfax*, 27 May 2024, www.interfax.ru/business/962425 (accessed 27 May 2024).
87 'VTB provodit audit OSK, posle chego rasschityvayet na vlivaniya gosudarstva v kompaniy', *Moscow Times*, 11 September 2024, https://www.moscowtimes

.io/2023/09/11/povtor-vtb-provodit-audit-osk-posle-chego-rasschityvaet-na-vlivaniya-gosudarstva-v-kompaniyu-a106433 (accessed 12 September 2024).
88 'Russia's 20,000 Defense Workers "Missing In Action"; Its Capability to Produce Cutting-Edge Weapons Exhausted', *Eurasian Times*, 29 May 2023, www.eurasiantimes.com/russias-20000-defense-workers-missing-in-action-its-capability/ (accessed 30 May 2023).
89 'V 'Rostekhe' otsenili nekhvatku kvalifitsirovannogo personala', *Mil.Press*, 22 August 2023, https://xn--b1aga5aadd.xn--p1ai/2023/%D0%A0%D0%BE%D1%81%D1%82%D0%B5%D1%8545/ (accessed 25 August 2023).
90 'L'gotnuyu ipoteku rasprostranyat na sotrudnikov oboronnykh', *Mil.Press*, 11 October 2023, zavodov https://xn--b1aga5aadd.xn--p1ai/2023/%D0%A4%D0%B8%D0%BD%D0%B0%D0%BD%D1%81%D1%8B11/ (accessed 14 October 2023).
91 A. Monaghan and R. Connolly, *The Sea in Russian Strategy*. Manchester, Manchester University Press, 2023, p. 145.

8

Future defence engagement with Russia

Having examined the type of navy that Russia seeks to build, how might the UK, and its allies, engage with it? The interaction and cooperation between the RN and RFN between 1988 to 2014 and the lessons learned provide an important foundation and context to the nature of UK's defence engagement with Russia both now and in the future. That engagement comes in three forms, namely Defend (Confront), Deter (Confront/Compete) and Dialogue (Cooperate). The Royal Navy in the maritime environment has a key role to play in all three of these elements. The unique twenty-five-year period of face-to-face interaction with the RFN provided an insight to its culture and how it thinks and behaves; how it operates its ships and submarines; its approach to training its personnel; the material state of its platforms; Russia's aspirations to become a global maritime power; and its thinking behind their maritime doctrines and policies. It also showed what they learned from us about the broader utility and attributes of maritime power, expressed not only through the deployment of their navy but also through other state entities, both civilian and security, that make up the tapestry of Russia's maritime power. Since 2014, the focus of engagement with Russia has been on Defend and Deter, with Dialogue along pre-2014 lines suspended. The latter will at some stage need to be addressed, but for the foreseeable future, it is highly likely that the former two elements will remain the focus.

Defend

With the benefit of hindsight, the Euro-Atlantic community took its eye off the ball regarding the threat that Russia might pose after the Cold War and the requirement to defend against it. The UK, in particular, became a hub for rich Russian oligarchs in the 2000s, connected to the Russian state and who gained influence within the UK's political and social establishment. The vast sums of Russian money that poured into London were welcomed. It reinforced Russia's perception of the UK's hypocrisy towards its actions and about the UK's emphasis on and 'lecturing' about the importance of the Rule of Law. NATO member states also sought to benefit from the peace dividend on defence spending derived from the end of the Cold War. Russia was viewed by many as 'yesterday's' problem, amid the rise of international terrorism in the form of Al Qaeda and so-called Islamic State, and the West's liberal interventionist actions against 'rogue nations' such as Iraq and Afghanistan, that led to protracted conflicts and also deep disagreements with Russia. For sure, the chaos that Russia had lived through economically in the 1990s gave the sense of a country that had been brought to its knees by the Cold War. The world had moved on from Russia and the challenge it might one day present.

Its armed forces were perceived by many as weak and obsolete and none more so than in the maritime environment. Pictures of rusting nuclear-powered submarines, defunct and decrepit port infrastructure, incidents such as the loss of the *Kursk* submarine, together with first-hand experience between 1988 and 2014 of either visiting ageing RFN warships alongside or at sea, all gave the impression of a spent force. Indeed, this is not altogether untrue. However, as history has shown, Russia and its Navy have a habit of reconstituting and rebuilding. For the RFN, the 1990s and early 2000s was a very testing period, with difficult decisions required over what vessels to scrap and retain, while developing doctrines, and designing new platforms and weapons for a future naval force that was able to compete and challenge NATO and its allies on the world's oceans and defend the territorial integrity of Russia. By 2007, the direction in which Putin was taking the country and the defence of it was clear, articulated in his Munich Security Conference speech that year. He maintained that Russia had been badly treated, not listened to regarding its security concerns and that the US and NATO remained Russia's main adversaries. Accordingly, Russia began a massive modernisation programme of its armed forces in 2008, and the Navy and Aerospace Forces were the prime beneficiaries of the first State Armament Programme 2020. At the same time, in the UK, overseas counter-terrorism operations and the focus on the land environment, coincided with several rounds of cuts to the RN's force structure. By the time new Russian submarines and surface platforms were coming into service, the RN, with fewer, although increasingly more capable platforms, was becoming ever more stretched to deal with the increased tempo of Russia's maritime operations and to defend against it.

The pace of Russian maritime operations targeting the UK preceded the events of 2014. There has been no let up since then, and nor will there be in the medium term, despite a drop in the number of Russian assets tracked near the UK in 2022, due probably to Russia's focus on the conflict in Ukraine. Answering a written parliamentary question in August 2023, Baroness Goldie stated that 'In 2021 the Royal Navy escorted 66 Russian warships through UK waters; 41 such warships were escorted in 2022. During the same period the Royal Navy also located and tracked several Russian submarines in the UK's marine area to guard against intrusion into UK sensitive waters.'[1] Russia's losses in the conflict are largely confined to its land and aerospace forces, not the navy and especially its very capable underwater forces. The RN possesses the military capabilities and plays a leading role in operating and defending the three 'crown jewels' of the UK's defence and security. Although some of that defence effort is mitigated by collective security as a member of NATO under Article 5 or operating in coalitions, defending them in whatever structure will result in persistent engagement between the RN and RFN.

The first of those 'crown jewels' is the ultimate guarantor of the UK's security – the Continuous At-Sea Deterrent (CASD), currently provided by the four *Vanguard*-class strategic nuclear submarines armed with Trident II D5 ballistic missiles. The replacement Dreadnought-class programme is expected to start coming into service in 2030. It is the most important military task for the UK Ministry of Defence to deliver and defend and given its sensitivity is a non-discretionary task. Key to the effectiveness of the CASD is its undetectability, and the Russians make every effort to detect it. Admiral Yevmenov's astonishment expressed to the UK Naval Attache in November 2013 that the UK had withdrawn its Nimrod maritime patrol aircraft in the Defence Review 2010, followed by his tongue-in-cheek comment that 'it might make his life easier', could have encouraged further bolder attempts at tracking CASD in 2015. It was widely reported at the time that the UK had had to rely on NATO partners, namely the USA, to help detect and track a suspected Russian submarine operating in the vicinity of Faslane, home to the CASD submarines.[2] Given the sensitivity of the capability and the non-discretionary nature for its protection by the UK, this UK capability gap needed to be filled. The procurement of nine RAF-operated Poseidon Maritime Patrol Aircraft has now taken place, hopefully making Admiral Yevmenov's successors' lives a little less easy, but it will not diminish the RFN's attempts at detecting and tracking this strategic UK defence asset. Nor will it have gone unnoticed amongst UK analysts within the Russian system that the RN is possibly struggling with the manning of the CASD, with the frank admission by the First Sea Lord in June 2023 that recruiting for the submarine service was proving difficult.[3] This overstretch both in platforms and manning, will encourage Russia to continue to test and probe any weakness it perceives, and the CASD will be a priority to undermine.

The second 'crown jewel' of UK's defence and security to Defend within the maritime environment is its Critical National Infrastructure (CNI), in particular subsea cables, but also wind farms and oil and gas platforms. The Russian naval research vessel *Admiral Vladimirsky* operated much closer to the UK in 2022/2023,[4] allegedly collecting data on a variety of CNI assets such as wind farms, gas pipelines, power and subsea cables. Former Prime Minister Rishi Sunak recognised the critical importance of CNI subsea cables when as a backbencher in 2017 he stated[5] that 'Undersea cables are the indispensable infrastructure of our time, essential to our modern life and digital economy, yet they are inadequately protected and highly vulnerable to attack at sea and on land, from both hostile states and terrorists.' The UK has attempted to address the capability gap to Defend its CNI through various measures, including the procurement of specialised Multi-Role Ocean Surveillance Ships. However, progress has been far from smooth. The first, RFA *Proteus*, entered service late due to engineering defects and manning shortages[6] and a decision on the intended second vessel is now under consideration pending the outcome of the UK's Strategic Defence Review in 2025. Operating remote and autonomous offboard systems for underwater surveillance and seabed warfare, these platforms would be a key asset to Defend UK's CNI, and in conjunction with the UK's submarine platforms, could provide a challenge to Russia's persistent attempts to target theUK's and other nations' CNI with assets both below and above water. Other recent initiatives to protect the UK's and allies' CNI include: a naval deployment at the end of 2023 by members of the UK-led Joint Expeditionary Force (JEF), which included Denmark, Estonia, Finland, Iceland, Latvia, Lithuania, Netherlands, Norway and Sweden;[7] and the opening in May 2024 of NATO's new Maritime Centre for Security of Critical Undersea Infrastructure (CUI), based at NATO Allied Maritime Command (MARCOM), Northwood, UK. This new centre is described as 'the operational hub, with a strategic hub based at NATO Headquarters in Brussels, to coordinate efforts between NATO Allies, Partners, and the private sector' and 'assists Commander MARCOM in making decisions, deploying forces and coordinating action' to protect allied CUI.[8]

The third 'crown jewel' of UK's defence in the maritime environment are the HMS *Queen Elizabeth*-class aircraft carriers, operating the F-35B Lightning aircraft, and projecting UK's power around the world. Russia made its views of the ship quite clear in 2017 – the ship was nothing more than a large convenient target for the RFN. The remarks followed comments by the then UK Defence Secretary, Michael Fallon, who thought the Russians would look at the ship 'with a little bit of envy', while referring to Russia's *Admiral Kuznetsov* sole aircraft carrier as being 'dilapidated'.[9] While *Admiral Kuznetsov* is not without its problems, it is nevertheless due to emerge from an extended refit in 2025. This war of words between the UK and Russia about respective capabilities is also not useful, especially given the UK's aircraft carrier, HMS *Prince of Wales*, suffered a catastrophic defect to its starboard shaft in August 2022, putting it out of service for over a year. Furthermore, in February 2024, HMS *Queen Elizabeth* was forced to withdraw from a major NATO exercise, Steadfast Defender, since the risk of failure of its propeller shafts was deemed too high and the work originally scheduled for 2025 was brought forward by a year.[10] Aircraft carriers represent one of the key threat concerns for Russia, given their ability to conduct long-range attacks against Russia, and their global reach. Thus it is no surprise that they represent a key target for the RFN, against which the UK will need to Defend, not just in the Euro-Atlantic but also in the Indo-Pacific region. Russia's Pacific Fleet orbat is being strengthened with new submarines, including potentially the special-purpose submarine *Belgorod*, and surface platforms, complemented with new base support infrastructure. Moreover, the RFN is exercising with navies of regional partners such as Iran, China and Myanmar, the latter in November 2023 being the first Russian-Myanmar naval exercise in modern history.[11] The then C-in-C RFN Admiral Yevemnov's visits to Tehran in May 2023, China in July 2023, including Chinese shipbuilding yards[12] and Myanmar in November 2023 also underlined the growing relationship with all three countries. Defence of the UK's aircraft carriers will become more challenging, globally, and Russia will be a key element of that threat.

Deterrence

The second area of engagement in the maritime environment between Russia and the UK and their respective navies is Deterrence. The UK's military doctrine adopts the NATO definition of deterrence as being 'the convincing of a potential aggressor that the consequences of coercion or armed conflict would outweigh the potential gains. This requires the maintenance of a credible military capability and strategy with the clear political will to act.'[13] Against this definition, Russia's invasion of Ukraine in February 2022, represented a failure of deterrence and underlined the deep complexities of what is and isn't deterrence and what deters and does not deter a potential adversary. Since Russia's annexation of Crimea in 2014, the Euro-Atlantic community has wrestled with the concept of deterring Russia. Through NATO it took proactive steps at the 2014 summit in Wales to bolster NATO's military readiness and responses to the security challenges presented by Russia, with the development of the Readiness Action Plan and Enhanced Forward Presence, primarily in the Baltic States and Poland. It called for a greater commitment from member states to meet the guideline of 2 per cent GDP spending on defence. Tough economic sanctions were also introduced to impose a cost on Russia for its actions. Military cooperation and dialogue were suspended, except for occasional high-level conversations or meetings, designed ostensibly to reduce the risks of miscalculation and misunderstanding.

Yet, while these actions might have deterred Russia from attacking NATO, assuming Russia has ever planned to do so, none of these actions, together with other initiatives such as high-level diplomacy and the threat of economic sanctions, deterred Vladimir Putin from launching his 'special military operation' in Ukraine. Western deterrence failed. The political rupture between Russia and the West was too deeply embedded. Fundamental disagreements on subjects such as future global security architectures, NATO expansion, 'colour revolutions' in Russia's near abroad, Western interference in the sovereignty of other countries, differences on moral values, human rights and other perceived hostile actions towards each other in the preceding twenty years, have come together in the struggle over Ukraine. On the one hand, Ukraine's rightful desire to pursue its own national, sovereign path, and on the other Russia's desire to keep Ukraine within its sphere of influence and not to allow it to become, as Russia perceives it, a stepping stone for 'further aggression' by the West towards Moscow. Furthermore, for Russia which has historically sought to gain and maintain access to the sea, the threat in 2014 of the potential loss of access to Crimea and Sevastopol should Ukraine join NATO, was one of the key drivers for Putin's decision to annex the peninsula.

More often than not, deterrence and dialogue are viewed as separate policies. Yet they should not be. Deterrence is largely about the psychological impact on an adversary of one's actions, of demonstrating what consequences an adversary might incur, if a particular course of action is adopted. However, without some form of dialogue, deterrence actions can be misinterpreted or misunderstood, leading to a response, which if conducted in a confrontational way, risks further escalation of mutual hostility.[14] Without dialogue, opportunities are lost to either emphasise and explain what costs might be incurred for any given action, or to understand particular points of view and to gain insight into political and military strategic thinking and planning. Russia's sense of perceived injustice and victimhood pervades the interpretation of most actions it believes are directed against it. Russia frequently accuses the West of 'lecturing it' and applying double standards when attempting to adopt a firm approach towards Russia (Constrain), while wanting to keep open channels of dialogue. This makes the application of deterrence measures challenging, since there always exists the fear of provocation and subsequent escalation to confrontation between the two sides.

The maritime environment provides both Russia and the UK the opportunities to deter each other, either through nuclear or conventional deterrence capabilities. The attributes of maritime power,[15] which include Poise, Mobility, Persistence, Versatility and Access, lend themselves to the aim of deterrence; to exert influence and to change the behaviour of an adversary through the projection of military power, in combination with other non-military measures of deterrence. Both Russia and the UK will continue to procure maritime capabilities that will seek to bring credibility to its deterrence posture and this will mean increasing interaction, often friction, between the two on the high seas and in regions of competition, such as the Arctic and Indo-Pacific. An example of creating friction was the incident involving the transit of the Type 45 destroyer, HMS *Defender*, in June 2021 off the Crimean peninsula, the aim of which was to assert Freedom of Navigation rights in the Black Sea in support of Ukraine. It led, unsurprisingly, to a diplomatic and military dispute between Russia and the UK with each side using the incident to underpin their respective narratives. Putin on the one hand claimed it was a provocation that brought the risk of confrontation to a new level. He argued that Russians 'are fighting for ourselves and our future on our own territory. It was not us who covered thousands of kilometres by air and sea towards them; it was them who approached our borders and entered our territorial sea.'[16] On the other hand the UK said that it acted under the premise of Freedom of Navigation, exercising its rights of innocent passage through an internationally recognised traffic separation corridor. As tensions continue to escalate between Russia and the West we can expect more friction in the maritime environment as both sides seek to use this element of military power to make political points and to deter one another.

Dialogue (cooperation)

Defence and Deterrence against Russia since 2014 has been the main effort for the UK and its allies and this is unlikely to change in the medium term. It has driven national strategies, policies and capability procurement and led the US and the West into a proxy conflict in Ukraine against Russia. This focus has driven the third element of defence engagement with Russia, Dialogue, further into the past and consequently a lesser part of the collective memory in how to deal with Russia and the Russians. In large part this is due to the UK's and other allies' decision to suspend military dialogue with Russia in the immediate aftermath of the annexation of Crimea. For the UK this mirrored UK policy that all dialogue, for example political and economic, should only be conducted so long as Russia in essence behaved and acknowledged the error of its ways.[17] This was encapsulated in the UK government's (and NATO's)[18] term of 'no return to business as usual' until Russia's behaviour changed. This missed the point that from a Russian perspective the West's 'business as usual', such as NATO expansion, was a fundamental reason for bringing the relationship to this point of confrontation. Russia had, nor does it have, any intention of returning to business as usual. For the UK, this suspension of military dialogue represented a real failure to capitalise on the close relationships, and mutual understanding, built up during a twenty-five-year period of dialogue and cooperation between high-ranking UK and Russian defence officials, as well as personnel from all branches of the respective armed forces, and especially between the two navies. The flipside of the deterrence coin was undermined and opportunities to support the political and diplomatic levers of power by messaging the Russian military at all levels, face to face and to gain insight, were lost.

Re-establishing military dialogue and cooperation with Moscow will not be easy, in whatever scenario exists after the present conflict in Ukraine, but for the UK the maritime environment and the RN will most likely take the lead on any re-engagement with the Russian armed forces. Such was the case in 1997. The election of a New Labour government in May that year heralded a new policy initiative in the UK Ministry of Defence, namely Defence Diplomacy, the mission of which was 'to provide forces to meet the varied activities undertaken by the MoD to dispel hostility, build and maintain trust and assist in the development of democratically accountable armed forces, thereby making a significant contribution to conflict prevention and resolution'.[19] Russia was a key country upon which to 'test' this new policy, and the already close relationship between the RN and RFN, which had been re-established in 1988, acted as the spearhead for the initiative and turbo-charged navy-to-navy activity, including the signing of the MoU on naval cooperation in 1998.

However unlikely it might seem, as the conflict continues between Russia and Ukraine, and from a Russian perspective with the West, the question of how we might re-establish defence dialogue and even cooperation with Russia, will, at some stage, need to be addressed. In all likelihood this will be several years away but it could be sooner, if the political conditions inside Russia were to suddenly change. Unexpected and dramatic political change in Russia is not without precedent and Russian history has many examples. The twentieth century alone saw two such events of political turmoil, namely the 1917 October Revolution and the fall of the Berlin Wall in 1989 and subsequent demise of the Soviet Union. Thus, the political context will be key and the Ukraine conflict, whatever the outcome, will have a profound effect on that military re-engagement process. The period coming out of the Cold War, however, was very different to what we are witnessing now and it could become even worse. At that time, although there was an ideological clash between the West and the USSR and deep suspicion, there was no direct conflict between the two as Russia perceives there to be now, and *fora* existed in which the Soviet and Western militaries met. Furthermore, history played an important role in bridging and improving the relationship between militaries, drawing heavily on and regularly commemorating the common struggle of Russia and the Western Allies against the Nazis and the spread of fascism. Now the Western alliance is considered by Russia as a neo-Nazi sympathiser for its support to the Ukrainian government and although the West is technically not in direct conflict with Russia, its political, military and economic support to Ukraine makes it, as the Kremlin views it, a party to the conflict, with the UK leading from the front. The latter was further exemplified in November 2023 by the announcement of a UK–Norway initiative to co-lead a maritime capability coalition to develop Ukraine's Navy.[20] The irony of twenty-five years of naval cooperation with Russia with the now strong support for the Ukrainian Navy will not be lost on the Russians. Justifying to Ukraine any defence re-engagement with a country that is responsible for the destruction and misery caused by its invasion will also be extremely difficult, and should Ukraine join NATO, then even more so from a Russian perspective. A further obstacle to defence engagement will be that many of the key interlocutors that might be instrumental in setting Russian defence re-engagement policy are likely to have been sanctioned or worse, under investigation for possible war crimes.

The landscape for future defence dialogue and cooperation between the UK and Russia will thus be complicated and extremely challenging. Even before the annexation of Crimea in 2014, it was not a smooth process, as already indicated. First, the UK will need to consider how and when to conduct military re-engagement with Russia which will need to be done both in support of the UK's national interest and also in negotiation with close partners in NATO and with EU members to ensure a common approach. Whatever re-engagement policy is determined, Moscow will most likely seek to exploit fissures within Western alliances, as it always has done in virtually any policy towards it, in an attempt to gain both economic advantage and security-technology to support its defence industry. Thus, the type of military engagement with Russia that is sought by the UK will need to be clearly defined as well as having a clear understanding of how Moscow perceives that engagement.

From a UK perspective there are two distinct aspects in a bilateral military relationship. The first is Defence Cooperation. This can be summarised as sharing capability, operating concepts, doctrine and technology, with a view to developing access, influence and interoperability, in order to allow the conduct of combined operations against a common threat. Typically these include UN mandated peace-keeping, counter-terorrism and counter-piracy operations. The second is Defence Engagement. This element focuses on dialogue and is intended to maintain lines of communication with military counterparts to enable insight into capability, intentions and key decision-makers, with a view to encouraging transparency and trust, but more significantly preventing strategic surprise. It is also important that defence engagement should be complementary to political engagement. Military dialogue, except for one or two very high-level meetings, was non-existent between the annexation of Crimea in March 2014 and Russia's invasion of Ukraine in February 2022. It would be naive to suggest that had there been more defence engagement and dialogue the invasion could have been prevented, but its suspension probably precluded important messaging both to and from the Russian military and hence thwarted a better insight to both sides' policies and thinking.

Russia's perspectives of defence cooperation and engagement are quite different and the all-embracing Russian term used, Military-Technical Cooperation, provides the clue. The main objective of this cooperation is the desire to improve the operational capability of the Russian armed forces, driven at times by a lack of competitive indigenous military technology. The conflict in Ukraine has shown the pragmatic, transactional nature of this cooperation as Russia seeks to obtain military equipment and weaponry from, for example, North Korea and Iran. It is axiomatic, therefore, that the reconstitution of the Russian armed forces after the Ukraine conflict will be a key driver to Russia's future military-technical cooperation programme and their partners are likely to be prioritised accordingly. Even before the events in Crimea in 2014, the Russian military was less interested in dialogue for dialogue's sake unless it had a measurable output, which meets their three broad goals for Military-Technical Cooperation:

- To transfer technology to the Russian Military Industrial Complex and armed forces.
- To transfer doctrine and operating processes which can enhance Russia military capability.
- To develop an awareness of a competitors' readiness and capability for conflict.

Taking these subtle but important differences in the UK and Russia's approach to military cooperation, the UK's aim needs to focus on its principles of Defence Engagement. In the first instance, this should be to improve dialogue to avoid any further strategic surprises, misunderstandings or miscalculations and to better understand future Russian capability and intent, while ensuring that the dangers of meeting Russia's objectives, in particular capability transfer, are not met. However, even establishing a meaningful dialogue will be challenging given the hugely significant damage done by Russia's invasion of Ukraine to trust, confidence and indeed respect between the two militaries. Although the Russian military contains some of the deepest strategic thinkers in Russia, they are also amongst some of the most paranoid about the West's intentions towards the country. That will not dissipate any time soon and is further compounded by the UK's and other allies' vital support to Ukraine, which, as Russia is likely to view it, has been responsible for the deaths of thousands of Russian armed forces personnel.

This fact will make military re-engagement extremely challenging but not impossible. The last time that Russia and the West emerged from a period of confrontation, the Cold War, both sides, although not in direct conflict, had threatened each other with nuclear armageddon and the USA and its allies had a significant military footprint based in Europe. Moreover, in the period prior to the collapse of the Soviet Union, the USA, the UK and other allies had provided significant military support and equipment to the Mujahideen of Afghanistan during the Soviet-Afghan war, tipping the balance of the conflict and forcing the USSR to withdraw between May 1988 and February 1989. Yet it was during this same period that the first set of Adderbury talks took place, which sought to develop confidence-building measures through dialogue on naval matters, building on the INCSEA treaty that had been signed in 1986.

While it is dangerous to draw parallels between events of thirty-five years ago with their differing political contexts, it does at least demonstrate a pathway, however unlikely it seems, towards dialogue. There will need to be high-level political and defence meetings, bound within the framework of the government's guiding principles for any military re-engagement and in coordination with other Western allies. The establishment of those political principles in itself will be profoundly challenging, as leaders seek to strike the balance between any sign of re-engagement being interpreted as indifference towards Russia's action in Ukraine, while developing a relationship with Russia that rebuilds shattered trust and understanding, and challenges or informs future Russian thinking.

Part of that balancing act should be to enable contacts to be established at a working level, below the political radar and out of the media spotlight. It is here that a future Defence Engagement policy should focus on utilising the navy-to-navy relationship established between 1988 and 2014 as a route towards some sort of new military relationship with Russia post-Ukraine, drawing on what was achieved in the twenty-five years of that engagement. Experience showed that a common historical bond extending from Peter the Great's founding of the Russian Navy to Allied support in the Arctic Convoys to the USSR in the period 1941–45, really did matter and enabled a cordial atmosphere both at high-level meetings and at sea between ships.

Time and time again the importance of the bond generated by the brotherhood of the sea was expressed by the Russians. This might sound trite but it is important. The sea is a naturally hostile environment in which to operate and at a practical level, discussions were always first and foremost about the challenges of operating in that environment, about keeping mariners safe and keeping politics out of it. Over and above the rescue of the *Priz*, in 2005 there were several other practical examples, as when HMS *Glasgow*'s helicopter airlifted a Russian sailor suffering from appendicitis from a Victor III nuclear submarine at sea to hospital in Scotland in February 1996. The High North and Northern Sea Route (NSR) is a region of increasing tension between Russia and the West but is also one of the most hostile maritime environments in the world. Paradoxically, therefore, the region could offer a route to cooperative interaction in the field of maritime search and rescue, as the volume of marine traffic increases in the coming years along the NSR.

The achievements made during the period of 1988 to 2014 offer a useful template for future navy-to-navy engagement, which could then lead to broader defence engagement. The annual treaty obligating face-to-face

Figure 8.1 Admiral Sir Jock Slater, First Sea Lord, greets Admiral Igor Kasatonov, First Deputy Commander-in-Chief Russian Federation Navy, in the Mall House Flat, 5 March 1996. Kasatonov had just handed over a letter from C-in-C RFN Admiral Feliks Gromov, thanking the Royal Navy for airlifting a sailor suffering from appendicitis from a Victor III SSN off Scotland earlier that month.
© Crown Copyright.

meetings under the 1986 INCSEA agreement offers an obvious pathway to renewing some form of dialogue. Other confidence-building measures could include establishing Track 2 dialogue[21] between academics and retired naval personnel, akin to the Adderbury talks in the late 1980s. They could be established and facilitated through linkages between think-tanks such as the Royal United Services Institute (RUSI) and the Russian International Affairs Council (RIAC), who have collaborated in the past on work that offers ways of finding a pathway back to dialogue.[22] Another venue to consider for broader and discreet defence and security dialogue between retired personnel, who nevertheless remain well connected to their respective government organisations and might have met before, is the Club of Military Leaders of the Russian Federation (*Klub voyenachal'nikov Rossiyskoy Federatsii*') in Moscow.[23] The Club was founded in 2005 and includes more than one thousand active and retired senior officers of the Ministry of Defence, the Ministry of Internal Affairs, the FSB, the Foreign Intelligence Service, the Ministry of Emergency Situations and other law enforcement agencies. It exerts considerable influence through its members acting as experts on relevant committees of the State Duma and the Federation Council. The Club also conducts international cooperation in matters of collective security, countering terrorism, counter-narcotics and smuggling.

Initial dialogue, in whatever *fora*, is determined to be the most beneficial, should also lead to re-opening the important FRUKUS forum, drawing on what was achieved until 2014, thereby resuming the dialogue between serving naval personnel from France, Russia, the UK and the US. On the practical side, taking into account the challenges and dangers of operating at sea, the topic of submarine search and rescue, reflecting UK and NATO's experience with Russia up to 2014, should become a priority to revitalise. Interactions at sea, over the horizon and out of the gaze of media scrutiny, also offer a further conduit for dialogue and confidence building exercises. Port visits offer a more tangible and stronger political and diplomatic signal of both sides wanting to re-establish not just defence but also political re-engagement too. That might seem fantastical at present but so too in November 1989 when the Berlin Wall fell. Eight months later the Soviet destroyer *Bezuprechny* sailed into Portsmouth harbour.

The commemoration of the Arctic Convoys will probably be the main conduit to the re-establishment of historical connections between the two navies, as well as maintaining a focus on the Commonwealth War Grave Commission (CWGC)[24] sites that exist across Russia. These sites were frequently part of bilateral ships which saw personnel from the ships helping to check, clean and tidy the sites. Even since 2014, interaction has taken place, for example during the seventy-fifth anniversary of Operation Dervish in 2016 in Arkhangelsk and St Petersburg, attended by HRH the Princess

Royal, Vice Admiral Sir Timothy Laurence and the then Assistant Chief of Naval Staff, Vice Admiral Sir Nick Hine. However, 2017 marked the last real point of cooperation with the Russian Northern Fleet when there was a joint project with the CWGC to mark the graves of two naval airmen on the Rybachiy Peninsula. The attempted poisoning of Skripal in March 2018 and the subsequent closure of the British Consulate in St Petersburg finally put an end to in-country bilateral activity related to the Arctic Convoys. Future engagement will require cooperation with the Northern Convoys' International Centre (NCIC)[25] established in 2018 in St Petersburg, which is the conduit to Russia's Polar Convoy Club, with whom the UK once enjoyed a good relationship, and attended their twentieth anniversary exhibition in the Peter and Paul Fortress in April 2015.[26] The Russian Arctic Convoy Museum,[27] based in Poolewe, signed a cooperation agreement with NCIC at the end of 2021, with the idea of possibly exchanging some exhibits but since the invasion in February 2022 there has been little contact. Other linkages established between museums include the Arkhangelsk Northern Maritime Museum[28] and the Western Approaches Museum in Liverpool.[29]

Future defence dialogue between Russia and the UK will pose significant political risks and challenges. If the conflict between Russia and Ukraine becomes protracted, then even more so, given the significant political, economic and military support provided by the UK, and the Western alliance, to Ukraine. Important achievements in the bilateral relationship were made between the RN and RFN from 1988 until 2014 and should inform the future direction of military re-engagement. Defence re-engagement is not, however, the sole reason for focusing on what was learned about the RFN during that period. Russia's maritime ambitions, and indeed the UK's, are global from the High North to the Indo-Pacific region, around the African continent and elsewhere. Thus, the world's oceans will likely be one of the key environments in which the UK and Russia will continue to confront each other, to compete and maybe to cooperate.

Notes

1 B. Glaze, 'Royal Navy Ships Scrambled to Shadow More Than 100 Russian Warships in Two Years', *Mirror*, 13 August 2023, www.mirror.co.uk/news/politics/royal-navy-ships-scrambled-shadow-30692641 (accessed 25 August 2025).

2 V. Ward, 'A Suspected Russian Submarine Is Lurking off of the Scottish Coast', *Insider.com*, 9 January 2015, www.businessinsider.com/a-suspected-russian-submarine-is-lurking-off-of-the-scottish-coast-2015-1?r=US&IR=T (accessed 14 May 2024).

3 D. Haynes, 'Royal Navy Boss Reveals Fears over Staffing of UK's Nuclear Deterrent', *Sky News.com*, 19 June 2023, https://news.sky.com/story/royal-navy-boss-reveals-fears-over-staffing-of-uks-nuclear-deterrent-12905148 (accessed 24 June 2023).
4 C. Bueger, 'Russian "Spy Ship" in North Sea Raises Concerns about the Vulnerability of Key Maritime Infrastructure', *UK Defence Journal*, 22 April 2023, https://ukdefencejournal.org.uk/russian-spy-ship-raises-concerns-about-vulnerability/ (accessed 15 May 2024).
5 R. Sunak, 'Undersea Cables: Indispensable, Insecure', *Policy Exchange.org*, 1 December 2017, https://policyexchange.org.uk/publication/undersea-cables-indispensable-insecure/ (accessed 15 May 2024).
6 'Setbacks in the Royal Navy's Effort to Get Newly Acquired Auxiliary Ships into Service', *NavyLookout*, 27 August 2024, https://www.navylookout.com/setbacks-in-the-royal-navys-effort-to-get-newly-acquired-auxiliary-ships-into-service/ (accessed 13 November 2024).
7 J. Beale, 'Royal Navy Sends Second Warship to Gulf', *BBC News*, 30 November 2023, www.bbc.co.uk/news/uk-67572536 (accessed 30 November 2023).
8 NATO, 'NATO Officially Launches New Maritime Centre for Security of Critical Undersea Infrastructure', *Public Affairs Office at MARCOM*, 28 May 2024, https://mc.nato.int/media-centre/news/2024/nato-officially-launches-new-nmcscui (accessed 5 June 2024).
9 A. Osborn and D. Solovyov, 'Russia Calls Britain's New Aircraft Carrier "a Convenient Target"', *Reuters*, 29 June 2017, www.reuters.com/article/cnews-us-russia-britain-aircraft-idCAKBN19K0XT-OCATP (accessed 15 May 2023).
10 'HMS Queen Elizabeth Dry Docking Period in Rosyth Extended', *Navy Lookout*, 31 May 2024, https://www.navylookout.com/hms-queen-elizabeth-dry-docking-period-in-rosyth-extended/ (accessed 11 June 2024).
11 'The Active Phase of Exercises between Russian and Myanmar Ships with Firing Begins in the Andaman Sea', *Interfax*, 7 November 2023, www.militarynews.ru/story.asp?rid=0&nid=605718&lang=RU (accessed 8 November 2023).
12 'Glavkom VMF Rossii posetil kitayskiye verfi', *Flotprom.ru*, 10 July 2023, https://flot.com/2023/%D0%9C%D0%B5%D0%B6%D0%B4%D1%83%D0%BD%D0%B0%D1%80%D0%BE%D0%B4%D0%BD%D0%BE%D0%B5%D0%A1%D0%BE%D1%82%D1%80%D1%83%D0%B4%D0%BD%D0%B8%D1%87%D0%B5%D1%81%D1%82%D0%B2%D0%BE33/ (accessed 12 July 2023).
13 'Joint Doctrine Publication 0–01 UK Defence Doctrine – 6th Edition', *Ministry of Defence London*, November 2022, p. 49.
14 A. M. Monaghan, *Dealing with the Russians*. Cambridge, UK, Polity Press, 2019, p. 83.
15 'Joint Doctrine Publication 0–10 UK Maritime Power (5th Edition)', *Ministry of Defence London*, October 2017, p. 36.
16 D. Gorenburg, 'The HMS *Defender* Incident: What Happened and What Are the Political Ramifications?', *Russia Matters*, 1 July 2021, www.russiamatters

.org/analysis/HMS-defender-incident-what-happened-and-what-are-political-ramifications (accessed 16 May 2023).
17 H. Stewart, '"Despicable Act": May Confronts Putin over Salisbury Poisoning', *Guardian*, 28 June 2019, www.theguardian.com/politics/2019/jun/28/theresa-may-exchanges-cool-handshake-with-vladimir-putin#:~:text=%E2%80%9CIt's%20not%20business%20as%20usual,on%20the%20streets%20of%20Salisbury (accessed 13 June 2024).
18 N. Walker and B. Smith, 'Russian Annexation of Crimea', *House of Commons Library*, 18 April 2019, https://researchbriefings.files.parliament.uk/documents/CDP-2019-0093/CDP-2019-0093.pdf, p. 14 (accessed 12 June 2024).
19 Select Committee on Defence, 'Security Policy in a New World Order', *UK Parliament*, 1998, https://publications.parliament.uk/pa/cm199798/cmselect/cmdfence/138/13812.htm (accessed 5 April 2023)
20 'UK and Norway Will Co-Lead a Maritime Capability Coalition to Develop Ukraine's Navy', *Naval News*, 11 December 2023, https://www.navalnews.com/naval-news/2023/12/uk-and-norway-will-co-lead-a-maritime-capability-coalition-to-develop-ukraines-navy/ (accessed 13 December 2023).
21 Track 2 dialogue, which avoids direct government official or ministerial engagement with Russia, has been discussed frequently since 2014 but UK policy was always at best lukewarm about the idea.
22 A. V. Kortunov and S. Lain, 'Defining Dialogue: How to Manage Russia–UK Security Relations Part 1', *RIAC/RUSI*, May 2017, www.slideshare.net/RussianCouncil/defining-dialogue-how-to-manage-russiauk-security-relations-76524175 (accessed 15 June 2023) and A. V. Kortunov, M. Chalmers, S. Lain and M. Smekalova, 'Defining Dialogue: How to Manage Russia–UK Security Relations Part 2', *RIAC/RUSI*, March 2018, https://russiancouncil.ru/en/activity/publications/defining-dialogue-how-to-manage-russia-uk-security-relations-part-2/ (accessed 15 June 2023).
23 The club was visited by the British Defence Attache, Naval Attache and First Political Secretary in 2015. Further information is at http://kvrf.milportal.ru/o-klube/ (accessed 23 July 2023).
24 CWGC, www.cwgc.org/visit-us/find-cemeteries-memorials/ (accessed 22 July 2023).
25 NCIC, https://north-convoys.com/en/home.html (accessed 22 July 2023).
26 'Arctic Convoys Exhibition Opens in St Petersburg', *Gov.uk*, 28 April 2015, www.gov.uk/government/news/arctic-convoys-exhibition-opens-in-st-petersburg (accessed 15 May 2023).
27 RACP, https://racmp.co.uk/ (accessed 22 July 2023).
28 Northern Maritime Museum, https://northernmaritime.ru/main_engl (accessed 22 July 2023).
29 Liverpool War Museum, https://liverpoolwarmuseum.co.uk/ (accessed 22 July 2023).

Conclusion

Russia continues to strive towards becoming a maritime power, one which is not constrained to operating in the Euro-Atlantic region, but one that is able to compete in the global commons politically, economically and militarily. Despite some difficulties and constraints, Russia has instigated an ambitious naval ship and submarine building programme, as well as employing LACMs, that both defend Russia and project its power worldwide. Interaction with the RN and other western navies in the post-Soviet era taught the RFN about the wider utility of maritime power, how those navies operated and also about their capabilities and doctrines. Whether through defence, deterrence or dialogue, the RN and RFN will continue to interact and engage for the foreseeable future. The period of naval cooperation between 1988 and 2014, which included the signing of a MoU between the two navies in 1998, offered unparalleled insights to the RFN and its people. Whilst the focus for now is on defence and deterrence against Russia as the Ukraine crisis develops or resolves, there is every possibility that the RN could be used as a conduit for re-establishing the third pillar of defence engagement, dialogue. In this regard, remembering that this period of cooperation existed and the ways in which it did will be crucial if dialogue is to be anything more than superficial.

Since the founding of the Russian Navy by Peter the Great in 1696, the development of the Russian and Soviet navies has been affected by political upheavals and military setbacks and even defeats. Inter alia, these have included military defeats in the Crimean War of 1853–56, the Russo–Japanese War in 1904–5, and profound political events such as the October 1917 revolution and the collapse of the Soviet Union in 1991. Yet, much like the Russian state itself, the navy has consistently found a way to get 'back on its feet', to learn lessons, to reconstitute itself and to recover from what, for any nation or navy, would represent significant, even cataclysmic, events. The most notable example of this phenomenon in more recent history, was the period immediately following World War II. Admiral Gorshkov argued the case for the Soviet Union to become a Great Maritime

Power (*Velikaya morskaya derzhava*) and to create a fleet that was capable of reliably protecting the Motherland and guaranteeing its state interests worldwide. By the mid-1970s the Soviet Navy had a very large number of naval assets at its disposal. By 1991, the USSR no longer existed, and much of Gorshkov's fleet lay obsolete and rusting, having been subjected to years of chronic underinvestment as the Soviet economy collapsed.

The 1988–2014 period of close interaction and cooperation between the RN and first the Soviet Navy and the RFN, offered a unique opportunity to witness one of the cycles that Russia's navies had been subjected to over the preceding nearly three hundred years – the rise and fall and rise again of Russia's maritime power. Under Putin's leadership, the drive in recent years for Russia to become a great maritime power has manifested itself through two key policy documents. The July 2022 Maritime Doctrine, focused on the geo-economic challenges, and the 2017 Naval Policy focused on the Navy itself, underpinned by an ambitious ship and submarine building programmes and global operational deployments. Putin has consistently used his annual Navy Day address at the end of July, to emphasise the importance of the sea in Russian strategy, and the RFN's role both to defend Russia and also to project its power on the world oceans and protect its national interests.[1] Russia's Navy Day parade was, for many years, a fixed event to attend in the RN's calendar and a highlight in the annual bilateral and multilateral programme of events. It also acted as a useful reference point in gauging the state and development of the RFN following the collapse of the USSR. Two things were noticeable at the 2023 event. First the guest list which has been steadily changing since 2014. Where once there were UK and NATO ships moored on the River Neva alongside their Russian colleagues to celebrate Navy Day, with a galaxy of heads of navies attending the ceremonies, now the list is confined to Global South leaders, and fewer of those attended in 2023. Second was the reflection of the modest progress the RFN has made, in that the majority of the ships and submarines on display were delivered in the last ten years and equipped with *Kalibr* missiles.

However, the interaction between the two navies did not only allow an insight into the material state of the RFN and the regeneration of capability, but also into the thinking of its leaders about the importance of maritime power and the RFN's role in delivering it. Early ship visits and staff talks quickly revealed both the poor material state of the RFN in the 1990s, as well as its doctrine concerning the role of warships and submarines in delivering maritime power. On the latter, it was anathema to RFN senior commanders that warships could, for example, be used for anything other than primarily war-fighting. The multilateral FRUKUS forum, as well as bilateral staff talks, demonstrated to the RFN the broader utility of maritime power, for example, in constabulary operations and defence diplomacy. Examples include enforcing embargoes and counter-piracy operations, which have led the RFN to operate off the Horn of Africa region countering Somali piracy in the late 2000s, and in the current conflict with Ukraine, the deployment of the corvette *Sergey Kotov* to the southern Black Sea, following the collapse in July 2023 of the Black Sea grain initiative, ostensibly to intercept commercial vessels as required en route to Ukraine.[2] Defence diplomacy activity, which in the early years was frowned upon by our RFN interlocutors, has markedly increased, as demonstrated by the large number of ship visits to and exercises with, for example, China, Iran and many others in the Indo-Pacific region.

The overriding impressions, and indeed surprise, from those first meetings in 1988, and which were prevalent throughout to 2014, were the respect in which the RN was held by our Russian counterparts and the warmth of Russian naval hospitality. We had assumed during the Cold War they were our sworn enemies focused solely on our destruction. It did not feel like that. We also discovered a great sense of humour amongst our opposite numbers, which could nevertheless be countered by the Russian tendency to low mood swings, obduracy, bureaucracy and frequent lying or its peculiar close relative, *vranyo*. Despite the turbulent political periods after Putin came to power in 2000 and the sharp disagreements between the UK and Russia, the navy-to-navy relationship remained courteous and respectful, founded on history, mutual respect and, although strange to some but understandable to mariners, a bond generated by operating in the hostile environment of the sea. We discovered, however, a very conservative Russian approach to managing and dealing with their people, a system that reflected wider society. Commanders relied on a 'vertical power' system to achieve their aims, who tolerated neither dissent nor questioning back up the chain of command. This led to a lack of freethinking and freedom of action by subordinates, a weakness that can be exploited by a more agile, mission-command focused opponent. The sinking of the *Slava*-class cruiser *Moskva* might have been an example of this but in any event it was also likely an example of the other key lesson learned. The standard of RFN training driven more by the timely achievement of a serial rather than the quality of its output, especially in damage control and firefighting, could also have been a factor in the loss of the *Moskva*.

While there were successes in the naval relationship, such as the signing of a MoU in 1998, the rescue of the personnel from the *Priz* submersible in 2005, together with the large number of ship and Flag Officer visits generating goodwill and some limited practical interoperability, the interaction was nevertheless uneven. Largely confined to the surface fleet, the same depth of interaction with the RFN's submarine fleet was not achieved. The failed attempts to achieve a MoU on the safety of dived submarine navigation pointed to the underlying suspicions of each other in this particular field of maritime operations, an activity which relies on secrecy and is focused on the protection of the 'crown jewel' of each other's defence – the at sea nuclear deterrent – as well as the projection of military power worldwide. Thus, we should be cautious of applying the lessons we learned primarily about the way the surface fleet operates, to how the submarine fleet operates and which on a daily basis demonstrates its operational prowess both in conflict and on global deployments. There were also other areas of uneven cooperation. The early interaction between the Royal Marines and Russian Naval Infantry promised much but delivered little and likewise the early relationship between hydrographic departments did not lead to the output envisaged in the 1995 Hydrographic Bilateral Arrangement.

As well as learning lessons about the RFN from this period of cooperation, they too learned much from us. The Naval Policy of 2017, whose key architect was an interlocutor with the RN in the 1990s, Admiral Igor Kasatonov, brings together those lessons learned about the utility of maritime power and provides a set of objectives for the RFN not too dissimilar from those for the RN. Through the various visits and exercises, we provided the RFN with a real insight to the RN and most importantly to its future structures and capabilities. This openness is something to beware of in the future. While certainly there was a genuine friendship and professional relationship between the two navies, equally there were frequent signs of darker forces at play. These included the FSB, the GRU and a political leadership, less prone to support closer cooperation in an era of worsening political relations with the West from the early 2000s, but who nevertheless benefited from the insights the RFN was providing about us. It is highly unlikely that the sharp reduction in maritime platforms for the RN over the period of cooperation, which were openly discussed at various meetings, will have gone unnoticed, as Russia sought to restructure its own Navy against future threats and challenges, notably the UK. Admiral Yevmenov's astonishment at the withdrawal of the UK's organic Maritime Patrol Aircraft capability in 2010 is but one example. More recently in November 2023, a Russian defence analyst described the reduction of RN platforms and capability over the last few decades as 'catastrophic' for a once global maritime hegemon[3] and the RN's reported challenges in manning its new warships are also likely to contribute to Moscow's schadenfreude.[4]

Irrespective of the outcome of the current conflict in Ukraine, the RFN is set to be a persistent challenge and competitor for the RN and its allies, one which will need to be both defended against and deterred around the world. It is a navy that has risen from the ashes of the post-Soviet era, operating a broad range of assets from nuclear strategic ballistic-missile submarines, conventional submarines and sub-surface assets that can target

CNI, to frigates armed with hypersonic missiles and land-attack cruise missiles and corvettes, which pack a far greater punch than their equivalents in the RN. Naval bases are being upgraded in all fleets and ice-capable platforms procured to enable better operations in the High North. The RFN has largely validated its 2017 Naval Policy through its operations not only in Ukraine but also in support of its land operations in Syria, gaining valuable operational experience and learning lessons that can be incorporated into future platforms and tactics. It has demonstrated an operational tempo against Ukraine and platform availability which has been remarkable and a testament to the prowess of their engineers and maintainers to keep their platforms operational.

For sure, there are constraints and weaknesses to ship and submarine delivery schedules, as well as ongoing debates about procuring larger platforms, such as aircraft carriers and large amphibious shipping. The reliance on host-nation support for deployed units and the lack of robust at-sea logistic support is also an Achilles heel that can be exploited. The full impact of the Ukraine war on Russia's future maritime procurement is also uncertain, as is the effect of the sanctions imposed. But measures are being put in place to ensure Russia's 'technological sovereignty', with shipbuilding being one of the target sectors for investment. Submarine building has been less affected by the war due to the fact that it is far less reliant on imported goods. The steady drumbeat of production of conventional submarines, in particular, continues and the next six *Kalibr*-armed Project 636.3 Varshavyanka (NATO: *Kilo*) are due to be based either in the Northern Fleet or the Baltic Fleet.

While the RFN has not lost platforms on the scale that land forces have, the biggest impact of the war on the RFN has been the expenditure of *Kalibr* missiles which has been extremely high, with some analysts suggesting that stocks in June 2023 amounted to 88 remaining out of 689 at the start of the war.[5] However, what has become evident is that Russia, used to operating under a sanctions regime since 2014, had built up sufficient stocks of domestically produced military goods and foreign produced 'dual-use' goods, especially microelectronics, to continue producing what it needs to sustain its war effort and to import through third parties and other illicit trade routes. Despite the high usage of *Kalibr*, it is now assessed that Russia is producing about twenty-five per month, which is at least double pre-war production rates, although possibly not as good quality.[6] The challenge though will not only be to replenish current in-service platforms but also to equip those planned to enter service in the coming years.

The Ukraine conflict, therefore, is unlikely to affect the intended trajectory of the development of the RFN, nor Russia's ambition to be a global maritime power. There might be balance of investment decisions to be made as Russia re-constitutes its armed forces, which may affect the scale of naval procurement, although we should be mindful that spending on defence and security is often prioritised over expenditure on other federal government departments. In essence, what we see now is a navy modelled on Gorshkov's vision of a force centred on submarines, supported by surface ships and naval aviation but with important differences. It now has at its disposal the capability to launch long-range land-attack cruise missiles, providing Russia with a potent capability it lacked in Gorshkov's time. It is also a navy that is fostering relations with nations of the Global South and which regularly operates with partners, in particular China, with whom it conducts regular joint patrols in the Pacific region[7] and beyond. It is a navy that the RN and other Western navies will be regularly defending against and deterring whether it be in the High North, the Mediterranean or the Euro-Atlantic and Indo-Pacific regions.

It is also a Navy with which dialogue might be re-established as part of a wider UK and Western defence re-engagement effort with Russia. The notion of defence dialogue leading to cooperation with a country that has invaded its neighbour and unleashed untold misery, death and destruction may seem far-fetched at best and at worst, impossible. Similar views were held at the end of the Cold War, especially in light of the USSR's invasion of Afghanistan in the 1980s and the heavy military support provided by the West to the Mujahideen that led to the Soviet withdrawal in 1989. That said, the present political rupture between Russia and the West and their allies, the fundamental disagreements in foreign and security policies, war crime indictments against Putin and other senior military officials, and the massive Western military and economic support provided to Ukraine by the West is without precedent. Trite though it sounds, a process of re-establishing defence dialogue will not be easy, but it will be necessary. Whatever the outcome of the Ukraine conflict, Russia will continue to assert its place as a ubiquitous and indispensable player in international affairs, often pursuing policies that conflict with the Euro-Atlantic community.[8] The focus on Putin and his regime's demise misses the point that Russia systemically has a different world view and its place within it, and its long held grievances against the West, legitimate or otherwise, will continue.[9] To some extent that sense of victimhood and grievance has changed little in the last few hundred years. Short of going to full-scale war with Russia, its total defeat in the Ukraine conflict is unlikely to be achieved, as called for by some, and thus it will still need to be dealt with.

As and when the political conditions are met, the RN–RFN relationship from 1988 to 2014 provides an example of the art of the possible and a model to consider in re-establishing defence dialogue with Russia. The sea provides an environment in which there is a common bond and mutual understanding, and the navies' historical links, together with what was achieved between the two in the post-Cold War era will provide a good starting point. The 1998 MoU and the annual talks obligated by the 1986 INCSEA Agreement provide an official foundation on which to begin building dialogue. Informal talks, such as those started at Adderbury in 1988, should also be considered, in particular with retired personnel from this period of naval cooperation, who remain well connected with their respective defence and security organisations. These early talks between former colleagues should be aimed at rebuilding trust and confidence, which will be in short supply, before any consideration is given to wider, official defence dialogue and cooperation. Preparation for this future period of dialogue should begin now with a greater focus on cultural and language training, such that a body of RN Russian specialists exists when the time comes. Dialogue is a key component of deterrence, and indeed defence, but it requires people with a sophisticated understanding and knowledge of Russian defence and security thinking, of the language and the naval capabilities being procured.

For those involved in future navy-navy dialogue with the Russians what will you discover? Once the fear of using a difficult language that you might have learned is overcome, you can expect a blunt, challenging, suspicious, even hostile environment in which negotiations and talks will take place. The generation that will be met has been indoctrinated with anti-Western rhetoric, brought up in an education system that focuses on this and glorifies military service in defence of the Motherland. Although the former Soviet Zampolit officer system has been removed, which was designed to ensure personnel in ships and submarines adhered to the Communist creed, there still nevertheless exists a system of what are now called military political officers, who provide patriotic lectures to captive audiences. Paradoxically, you will also discover an unexpected warmth of hospitality, fuelled by vodka, and a certain, almost naive, bewilderment that the West hates Russia so much. This in turn is likely to generate a sense of euphoria that 'the Russians are not as bad as we thought' and even have a sense of humour. But beware the other forces within the Russian system, never to be resigned to accommodating the West and its liberal values and seeking to ensure that Russia remains a key player in international affairs, that is not governed, as the Russians see it, by the West's imposed rules-based system.

Activity in the maritime environment has consistently, almost daily, underpinned the three pillars of UK's defence engagement with Russia, namely Defend, Deter and Dialogue. The latter, although in abeyance since 2014, will in time return. The experience of the RN–RFN engagement between 1988 and 2014 also highlights another notion that should be considered more broadly after the present political crisis is resolved – seeking coexistence with Russia. That is hard to contemplate and difficult to achieve but the idea is nothing especially new in the debate of how to deal with the Russians. In 1951, Edward Crankshaw,[10] in writing about how to try to find coexistence with then Communist Russia, noted that:

> We have to make every effort to break down the present paralysis of the brain which allows us to confuse coexistence as such, which is attainable, with coexistence on our own terms which is not attainable. It is the job of our statesmen to find out what terms we can impose at any given time and push them to the limit of the possible. It is the job of ordinary people to remember that from its first beginnings the world has been full of menace.

Whatever happens in the Ukraine conflict and whoever may or may not come after Putin, political consideration will need to be given by both sides on how to coexist, without the imposition of each other's own terms of how to do so. That will take huge courage in the face of accusations of appeasing Russia, compromise and deal making, and, most importantly, a better understanding of each other. In spite of recent history, things will need to be done differently, if we want to avoid perpetuating the present discord between Russia and the UK and the rest of the Euro-Atlantic community and break the historical 'cycle of clash and entente' with Russia. Finding a degree of coexistence with a country like Russia that has a different set of values to the West's liberal democratic values would not be without precedent. The UK, driven in the main by economic necessity, has found ways to coexist with China, manifested by the visit of then British Foreign Secretary, James Cleverly, to China in August 2023. He stated that his visit was an opportunity 'to speak directly and unambiguously' on areas of disagreement and 'work together where it is in our mutual interest to do so'.[11] Just over a year later, the new Labour government has adopted the same approach. A two-day visit to China by the new Foreign Secretary, was described as 'a reflection of the consistent, strategic and pragmatic approach the UK government will take to managing the UK's relations with China; *cooperating* where we can; *competing* where we need to; and *challenging* where we must'.[12] These three italicised words when put together are a reasonable definition of coexistence. Moreover, this dialogue has happened despite China's human rights record and belligerence in the South China Seas and towards Taiwan. It has also occurred despite the fact that, according to the UK's refreshed 2023 Defence Command Paper, China 'poses an enduring and epoch-defining global challenge to British interests, including Defence interests, through its increasingly assertive and coercive behaviour as it seeks to rewrite the international order that has provided stability and prosperity for generations'.[13] The UK's relationship with Saudi Arabia is a further example of pragmatic coexistence with a country that has at best a

Conclusion

dubious human rights record but is nevertheless a key nation in the Gulf Cooperation Council. It also has an attractive trillion pound investment fund to diversify its economy away from oil, which offers significant investment opportunities to the UK economy.[14] The RN's relationship with the RFN between 1988 and 2014 reflected, to a certain extent, a pragmatic way of coexisting. On any given day during that period the RN was using its assets either to confront (defend), to compete (defend/deter) or to cooperate with the RFN, albeit not always in equal measure. The *fora* that were established for dialogue provided opportunities in which to agree or disagree and to message robustly, i.e. deter, while finding common ground on which to cooperate.

The RN's experiences with the RFN over a twenty-five-year period, also proved there was a Russian willingness at a personal level to interact with the West and their former adversaries. We should not lose sight of that in these difficult times. It is hoped that the nascent relationship between the RN and RFN, laid down in the years following the end of the Cold War, was not in vain and could still be built upon to re-establish mutually beneficial lines of communication. It will be a significant challenge.

Notes

1 'Glavnyy voyenno-morskoy parad', *Kremlin.ru*, 30 July 2023, http://kremlin.ru/events/president/news/71848 (accessed 31 July 2023).
2 D. Axe, 'Harried by Ukraine's Drone Boats, a Russian Navy Warship Goes Hunting for Grain Ships', *Forbes*, 26 July 2023, www.forbes.com/sites/davidaxe/2023/07/26/harried-by-ukraines-drone-boats-a-russian-navy-warship-goes-hunting-for-grain-ships/ (accessed 31 July 2023).
3 A. Khramchikhin, 'Tak prokhodit morskaya slava', *Nezavisimoye Voyennoe Obozrenie*, 23 November 2023, https://nvo.ng.ru/forces/2023-11-23/6_1263_fleet.html (accessed 30 November 2023).
4 D. Sheridan, 'Navy Has So Few Sailors It Has to Decommission Ships', *Telegraph*, 4 January 2024, www.telegraph.co.uk/news/2024/01/04/royal-navy-few-sailors-decommission-ships-new-frigates/ (accessed 5 January 2024).
5 O. Bilousova, O. I. Gribanovskiy, B. Hilgenstock, E. Ribakova, N. Shapova and V. Vlasiuk, 'Russia's Military Capacity and the Role of Imported Components', *KSE.ua*, 19 June 2023, https://kse.ua/wp-content/uploads/2023/06/Russian-import-of-critical-components.pdf (accessed 2 July 2023).
6 'Predstavitel' GUR MO Ukrainy nazval kolichestvo vysokotochnykh raket, kotoroye Rossiya yakoby proizvodit za mesyats', *TopWar*, 9 May 2023, https://topwar.ru/217397-predstavitel-gur-mo-ukrainy-nazval-kolichestvo-vysokotochnyh-raket-kotoroe-rossija-jakoby-proizvodit-za-mesjac.html (accessed 15 May 2023).

7 'Russian, Chinese Warships Begin Third Joint Patrol in Pacific Ocean', *TASS*, 28 July 2023, https://tass.com/defense/1653245 (accessed 1 August 2023).
8 A. M. Monaghan, *Dealing with the Russians*. Cambridge, Polity Press, 2019, p. 122.
9 These include, inter alia: Russian desire for a new European Security architecture which takes Russia's concerns into account; NATO enlargement; Ballistic Missile Defense; Western interventions in the Middle East.
10 E. Crankshaw, *Putting Up with the Russians*. London, Macmillan, 1984, p. 39.
11 S. McDonell and K. Whannel, 'Disengaging with China Not Credible, Says James Cleverly', *BBC News*, 30 August 2023, www.bbc.co.uk/news/uk-politics-66656443 (accessed 5 September 2023).
12 'Foreign Secretary Visits China', *Foreign, Commonwealth & Development Office London*, 18 October 2024, https://www.gov.uk/government/news/foreign-secretary-visits-china--2 (accessed 13 November 2024).
13 'Defence's Response to a More Contested and Volatile World', *Ministry of Defense London*, 18 July 2023, p. 6 https://assets.publishing.service.gov.uk/government/uploads/system/uploads/attachment_data/file/1171269/Defence_Command_Paper_2023_Defence_s_response_to_a_more_contested_and_volatile_world.pdf (accessed 5 September 2023).
14 M. Oi, 'Saudi Investment Fund to Buy 10% Stake in Heathrow Airport', *BBC News*, 29 November 2023, https://www.bbc.co.uk/news/business-67562523 (accessed 18 March 2024). In November 2023, Saudi Arabia's Public Investment Fund (PIF) agreed to buy a 10 per cent stake in Heathrow airport from Spanish infrastructure giant Ferrovial. The fund is controlled by Saudi Arabia's Prince Mohammed bin Salman Al Saud.

Bibliography and suggested reading

Bibliography

E. Crankshaw, *Putting Up with the Russians* London, Macmillan, 1984
A. Gordon, *The Rules of the Game*. London, John Murray, 1996
L. Hughes, *Peter the Great – A Biography*. New Haven, CT, Yale University Press, 2004
F. T. Jane, *The Imperial Russian Navy*. London, Conway Maritime Press Ltd, 1983
V. F. Kupreyenkov and I. V. Solov'yov, *Morskiye operativniye karty*. St Petersburg, 1996
D. W. Mitchell, *A History of Russian and Soviet Sea Power*. London, André Deutsch, 1974
A. Monaghan, *Dealing with the Russians*. London, Polity Press, 2019
A. Monaghan and R. Connolly, *The Sea in Russian Strategy*. Manchester, Manchester University Press, 2023
Peter the Great, *Kniga ustav morskoi (Naval Regulations)*. St Petersburg, 1720
F. Pope, *72 Hours*. London, Orion/Hachette UK, 2012
B. Ranft and G. Till, *The Sea in Soviet Strategy*. London, Macmillan, 1983
S. Roskill, *Admiral of the Fleet Earl Beatty – An Intimate Biography*. London, Collins, 1980
M. E. Sarotte, *Not One Inch: America, Russia and the Making of the Post-Cold War Stalemate*. New Haven, CT, Yale University Press, 2021
B. W. Watson, *Red Navy at Sea Soviet Naval Operations on the High Seas 1956–1980*. London, Arms and Armour Press, 1982

Suggested reading

K. Bogdanov and I. Kramnik, *The Russian Navy in the 21st Century: The Legacy and the New Path*. Arlington, CNA, 2018
C. A. G. Bridge (editor), *History of the Russian Fleet during the Reign of Peter the Great by a Contemporary Englishman (1724)*. London, Navy Records Society, volume 15, 1899

M. Mitchell, *The Maritime History of Russia 848–1948*. London, Sidgwick & Jackson, 1949

M. Mitchell, *The Red Fleet and the Royal Navy*. London, Hodder & Stoughton, 1942

E. J. Phillips, *The Founding of Russia's Navy: Peter the Great and the Azov Fleet 1688–1714*. Westport, CT, Greenwood Press, 1995

N. Polmar, *The Naval Institute Guide to the Soviet Navy*. Annapolis, MD, United States Naval Institute, 5th edition, 1991

B. W. Watson and S. W. Watson, *The Soviet Navy: Strengths and Liabilities*. London, Arms and Armour Press, 1986

D. Woodward, *The Russians at Sea*. London, William Kimber, 1965

Index

Note: 'n.' refers to chapter endnotes. Page numbers in *italic* refer to photographs, those in **bold** refer to tables. All ships without a country designation (e.g. HMS) can be assumed to be Russian. Titles with acronyms appear in full, unless more commonly known under initials.

Abramov, Admiral Mikhail 96–97
accidents 142
Adderbury talks 18–25, 27, 36–39, 43, **110**, **128**, 203
Admiral Chabanenko (destroyer) *101*, 163
Admiral Chichagov (frigate) 168, 175
Admiral Golovko (frigate) 168, 174–175
Admiral Gorshkov-class frigates 157, 163, 168, 169, 174
Admiral Kuznetsov (aircraft carrier) 98–99, 142, 163, 165, 196
Admiral Levchenko (destroyer) 34, 54, *55*, 163
Admiral Nakhimov (cruiser) 163, 170
Admiral Panteleyev (destroyer) *56*, 157
Admiral Tributs (destroyer) 157
Admiral Vinogradov (destroyer) 14, 163
Admiral Vladimirsky (naval research vessel) 196
Admiral Zakharov (destroyer) 7, 11–13, *12*
Adventure (yacht) 78, 106
Afghanistan 203, 214
aircraft carriers 105, 153, 165–166, 196–197
Akademik Pashin-class tankers 163, 176
Albion, HMS (landing platform dock) 94–95, 99
Aleksandrit-class minesweepers 172–173

Aleksandr Suvorov (cruiser) 7
Alrosa (submarine) 91
amber (commodity) 62
Amel'ko, Admiral Nikolai 18, 37, 76n.2, 138–139, 143–144, *146*, 147
American Committee for US–Soviet relations 18, 19
amphibious capability 94–95, 140, 166–168, **167**, **168**
Andreyenkov, Captain First Rank V. Ye 44, 145
Andromeda, HMS (frigate) 7, 10–15
Apollo, HMS (minelayer) 7
Arab Spring (2011) 103
Arctic Convoys 5–6, 54, 78, 133–134, 205–206
Arctic Military Environmental Cooperation programme (AMEC) 84–85
Arctic Star medal 6
Argyll, HMS (frigate) 24
Arkhangel'sk (previously HMS *Royal Sovereign*) (battleship) 5
arms control (Adderbury talks) 20–22
AUKUS security pact 153
Avdoshin, Vice Admiral V. V. 87, 96–97, 100
Avenger, HMS (frigate) 22, 139, 143
Avery, Robert 25, 39, 43, 48, 68–69, 80, 95, 144, *146*
 first-hand account 39–42, 44–47, 95–100

Index

Baltic Fleet 2–3
Baltiysk, Russia 32, 56, 58–61, 65–68, 70–71
Band, Admiral Sir Jonathan 95
banyas (saunas) 142, 143
Battleaxe, HMS (frigate) 56, *56*, 57–58
Belfast HMS (cruiser) 6, 16n.4, 133
Belgorod (special purpose submarine) 158, 160, 197
Berlin Wall, fall of 19
Bespokoiny (destroyer) 47, *48*, *50*, 147
Bessonov, Rear Admiral V. F. 37, 39–40
Bezuprechny (destroyer) 7, 205
Black Rover, RFA (tanker) 24, 34
Black Sea Fleet 3, 156
Borei-class submarines 160, 163
Borisov, Yuri 166
Boyce, Vice Admiral Michael 10, 143
Brigstocke, Vice Admiral John 37, 52
Bristol, HMS (destroyer) 7
Britannia, HMY (Royal Yacht) 16, 47–48, *48*, *49*, *50*, *51*, 141
Britannia Royal Naval College (BRNC) 48, 78, 93–94, 106
Brown University, Adderbury talks 22–23
bureaucratic inflexibility 53, 140–141, 180–181

Cameron, David 103–104
Campbeltown HMS (frigate) 14–15, 136
CBMs *see* confidence-building measures (CBMs)
Chevron, HMS (destroyer) 7
Chieftain, HMS (destroyer) 7
China 95, 99, 197, 214, 216
Chirkov, Admiral Viktor Viktorovich 105, 106
Cleverly, James 216
Club of Military Leaders of the Russian Federation 205
Cold War 3, 7, 11, 39, 62–63, 81, 132
'colour revolutions' 94, 198
command and control
    mission command approach (RN) 138, 151n.9
    ship-command ranks (RFN) 141
    top-down approach (RFN) 26, 27, 35, 138, 211

Commonwealth War Graves Commission (CWGC) sites 107, 205–206
communications 25, 38, 140, 202
competition 194–195, 209, 212–213
    see also deterrence
confidence-building measures (CBMs) 17, 18, 20–21, 36, 106, 108, 203, 205
confrontation
    Cold War 7, 17
    future 153–157, 198–200, 203
    historic 5, 15
    return to 77–79, 103, 132
    see also defence engagement
conscription 140, 149, 183
Continuous At-Sea Deterrent (CASD) 195
cooperation
    between 1988 and 2014 15–16, 47–48, 51–53, 78–79, 94–95, 102, 209–212
    collapse of 103–109, 132–134
    dialogue as 16, 18, 36–39, 132–134, 198–206, 214–217
    historic 1–2, 5–7, 209–210
    hydrographic departments 72–75
    political headwinds 94–102
    training establishments 92–94
Cornwall, HMS (frigate) 79–82, 137
corvettes 163, 169, 171–172, **172**, **173**, **174**, 175
Crabb, Commander Lionel 'Buster' 7
Crimea
    annexation of 38, 95, 103, 132, 167, 197–199
    Morye shipyard **173**
    Zaliv shipyard **168**, **173**
Crimean War (1853–56) 2, 5, 209
Critical National Infrastructure (CNI) 155–156, 195–196
culture 25, 38–39, 53, 136, 141–142, 147
Cunningham, First Viscount of Hyndhope, Admiral Andrew Browne 43, 45

damage control 102, 138, 139, 149, 151n.11, 211
decision-making 27, 30, 135, 138
Decoy, HMS (destroyer) 7

Defence Centre for Languages and Culture (DCLC) 150–151
Defence Command Paper (2023) 153, 216
defence cooperation 77, 94, 201–202
defence dialogue 16, 18, 36–39, 132–134, 198–206, 214–217
defence diplomacy 26, 54, 155, 157, 200, 210–211
defence engagement 25, 38, 94, 102, 104, 134, 193–197, 202–206, 209, 215–217
Defence Review (2010) 108, 195
defence spending 181–183
Defender, HMS (destroyer) 199
Demyanchenko, Rear Admiral Oleg 51–52, 76n.11
Derzky (corvette) 171
destroyers 169
deterrence 132, 133, 195, 197–199
Devonshire, HMS (destroyer) 7
Di Paola, Admiral Giampaolo 91–92
dialogue 16, 18, 36–39, 132–134, 198–206, 214–217
Diana (destroyer) 7
disaster-relief training 139, 149
drones 156–157
Dryad, HMS (shore establishment) 48, 92

economy (Russia) 181–184
Elizabeth II, Queen 16
EnergoMashSpetsStal plant, Donetsk 178
Essenhigh, Rear Admiral Nigel 73–75, 74, 75, 76n.15
exercise planning 137

Falkland Islands 81, 144, 149
Fallon, Michael 196
Far East
  Amur shipyard 169, **174**
  Zvezda shipyard 166, **179**
Fields, Lieutenant Commander David 27, 53, 132
  first-hand account 28–33
flag officers 15, 47, **117**, 135, 137
Fleet Operational Sea Training (FOST) (previously Flag Officer Sea Training) 102n.7, 105, 137
Fort Victoria, RFA (solid stores support ship) 177

Foundation for International Security (FIS) 18–21
France–Russia–UK–US (FRUKUS) 54, 79, 83, 93, 102, 105, 106, **128**, 205, 210
Fraser, Admiral Sir Bruce 6–7
Freedom of Navigation (FoN) 180–181, 199
frigates 140, 150, 163, 168–169, **170**, 174–175
future prospects (Russian Navy) 153–158, 181–185

G8 Global Partnerships Programme (G8GPP) 84
gaming 24–25
Germany 2–3
Glasgow, HMS (destroyer) 50, 143, 204
Gloucester, HMS (destroyer) 34, 37
Gorbachev, Mikhail 7, 15, 36
Gordon, Andrew
  Rules of the Game, The 146
Gorshkov, Admiral S. G. 3–4, 45, 137, 139, 154, 158, 209–210, 214
Great Patriotic War *see* World War II
Greig, Admiral Samuel 1, 43, 45
Gremyashchy (destroyer) 135, 137, 144
Gromov, Admiral Feliks 40–41, 45, 73, 97, 145, 147, 148, 149, 204
GRU (Russian military intelligence) 39, 42, 93
Guillot, General Gregory M. 181
Gulnev, Captain First Rank Konstantin 132–133

helicopters 13–14, 30–31
Herald, HMS (hydrographic vessel) 71, 72
High North 177, 180–181, 204, 213
history (Russian Navy) 1–10, 43, 45, 78–79, 145, 200–201, 209–210
Hogland, Battle of (1788) 1
Holloway, Captain Jonathan 84, 86, 86, 140–142
  first-hand account 87–90
human connections 143–145
hydrographic departments cooperation 72–75, 134, 212

icebreakers and ice-class patrol ships 177–181, **179**, **180**

Illya Muromets (icebreaker) 178–179
Imperator Aleksander III (submarine) 160
Incidents at Sea Agreement (INCSEA) 16–18, 20, 21, 36, 92, 133, 205
'On Inland Sea Waters, the Territorial Sea and the Russian Federation's Owned Zone' 180–181
Integrated Review (IR) (2021) 153
Invincible, HMS (aircraft carrier) 139
Iraq 77, 94
Irkutsk (submarine) 162
Ivan Gren-class landing ships 163
Ivan Kruzenshtern (oceanographic ship) 72
Ivan Papanin (ice-class patrol ship) 179–180
Ivan Rogov (landing ship) 163, 167

Japanese Navy 2

K-159 (submarine) 83–84
K-291 (submarine) 85
Kalibr missiles 155–156, 163, 166, 171, 187n.31, 213
Kaliningrad
  airport 68
  Yantar shipyard **167**
Karakurt-class corvettes 175
Kasatonov, Admiral Igor 35, 36, 37, 40, 46, 52, 73, 97, 147, 154, 168, 204, 212
Kazan, Zelenodol'sk shipyard **172**
Kerch (cruiser) 19, 21, 142
Key, Admiral Sir Ben 106, 153
Khabarovsk (special purpose submarine) 160
Kiev (cruiser) 7, 10
KIL 27 (support vessel) 88–90, 141
Kilgour, Rear Admiral Niall 92
Kilo-class submarines 5, *100*
Kirov-class cruisers 163
Kola Peninsula 84, 85, 108
Komaritsyn, Vice Admiral Anatoly 73–75, *74*, 75
Komoyedov, Admiral V. P. 143
Konusov, Captain First Rank Victor 79, 93
Kostin, Andrei 182–183
Krutskikh, Mr A. 40–42
Kupreyenkov, Captain First Rank Vladimir 39, 40, 41
Kuroyedov, Admiral Vladimir Ivanovich 41, 43, *44*, 44–47, 91, 97
Kursk (submarine) 79–83, 91, 142
Kuznetsov, Admiral Nikolai G. 7
Kuznetsov Naval Academy (KNA) 33, 40, 41, 45, 48, 92–93, 95, 106, 137, 149

Lada-class submarines 161
landing ships 163, 166–168, **167**, **168**
Lane-Nott, Commodore Roger *100*, 144
Laputskiy, Admiral Yevgeni Timofeevich 81–82, *82*
Lazarev, Rear Admiral O. N. 137, 147
Lenin (icebreaker) 145
Leningrad (icebreaker) 178
Leopard (*submarine*) 162
lessons learned 135, 147–151, 193, 212
Lider-class destroyers 169
Lider-class icebreakers 178
Lion HMS (battlecruiser) 5
Lippiett, Rear Admiral John 147, *148*
Lister, Vice Admiral Sir Simon 78, 85
Litvinenko, Alexander 85, 90–91, 94, 139
logistic support ships 165, 175–177, **176**, 213
Lower, Rear Admiral Iain 133
Lutsk (corvette) 136

MacDonald, Admiral W. 38
Main Directorate for Navigation and Oceanography (GUNIO) 72–75, 134
Makarov, Army General Nikolai 91
manpower resources 99, 183–184
Manturov, Denis 156, 183
Marat (battleship) 5
Maritime Doctrine (2022) 153–154, 157, 210
Maritime Warfare Centre (MWC) 48, 92–93, 96
Marshal Shaposhnikov (destroyer) 157
Marshal Ustinov (cruiser) 148
Masorin, Admiral V. V. 91, 95–100, 139
Massey, Captain Alan 136
McClement, Vice Admiral Sir Tim 79–80

first-hand account 80–82
Medvedev, Dmitry 94
Memorandum of Understanding (MoU) on Naval Cooperation between the RN and RFN 37, 43–47, 77–78
Michael of Kent, HRH Prince 38, 54, 55
military dialogue *see* dialogue
military expenditure (Russia) 182–183
Military Industrial Complex (MIC) 156, 183
military intelligence organisation (GRU) *see* GRU
military-technical cooperation 202
Military Technical Cooperation Agreement (MTCA) 104, 109
minesweepers 172–174, **174**
Ministry of Defence (MoD) (Russia) 77, 91, 169, 180
  External Relations Department (GUMVS) 39, 79, 87, 107
Ministry of Defence (MoD) (UK) 38, 83, 105, 195, 200
Ministry of Foreign Affairs (MFA) (Russia) 23, 39, 42
missiles 3, 19, 20, 156, 163, 168, 213 *see also* Kalibr missiles
mission command *see* command and control
Mitrofan Moskalenko (landing ship) 163, 167
modernisation programme of military 4, 194
Moloko, Captain First Rank 106–107
Moskva (cruiser) 138, 156, 211
Myres, Rear Admiral John 71, 72

Nance, Captain Adrian 51–52
Nastoichivy (destroyer) 47
National Defence Management Centre (NDMC) 106–107
NATO (North Atlantic Treaty Organisation)
  BALTOPS/PfP exercise 28, 52
  Bold Monarch exercise 91–92
  collective security 195
  deterrence 197–198
  expansion concerns 77, 94, 200
  incidents 17
  Maritime Centre for Security of Critical Undersea Infrastructure (CUI) 196

Partnership for Peace (PfP) programme 27, 52, 76n.5
Serbian bombing campaign 78
Submarine Rescue System (NSRS) 90–91
Naval Policy (2017) (Russia) 26, 154–155, 157, 168, 210, 212–213
Navarino, Battle of (1827) 2
Navy Day 47, 146, 210
Neustrashimy (frigate) 27–33, 54, 76n.6
New Zealand, HMS (battlecruiser) 5
Newcastle, HMS (destroyer) 7, 10, 30, 79
Nikolai Zubov (ice-class patrol ship) 180
Nimrod maritime patrol aircraft (MPA) 108, 195
Northern Convoys' International Centre (NCIC) 206
Northern Fleet 3, 105–107, 206
Northern Sea Route (NSR) 177–178, 180–181, 204
Norway 85, 177

Obama administration 102, 103
Obraztsovy (destroyer) 7
October Revolution 2, 5, 54
Oduvanchik drone 156
officer training and appointments 1–2, 14, 92–94, 137–141, 150–151
Operation Dervish *see* Arctic Convoys
Opossum, HMS (submarine) 97, 100, 101
Ordzhonikidze (cruiser) 7
OSK (United Shipbuilding Corporation) 169, 182–184
Oswald, Admiral Sir Julian 19, 35, 37

Pacific Fleet (Russia) 2, 80
Page, Captain Chris
  first-hand account 19–25
Patrushev, Vice Admiral Viktor V. 39, 40, 41, 42, 144–145, 147, 183
pay and conditions 32–33, 149
PD-50 (floating dock) 142, 165
'perestroika' 7
Perm (submarine) 160
Peter the Great 1, 145, 209
Piotr Morgunov (landing ship) 167
Piskunov, Captain First Rank A. 12–15

Podkopayev, Captain First Rank 142
Polar Convoy Club 206
pontoons 83, 85
Portland, HMS (frigate) 95–96, 100, *101*
Poseidon (unmanned underwater drone) 158, 160
Poseidon Maritime Patrol Aircraft 195
Pospelov, Vladimir 166
Prince of Wales, HMS (aircraft carrier) 197
Princess Royal, HMS (battlecruiser) 5
Priz (submersible) rescue 86–92, 140–142
propulsion plants 174–175
Proteus, RFA (support vessel) 196
Puchkov, Andrey 182
'purple' thinking 46
Putin, Vladimir Vladimirovich 6, 48, 48, 77, 79, 86, 86, 94, 103, 194, 198, 199
Pyotr Veliky (cruiser) 106, 108

Queen Elizabeth, HMS (aircraft carrier) 105, 153, 196–197
Queen Mary, HMS (battlecruiser) 5

ranks (Russia) 141
Rapid, HMS (destroyer) 6–7
rates system (Russia) 141
'reset' in relations with Russia 102–104
Revenge, HMS (submarine) 100
Riches, Commander Ian 86, 140
Rosatom 84, 177, 178
Rossiya (icebreaker) 178
Rostec 183
Royal Marines (RM) 34, 51, 53, 56–71, 97, 109
Royal Naval College (RNC) Greenwich 24, 35
Royal Naval Submarine Museum, Gosport 82
Royal Navy (RN)
  First Battle-Cruiser Squadron 5
  Russian impressions of 99–100
  Sixth Frigate Squadron 51–52
Royal Sovereign, HMS (battleship) 5
Rubin Design Bureau 83
Rules of Engagement (ROE) 26, 150
Russia, West's views of 193–194, 197–198

Russian Arctic Convoy Museum 206
Russian Federation Navy (RFN)
  Twelfth Division of Surface Ships 47, 51–52
  West's views of 193–194
Russian Naval Air Arm 139
Russian Naval Infantry (RNI) 34, 35, 55–71, 97, 109, 140
Russia–UK–US cooperation agreement (RUKUS) 25–27, 33–42, 37, 42, 48, 54, 79, **128**, 144
Russo–Georgia War (2008) 94
Russo–Japanese War (1904–5) 2

St Albans, HMS (frigate) 78
St Petersburg 1, 53–54
  Admiralty shipyard 106, 158, **162**, **180**
  Almaz shipyard **180**
  Baltzavod shipyard **179**
  English Embankment 49, 51, 54
  Pella shipyard **173**
  Severnaya Verf shipyard 6, 169, **170**, **172**
  Srednye-Nevsky shipyard **174**
Saint Petersburg Naval Institute (SPNI) (formerly M. V. Frunze Higher Naval School) 48, 93–94
Samuel B. Roberts, USS (destroyer) 34
sanctions 158, 167, 178, 182, 197–198, 213
Sankt Peterburg (submarine) 161
Saudi Arabia 216–217
Scorpio (unmanned underwater vehicle) 86–90, 140–141
Serbia 78
Sergey Kotov (corvette) 211
Severodvinsk 2, 142, **161**
Severomorsk 101, 107–108
ship building and construction 98, 157–158, 182–185, 194, 213
ship visits
  after 2014 157, 205–206
  between 1988 and 2014 15–16, 33, 47, 51, 53–56, 78–80, 94–95, 105–107, **110**, **117**, **128**
  hydrographic department cooperation 72–73
  pre-1988 5, 6–7, 8
Shkidchenko, Colonel-General V. 136
Shoigu, Sergei 139, 155, 168, 183

Sibiryakov (hydrographic vessel) 73
Sinope, Battle of (1853) 2
Skripal, Sergei 79, 132, 206
Skype link 106–108
Slater, Admiral Sir Jock 43, *44*, 145, *146*, 204
Smetlivy (destroyer) 7
Smotryashchy (destroyer) 7
Somerset, HMS (frigate) 51, *53*
Sorokin, Admiral Aleksei 40, 41, *146*
Southampton, HMS (destroyer) 137
Sovershenny (destroyer) 7
Soviet Committee for European Security and Cooperation 20–21
Soviet-era legacy units 140, 158, 161–163, **162**, 170, **171**, 177
Soviet Navy 3–4, 8, 17, 177, 210
Soviet Union
  collapse 4, 45, 203
Splendid, HMS (submarine) 80
Sposobny (destroyer) 7
Stanhope, Admiral Sir Mark 54, 105–106
Stark, Rear Admiral J. 42, *42*
State Armament Programme (GPV) 98, 105, 157, 166, 194
Strategic Defence Review (2025) (UK) 196
Style, Vice Admiral Charles 7
  first-hand account 10–15
submarines
  building 158–160, **159**, 160–163, **161, 162**
  escape and rescue 79–92
  failed attempts to achieve a MoU 82–83, 90–92, 211–212
  importance 3, 154
  role of Soviet 19, 21
  safe dived navigation 92, 211–212
Sunak, Rishi 196
Super-Gorshkov-class frigates 168, 169
surface platforms 163–165, **164**, 169, **171**
Sverdlov (cruiser) 7
Svyatogor (icebreaker) 179

Tatarinov, Admiral Aleksandr 96
'technological sovereignty' 182, 213
Tegentsev, Captain Second Rank Sergei 14, 15
telephone lines 106–107
Trafalgar Night 72, 76n.14

training establishments
  cooperation between 78, 92–94, 106, 135
  cultural and language 150–151, 215
  quantitative rather than qualitative 137–139
Triple Entente (1907) 5
'Triple Trust' exercise 24
Triumph, HMS (aircraft carrier) 6–7
Triumph, HMS (nuclear-powered submarine) 80
Tsirkon (hypersonic cruise missile) (anti-ship missiles) 155, 160, 168
Tsushima, Battle of (1905) 2

Udaloy-class destroyers 163
UK Hydrographic Office (UKHO) 72–75, 134, 142
UK Submarine Rescue Service (UKSRS) (James Fisher and Sons PLC) 86–90
Ukraine
  invasion of 132, 197–198, 201
  Maidan protests 103, 107
  'special military operation' 35, 55–56, 155–156, 160, 184, 198
Ukrainian Navy 90, 136, 201
United Kingdom, Russian views of 193–194
Universal Landing Ships (UDK) *see* landing ships
US Naval War College 22, 24–25, 39, 144
Ushakov, Admiral Fyodor 2, 6
Ushakov Medal 6
USSR *see* Soviet Union
Ustimenko, Vice Admiral Yu G. 135, 136, 144, 150

Vanguard-class submarines 100, 195
Varan (aircraft carrier) 165–166
Varshavyanka-class (submarine) 158, 160–161, 213
Varyag (cruiser) 45
Vasily Bykov-class corvettes 171, 175
Vasily Trushin (landing ship) 163, 167
Velikye Luki (submarine) 161
Victorious, HMS (submarine) 95
Victory, HMS (sailing ship) 105
Vidal, HMS (hydrographic vessel) 72
Vitse-admiral Kulakov (destroyer) 78, 106

Vizir-M (drone) 156
Vladimir Andreyev (landing ship) 163, 167
Vladivostok 80
vodka drinking 143
vranyo (making up tall stories) 144–145, 211
VTB Bank 182–183

warships, utility of 26, 210–211
West, Russian views of the 198, 214
White, Admiral Sir Hugo 36, *149*
Wilson, Colonel Charlie 56
  first-hand account 57–71
women, attitudes to 14, 141, 150
World War II 2–3, 5–6, 78–79

Yanukovych, Viktor 103, 107

Yasen-class submarines 160, 163
Yasnitsky, Rear Admiral Gennady 10
Yegorov, Admiral Vladimir 44–47, 52–53, *52*, *53*, 139, 147, *147*, *148*, 150
Yekaterinburg (submarine) 142
Yelovik, Colonel Maksim 133
Yevmenov, Admiral N. A. 107–109, 157, 165, 181, 195, 197, 212
Yevpatiy Kolovrat (icebreaker) 178–179
York, HMS (destroyer) 24, *104*, 105
Yury Dolgorukiy (submarine) 98

Zaikin, Captain First Rank Viktor 41, 42
Zakharenko, Admiral Mikhail 96
Zheglov, Vice Admiral Yuri 72, 73
Zvezda (manufacturer) 175